DIGITAL HEALTH CARE OUTSIDE OF TRADITIONAL CLINICAL SETTINGS

Health care delivery is shifting away from the clinic and into the home. Even prior to the COVID-19 pandemic, the use of telehealth, wearable sensors, ambient surveillance, and other products was on the rise. In the coming years, patients will increasingly interact with digital products at every stage of their care, such as using wearable sensors to monitor changes in temperature or blood pressure, conducting self-directed testing before virtually meeting with a physician for a diagnosis, and using smart pills to document their adherence to prescribed treatments. This volume reflects on the explosion of at-home digital health care and explores the ethical, legal, regulatory, and reimbursement impacts of this shift away from the twentieth-century focus on clinics and hospitals toward a more modern health care model. This title is also available as Open Access on Cambridge Core.

I. Glenn Cohen is Deputy Dean and James A. Attwood and Leslie Williams Professor of Law at Harvard Law School. He is one of the world's leading experts on the intersection of bioethics and the law, as well as health law. He is the author of more than 200 articles and book chapters and the author or editor of more than twenty books.

Daniel B. Kramer is a clinical cardiac electrophysiologist at Beth Israel Deaconess Medical Center and Associate Professor of Medicine at Harvard Medical School. His research focuses on bioethics, health policy, and clinical outcomes related to the use of cardiovascular devices and procedures.

Julia Adler-Milstein is Professor of Medicine at the University of California, San Francisco. Her work – more than 200 scholarly articles and book chapters – sits at the intersection of health policy and health informatics. In particular, she has examined how emerging technologies are shaping opportunities to improve diagnostic processes and outcomes.

Carmel Shachar is Assistant Clinical Professor of Law and the Faculty Director of the Health Law and Policy Clinic at Harvard Law School. She was previously Executive Director of Harvard Law's Petrie-Flom Center. Her work focuses on access to care and digital health.

Digital Health Care outside of Traditional Clinical Settings

ETHICAL, LEGAL, AND REGULATORY CHALLENGES AND OPPORTUNITIES

Edited by

I. GLENN COHEN
Harvard Law School

DANIEL B. KRAMER
Harvard Medical School

JULIA ADLER-MILSTEIN
University of California, San Francisco

CARMEL SHACHAR
Harvard Law School

Shaftesbury Road, Cambridge CB2 8EA, United Kingdom

One Liberty Plaza, 20th Floor, New York, NY 10006, USA

477 Williamstown Road, Port Melbourne, VIC 3207, Australia

314–321, 3rd Floor, Plot 3, Splendor Forum, Jasola District Centre, New Delhi – 110025, India

103 Penang Road, #05–06/07, Visioncrest Commercial, Singapore 238467

Cambridge University Press is part of Cambridge University Press & Assessment, a department of the University of Cambridge.

We share the University's mission to contribute to society through the pursuit of education, learning and research at the highest international levels of excellence.

www.cambridge.org
Information on this title: www.cambridge.org/9781009373241

DOI: 10.1017/9781009373234

© Cambridge University Press & Assessment 2024

This work is in copyright. It is subject to statutory exceptions and to the provisions of relevant licensing agreements; with the exception of the Creative Commons version the link for which is provided below, no reproduction of any part of this work may take place without the written permission of Cambridge University Press.

An online version of this work is published at doi.org/10.1017/9781009373234 under a Creative Commons Open Access license CC-BY-NC-ND 4.0 which permits re-use, distribution and reproduction in any medium for non-commercial purposes providing appropriate credit to the original work is given. You may not distribute derivative works without permission. To view a copy of this license, visit https://creativecommons.org/licenses/by-nc-nd/4.0

All versions of this work may contain content reproduced under license from third parties. Permission to reproduce this third-party content must be obtained from these third-parties directly.

When citing this work, please include a reference to the DOI 10.1017/9781009373234

First published 2024

A catalogue record for this publication is available from the British Library

A Cataloging-in-Publication data record for this book is available from the Library of Congress

ISBN 978-1-009-37324-1 Hardback
ISBN 978-1-009-37326-5 Paperback

Cambridge University Press & Assessment has no responsibility for the persistence or accuracy of URLs for external or third-party internet websites referred to in this publication and does not guarantee that any content on such websites is, or will remain, accurate or appropriate.

I. Glenn Cohen: To Uncle E and Uncle J, characters richer than any novelist could sketch and gone before their time.

Julia Adler-Milstein: To Daniel Yang and the team at the Gordon and Betty Moore Foundation, who are dedicated to fostering the achievement of diagnostic excellence; and to my family, who support my work in this and all areas of health system transformation.

Daniel B. Kramer: To Andrew and Emily, who always ask why.

Carmel Shachar: To IGC and the rest of the PFC team, past and present, for being a wonderful home for the last five years.

Contents

List of Figures	page xi
List of Tables	xiii
List of Contributors	xv
Acknowledgments	xvii

Introduction   1
Carmel Shachar, Julia Adler-Milstein, Daniel B. Kramer, and I. Glenn Cohen

PART I QUESTIONS OF DATA GOVERNANCE FOR DATA FROM DIGITAL HOME HEALTH PRODUCTS   11

Introduction   11
Carmel Shachar

1   In the Medical Privacy of One's Own Home: Four Faces of Privacy in Digital Home Health Care   15
Barbara J. Evans

2   Patient Access to Health Device Data: Toward a Legal Framework   27
Charles Duan and Christopher J. Morten

3   Challenges of Remote Patient Care Technologies under the General Data Protection Regulation: Preliminary Results of the TeNDER Project   38
Danaja Fabcic Povse

4   Renegotiating the Social Contract for Use of Health Information: Lessons Learned from Newborn Screening and Implications for At-Home Digital Care   50
Jodyn Platt and Sharon Kardia

PART II DIGITAL HOME DIAGNOSTICS FOR SPECIFIC
CONDITIONS   61

Introduction   61
Daniel B. Kramer

5   Patient Self-Administered Screening for Cardiovascular Disease
    Using Artificial Intelligence in the Home   65
    Patrik Bächtiger, Mihir A. Kelshiker, Marie E. G. Moe,
    Daniel B. Kramer, and Nicholas S. Peters

6   The Promise of Telehealth for Abortion   79
    Greer Donley and Rachel Rebouché

7   Monitoring (on) Your Mind: Digital Biomarkers
    for Alzheimer's Disease   92
    Claire Erickson and Emily A. Largent

PART III THE SHAPE OF THE ELEPHANT FOR DIGITAL
HOME DIAGNOSTICS   105

Introduction   105
I. Glenn Cohen

8   Physician and Device Manufacturer Tort Liability for Remote
    Patient Monitoring Devices   109
    David A. Simon and Aaron S. Kesselheim

9   Post-Market Surveillance of Software Medical Devices: Evidence
    from Regulatory Data   123
    Alexander O. Everhart and Ariel D. Stern

10 Labeling of Direct-to-Consumer Medical Artificial Intelligence
    Applications for "Self-Diagnosis"   139
    Sara Gerke

11 "Internet Plus Health Care" as an Impetus for China's Health
    System Reform   156
    Zhang Yi and Wang Chenguang

PART IV REIMBURSEMENT CONSIDERATIONS FOR DIGITAL
HOME HEALTH   169

Introduction   169
Julia Adler-Milstein

12 A Pathway for High-Value Home Hospital Care in the United States: Statutory, Reimbursement, and Cybersecurity Strategies in the Age of Hybrid Care   173
    Stephanie Zawada, Nels Paulson, Margaret Paulson, Michael Maniaci, and Bart Demaerschalk

13 Digitally Enabled Medicaid Home and Community-Based Services   185
    Kathryn Huber and Tara Sklar

14 EU In-Home Digital Diagnostics – Cross-Border Patient Reimbursement under Threat?   196
    Kaat Van Delm

Figures

5.1 Eko DUO smart stethoscope; patient-facing "bell" of stethoscope labelled with sensors; data flow between Eko DUO, user's smartphone, and cloud for the application of AI *page* 69
9.1 Proportion of devices with software by specialty over time 130
9.2 Two-year adverse event rates by specialty over time 131
9.3 Two-year class I and class II recall rates by specialty over time 132
10.1 Regulation of mobile health apps, including DTC medical self-diagnosing AI apps 148

Tables

3.1	Essential data protection requirements for RCTs: Preliminary results of TeNDER	page 48
8.1	Schematic of tort liability for manufacturers, physicians, and caregivers	111
8.2	Express preemptive effect of MDA on tort claims, by defect alleged	117
8.3	Express and implied preemptive effect of MDA on tort claims, by claim type	117
9.1	Two-year adverse event rates by specialty	133
9.2	Two-year class I and class II recall rates by specialty	134
9.3	Example recalls	135
11.1	A selection of legal and policy documents that impact IPHC	160
12.1	Frequent H@H program condition inclusion criteria	176
12.2	Example telehealth use cases	178
12.3	Scope of current H@H models	178
14.1	Regulation versus directive: Differences relevant for telemedicine	199
14.2	Member state functions	201
14.3	Stagnant patient versus patient insured abroad	201
14.4	Situations triggering application of regulation and/or directive	202

Contributors

Julia Adler-Milstein, University of California, San Francisco

Patrik Bächtiger, Imperial College London

Wang Chenguang, Tsinghua University School of Law

I. Glenn Cohen, Harvard Law School

Bart Demaerschalk, Mayo Clinic Center for Digital Health

Greer Donley, University of Pittsburgh School of Law

Charles Duan, American University Washington College of Law

Claire Erickson, Perelman School of Medicine, University of Pennsylvania

Barbara J. Evans, University of Florida

Alexander O. Everhart, Harvard Medical School

Danaja Fabcic Povse, Vrije Universiteit Brussel

Sara Gerke, Penn State Dickinson Law

Kathryn Huber, University of Colorado School of Medicine

Sharon Kardia, University of Michigan

Mihir A. Kelshiker, Imperial College London

Aaron S. Kesselheim, Brigham and Women's Hospital; Harvard Medical School

Daniel B. Kramer, Imperial College London; Harvard Medical School

Emily A. Largent, Perelman School of Medicine, University of Pennsylvania

Michael Maniaci, Mayo Clinic Florida

Marie E. G. Moe, Imperial College London; Norwegian University of Science and Technology

Christopher J. Morten, Columbia Law School

Margaret Paulson, Mayo Clinic Health System

Nels Paulson, University of Wisconsin

Nicholas S. Peters, Imperial College London

Jodyn Platt, University of Michigan

Rachel Rebouché, Temple University Beasley School of Law

Carmel Shachar, Harvard Law School

David A. Simon, Northeastern University School of Law

Tara Sklar, University of Arizona James E. Rogers College of Law

Ariel D. Stern, Harvard Business School

Kaat Van Delm, Katholieke Universiteit Leuven

Zhang Yi, Vanke School of Public Health of Tsinghua University

Stephanie Zawada, Mayo Clinic College of Medicine and Science

Acknowledgments

A book like this is the result of the hard work of many. We thank our student line editors for their meticulous work.[1] We are grateful to Laura Chong and Chloe Reichel for their administrative support in organizing the conference that gave rise to this book. We are also grateful for Laura Chong's hard work shepherding all the many pieces of this manuscript. We thankfully acknowledge the Petrie-Flom Center for Health Law Policy, Biotechnology, and Bioethics at Harvard Law School, with support from the Oswald DeN. Cammann Fund, for conference sponsorship. We also thank the Gordon and Betty Moore Foundation for their generous support of our *Diagnosing in the Home* project. Finally, of course, we thank the contributors for their thoughtful and important scholarly contributions.

---

[1] Olivia Staff (Lead Line Editor), Shing-Shing Cao, Noah Delwiche, and Scott Xiantao Wang.

Introduction

Carmel Shachar, Julia Adler-Milstein, Daniel B. Kramer, and I. Glenn Cohen

Even prior to the COVID-19 pandemic, health care delivery was already shifting away from the clinic and into the home, utilizing telehealth, wearable sensors, ambient surveillance, and other products. Patients often prefer the convenience and comfort of care in the home, and the health system can benefit in terms of the lower cost of care. The COVID-19 pandemic further crystallized the value that can be gained when "health care comes home." Trends such as facilitating aging at home for seniors, keeping patients out of the clinic as much as possible, and telehealth have only been accelerated by the pandemic. However, this transition is not without its risks and potential unintended consequences.

So, what does this post-pandemic new world of at-home digital health care delivery look like? Patients will increasingly interact with digital products from the start of their health care journey, using wearable sensors to monitor changes in temperature or blood pressure, conducting home or self-directed testing before virtually meeting with a physician for a diagnosis, and then using smart tools to document their adherence to the prescribed treatment. Some of these products may be direct-to-consumer, while others will be designed to be integrated into the existing models of health care delivery. Some medical care may be relatively easier to translate from the clinic to the home, due to factors such as pre-existing clinician/patient relationships. Other services, such as diagnostics, may prove more complicated to shift into the home, perhaps because the individual is unaware that they might be developing a condition or because there are no established care relationships. Consider the difference in translating diabetes detection into the home, with the challenges of educating individuals about why they should test without a previous history of diabetes, and translating ongoing diabetes care, with patients who have physicians monitoring them and experience in managing their conditions.

This volume reflects on the explosion of at-home digital health care and explores the ethical and legal challenges and opportunities of this shift. These issues are substantial and complex – in part because this care can straddle the line between consumer wellness products and medical devices – but also because moving care into the home raises privacy questions and the challenge of integrating home devices with medical practices, among other issues. The integration of this new category of products will depend on the thoughtfulness and insightfulness of the solutions to these ethical and legal questions. By characterizing (and in some cases offering solutions to) these complex issues, this volume offers new insights into what it would truly mean to leave the twenty-first century focus on the clinic and the hospital for a more modern model, one of medical "touching at a distance."[1] Our volume has a significant grounding in health law and public health law, with leading legal experts exploring topics such as post-market surveillance for digital health products and the role of the FDA in ensuring safety and efficacy. But this work is not exclusively legal in nature, with social scientists, physician leaders, and political scientists also providing their analysis of digital health opportunities, challenges, and changes. The goal of this interdisciplinary volume is to identify the right questions for readers looking to engage with the ethical and regulatory implications of developments in digital diagnostics and therapeutics outside of traditional clinical settings.

A NOTE ON THE SCOPE OF THIS VOLUME

A challenge of editing this volume was defining and categorizing the domain of digital at-home health that this project examines. Digital at-home health products are proliferating, and this rapidly expanding domain covers many different technologies. There is no settled definition for "at-home digital diagnostics," and yet, it is important to demarcate the scope of the inquiry. While others might arrive at slightly different definitions, for the purposes of this book project, the term "at-home digital diagnostics" is interpreted broadly, with each constituent part understood in the following way.

At-Home: Outside of traditional health care settings. Traditional health care settings include, for example, physician offices, brick-and-mortar hospitals, medical centers, and stand-alone testing facilities. When the product is used primarily or only in these settings or locations, the definition excludes them. An in-home sleep study device would, by contrast, qualify as "at-home," as would a smartphone application, like Hyfe, an app that produces a cough report by tracking user cough patterns whenever the user initiates the app. At the same time, for our purposes, "at-home" might also include a traditional health care service, such as an office visit, if performed remotely through video or telephone.

Diagnostics: Any device that can aid in the identification of a particular disease or condition, or an event associated with that disease or condition. This definition covers not only the initial diagnosis of a particular disease or condition, but also the "diagnosis" (or identification) of events caused by a particular disease or condition. Glucose monitors, for example, would fit within this definition because they can aid

---

[1] Robert D. Truong, Of Slide Rules and Stethoscopes: AI and the Future of Doctoring, 49 *Hastings Center Report* 3 (2019).

in the diagnosis of low blood sugar, even though a patient typically uses one only *after* an initial diabetes diagnosis. The majority of the contributions in this volume focus on diagnostics, but we have also included contributions across the entire care cycle, including monitoring and therapeutics, to provide the reader with a broader sense of the implementation of digital at-home health.

This volume's special emphasis on diagnostics stems from our belief that this is an especially exciting frontier for health care. Early attempts at digital health care have tended to focus on existing patient–provider relationships, such as using video conferencing for follow-up visits. Pre-diagnostic and diagnostic digital health products have the potential to integrate health care into daily living but also to move patients into treatment and care at earlier points, improving outcomes and saving on costs. To truly revolutionize health care, digital health needs to embrace the earlier portions of the medical cycle and deliver on monitoring and diagnostics.

Digital: Significantly incorporates a novel, technology-enabled component not traditionally found in health and medical devices. A self-testing kit that allows users to view their results online would not satisfy this definition of "digital," since the digital component does not significantly alter the analog self-test. By contrast, a self-testing kit that enables the user to run a tissue sample through a machine-learning application on a phone or tablet to process the results, or to assist the user in understanding and interpreting the results, would fall within this definition. This flexible definition captures the breadth of technologies where the digital component *significantly changes* the nature of the device.

A ROADMAP FOR READERS

The book is divided into four parts. Part I, "Questions of Data Governance for Data from Digital Home Health Products," dives into the digital side of this new products category. Introduced by Carmel Shachar, these chapters demonstrate how the digital aspect of these new technologies has revolutionized at-home care. But these chapters also address the challenges raised by using data gleaned from the home. In an age where digital data streams have turned into roaring rivers, how do we respect the privacy of consumers and patients? The authors of these chapters note that the products we focus on are embedded in the home, making the data more sensitive and privacy violations more concerning. Each of the chapters in Part I provides different approaches and solutions to the unique challenge of data governance when the data is both topically sensitive (health and medical data) and situationally sensitive (coming from the home).

Barbara J. Evans opens our volume with her chapter, "In the Medical Privacy of One's Own Home: Four Faces of Privacy in Digital Home Health Care." Evans's contribution is an expansive look at the concept of privacy. She contextualizes the unique privacy challenges raised by moving the medical panopticon into the home. We chose to open our volume with this contribution to remind the reader that digital at-home health products are not simply medical devices transplanted from the hospital to the home. Instead, because they are designed for and placed within our houses, worn on our bodies, or otherwise part of our daily lives, they are a new beast entirely. Evans suggests that there is a need for legislation specifically addressing these types of products to create a new data governance scheme for at-home digital health.

Charles Duan and Christopher J. Morten's chapter, "Patient Access to Health Device Data: Toward a Legal Framework," also articulates a new data governance framework for digital at-home health products. In this chapter, the authors focus on the problem of data silos, a data governance problem that appears time and time again in the digital at-home health field as developers purposefully design wellness products and medical devices to lock data away in manufacturers' cloud services. Duan and Morten argue that limiting access to data is especially problematic when that data is health and medical data. Additionally, they are concerned that this siloing undermines medical research by preventing researchers from building "real-world evidence" data sets. Duan and Morten argue for a patients' "bill of rights" with incentives for developers to build data interoperability into their products, technical standards to promote data sharing and access, and guidelines for data aggregation.

"Challenges of Remote Patient Care Technologies under the General Data Protection Regulation: Preliminary Results of the TeNDER Project," Danaja Fabcic Povse's contribution, provides a European-focused framing to questions of data governance for digital at-home health products. Povse aims to "bridge the gap between the high-level frameworks and practical, micro-level application of these technologies by providing an overview of the challenges under European Union (EU) law when developing and using" remote care technologies. She draws upon her experience with the TeNDER project, which builds technology that alerts caregivers when patients with complex diseases, such as Parkinson's and Alzheimer's fall. Povse's work is a great example of the challenge of distilling larger data governance principles and regulatory requirements into workable guidelines for those building innovative new technologies. She acknowledges that there are tensions between particular technologies and abstract legal frameworks in general, and that it is the work of lawyers and ethicists to determine how to bridge the gap.

Jodyn Platt and Sharon Kardia provide a different sort of case study in their chapter, "Renegotiating the Social Contract for Use of Health Information: Lessons Learned from Newborn Screening and Implications for At-Home Digital Care." Platt and Kardia analyze the experience of setting up the Michigan BioTrust for Health, which included Michigan's newborn screening bloodspots, to help guide the implementation of future technologies, including at-home digital health products. Platt and Kardia use consumer preferences and expectations for the BioTrust for Health to develop recommendations for the governance of at-home digital health care products. In doing so, they draw the reader's attention to the implicit and explicit social contract between patients, providers, and developers when it comes to data use.

Part II, "Digital Home Diagnostics for Specific Conditions," introduced by Daniel B. Kramer, focuses on the application of digital at-home health products to specific conditions, namely cardiovascular disease, reproductive health, and neurodegenerative diseases. Each chapter, on its own, provides a real-world case study of the challenges and opportunities of incorporating new technologies, such as sensors, data transmission, artificial intelligence (AI), and data science, to the diagnoses, treatment, and management of a particular condition. The chapters in Part II, when read together, allow the reader to consider the commonalities and contrasts in the ethical, legal, and regulatory questions raised when these products are used to address these conditions. What questions are universal when incorporating digital health technology into the home? What questions are specific to certain conditions?

Patrik Bächtiger, Mihir A. Kelshiker, Marie E.G. Moe, Daniel B. Kramer, and Nicholas S. Peters, in their chapter, "Patient Self-Administered Screening for Cardiovascular Disease Using Artificial Intelligence in the Home," explore the application of at-home digital technologies to cardiovascular disease, using data from a UK attempt to address late or missed diagnoses of congestive heart failure. Bächtiger and his co-authors explore questions of equity, agency, data rights, and responsibility. Drawing from the UK experience, they argue that the incorporation of digital at-home technologies with the monitoring and treatment of cardiovascular disease requires a rethinking of the roles and responsibilities of each stakeholder, including patients, providers, and regulators.

Greer Donley and Rachel Rebouché, in their chapter, "The Promise of Telehealth for Abortion," likewise consider questions of equity, agency, and data governance. In their case, these questions arise in their legal and regulatory analysis of medical abortion services provided without direct in-person care. This chapter was written at a very specific point in the timeline of reproductive care regulations, shortly after the US Supreme Court declared that there was not a constitutionally protected right to an abortion in *Dobbs v. Jackson Women's Health Organization*. The reader should consider their chapter as an early response to the upheaval caused by *Dobbs* and an attempt to flag the challenges and risks borne by patients seeking abortion care and providers of abortion services. Additionally, their contribution reminds us that inviting digital health into the home can mean inviting unwanted digital surveillance into our private lives as well. Are the benefits of digital at-home health worth the invasion of privacy? As such, Donley and Rebouché's chapter harkens back to Part I, with its broader discussions of privacy and data governance.

Claire Erickson and Emily A. Largent close this section with their contribution, "Monitoring (on) Your Mind: Digital Biomarkers for Alzheimer's Disease," which explores the complexity of using digital at-home health products with Alzheimer's disease. Erickson and Largent argue that some of the questions raised by incorporating these products into the diagnosis, care, and treatment of Alzheimer's are unique because Alzheimer's affects the mind. In contrast to physical ailments, using digital surveillance for people with preclinical or clinical dementia raises unique and challenging questions around consent. Alzheimer's is also differentiated from cardiovascular disease because of the absence of effective therapies for cognitive impairment. In light of the challenges of consent and the questionable value of early detection, how do we ethically incorporate these monitoring products into everyday life?

Part III, "The Shape of the Elephant for Digital Home Diagnostics," introduced by I. Glenn Cohen, reminds us that these technologies are designed to be products, sold on the market and bought by consumers. What happens when at-home digital health products are released into the wild? How should our legal and regulatory systems monitor and manage these technologies once they have passed the research and development stages? The chapters in Part III seek to illuminate the ways we can ensure the safety and efficacy of these products, both *ex-post* and *ex-ante*. Read together, these chapters remind the reader of the breadth of tools our regulatory system has to "keep an eye" on various at-home digital health products.

David A. Simon and Aaron S. Kesselheim open Part III with their contribution, "Physician and Device Manufacturer Tort Liability for Remote Patient Monitoring Devices." Simon and Kesselheim give the reader a whirlwind tour of the US tort system. They note the value of torts as "a major tool to hold these actors [device manufacturers and physicians] accountable for injuries they cause to patients." At the heart of this chapter is the question: How can torts be used to *ex-post* regulate at-home digital health products? To answer this question, Simon and Kesselheim evaluate various regulatory pathways that could be used to bring these products to market and their implications on subsequent tort claims. They also evaluate the application of the tort system to at-home digital health products by considering the application of US tort law to various stakeholders, including prescribing physicians, patients/consumers, and others who interact with the products, such as caregivers.

Alexander O. Everhart and Ariel D. Stern use a different approach to illustrate another approach to the *ex-post* regulation of at-home digital health products in their chapter, "Post-Market Surveillance of Software Medical Devices: Evidence from Regulatory Data." Everhart and Stern explore the FDA's post-market surveillance of remote patient monitoring devices that are categorized as medical devices. They use a dataset of all 510(k)-track and premarket notification approval medical devices approved by the FDA between 2008 and 2018 to demonstrate that "software-drive medical devices" had higher rates of adverse events and recall probabilities than devices that did not have a software component. They argue that this discrepancy suggests that post-market surveillance is not sufficient for software-drive medical devices and that our regulatory system needs further tools to ensure the safety of these products as they become more and more common.

While the first two chapters in Part III focus on *ex-post* regulatory mechanisms, Sara Gerke's chapter, "Labeling of Direct-to-Consumer Medical Artificial Intelligence Applications for 'Self-Diagnosis'" considers *ex-ante* regulatory mechanisms for at-home digital health products. Gerke focuses on direct-to-consumer medical self-diagnosing artificial intelligence apps. She argues that these apps have been largely mislabeled as "information-only" rather than diagnostic tools. The mislabeling is partially by design, because manufacturers have strong regulatory incentives to present their products as information-only, despite evidence suggesting that most consumers assume these apps are actually diagnostic. Gerke suggests that direct-to-consumer apps require better labeling, reducing user confusion, but that some apps should be prescription-only. Gerke provides suggestions for how the FDA can exercise leadership in this space but also calls for a new regulatory agency to be responsible for mobile health apps.

Zhang Yi and Wang Chenguang turn the focus of Part III away from the US approach to regulating digital at-home health products to the Chinese approach in their chapter, "'Internet Plus Health Care' as an Impetus for China's Health System Reform." Chinese regulation focuses on these products as being within the continuum of health care and, therefore, properly regulated within the context of health care regulation. China has created a regulatory category, "internet plus health care" (IPHC), for these products that the chapter describes in some depth. While the authors acknowledge that there are still many open questions when it comes to regulating these products, they also note that China has successfully integrated these technologies into their health care delivery and regulatory systems. This chapter will hopefully prompt US and European readers to consider whether the FDA and its European counterparts focus perhaps too much on digital health technologies as devices, rather than as integrated tools of medical practice.

Part IV, "Reimbursement Considerations for Digital Home Health," introduced by Julia Adler-Milstein, shifts the focus from regulation to reimbursement and financing for digital at-home health products. Despite the fact that digital at-home health products are an increasingly significant part of the health care landscape, American insurers and governmental programs are still struggling to articulate consistent reimbursement policies and approaches. As one chapter in this section makes clear, European regulators and policymakers likewise struggle to articulate clear and concise reimbursement pathways for these new care modalities. Clear and consistent pathways to reimbursement are important for this product category to continue to thrive, however. But what is a workable reimbursement approach for these new technologies? The authors of the chapters in Part IV agree that the current, scatter-shot approach risks undermining the impact that digital at-home health products can have on expanding access and improving quality of care.

Stephanie Zawada, Nels Paulson, Margaret Paulson, Michael Maniaci, and Bart Demaerschalk open Part IV with "A Pathway for High-Value Home Hospital Care in the United States: Statutory, Reimbursement, and Cybersecurity Strategies in the Age of Hybrid Care." The authors draw upon their experiences at the Mayo Clinic of building a hospital at-home (H@H) program to keep lower-acuity patients at home during the COVID-19 pandemic. Zawada and her co-authors describe a program that had many benefits, including increased access, lower utilization, and easier transitions to post-acute care. They note that a critical factor in establishing and expanding this program and in making it a success was payment parity. That is, patients within the H@H program were reimbursed as if they were inpatients at the Mayo Clinic. Payment parity for telehealth and other at-home digital care modalities has been hotly contested. Here, Zawada and her co-authors argue that, while some costs are lowered by home-based care, such as the physical infrastructure costs, the increased technology and staffing needs mean that these programs are only financially workable if reimbursement is at parity with inpatient programs. This chapter is informative to the reader because it dissects a real-world experience, delivering insights on what is needed to make at-home digital health care a success overall.

Kathryn Huber and Tara Sklar also consider the necessity of payment parity and other reimbursement incentives in building up at-home digital health care in their chapter, "Digitally Enabled Medicaid Home and Community-Based Services." Huber and Sklar focus on home and community-based services (HCBS) for older adults who otherwise might be candidates for skilled nursing facilities or other institutional settings. HCBS are currently limited, and demand far outstrips supply. Technology, such as remote patient monitoring, home telehealth, and self-administered diagnostics, could help bridge this gap and support aging in place. Huber and Sklar argue that leadership from the Centers for Medicare and Medicaid is vital, especially when it comes to innovative reimbursement policies to support the incorporation of at-home digital health technologies into long-term care. Huber and Sklar also flag challenges in the utilization of digital technologies to care for aging patients, such as ensuring equitable access, the mitigation of risks, and supported decision-making.

Kaat Van Delm then directs our attention to the need for united European reimbursement policies for these technologies in her chapter, "EU In-Home Digital Diagnostics – Cross-Border Patient Reimbursement under Threat?" Cross-border reimbursement for health care remains a challenge for the EU, where telehealth cross-border reimbursement is even more complicated and poorly defined. And cross-border reimbursement for digital diagnostics is almost entirely unmapped as of yet. Van Delm explains why cross-border reimbursement of telehealth remains such a challenge under the EU regulatory scheme that must attempt to harmonize its different member states' approaches. She warns that the status quo can discourage innovation by making it difficult for developers to achieve scale by operating across the EU. She also flags that EU policymakers should consider modernizing and simplifying the legal frameworks to better support the adoption and growth of digital health, including at-home diagnostics.

CONCLUSIONS

The authors of the chapters in this volume map out the opportunities of these new products alongside the ethical, legal, and regulatory challenges of integrating new technologies that have the potential to be so disruptive. We begin this volume with some of the questions that immediately come to mind when thinking of digital health products: questions of data governance, data ownership, and privacy. We then consider three case studies of different conditions, which demonstrate that digital at-home health products have the potential to be revolutionary for a variety of medical specialties. Our attention then turns to how to regulate these products when they are released to market, using both *ex-post* and *ex-ante* approaches. Lastly, we consider an aspect that is often overlooked when people consider how to integrate digital at-home health products into the health care landscape: The need for consistent and sensible reimbursement policies. Not every question raised in this volume has an answer, but, overall, the authors of this volume provide the reader with a roadmap toward a twenty-first-century model of medicine.

At-home digital health products are vital for moving health care from a twentieth-century model of care – largely based within the physician's office or the hospital – to a twenty-first-century modality in which monitoring, diagnosis, treatment, and follow-up are integrated into daily living. The development of at-home digital health products that can monitor and diagnose is especially exciting because, until recently, most at-home digital health care efforts have focused on translating ongoing, already-established care relationships. Bringing care into the home at earlier and earlier points in the medical cycle means making health care more accessible and delivering care at earlier intervention points. But whatever the medical cycle point, this product category has the potential to be transformative at a time when labor shortages, rising costs, and limited resources mean that health care can no longer be "business as usual."

PART I

Questions of Data Governance for Data from Digital Home Health Products

Carmel Shachar

INTRODUCTION

As Barbara J. Evans quotes from Daniel Solove in her chapter in this part, "[n]ot all privacy problems are the same." Digital home health products are exciting because they use the massive amounts of data that can be generated within the home to monitor, address, and improve our health. But this powerful leveraging of data means that digital home health products raise unique privacy problems, unlike those raised by most other medical devices. Not only are these products harnessing an ocean of data about their users, but they are also uniquely drawing that data from the most sacrosanct of settings, the home. This only heightens the importance of intentional, thoughtful, comprehensive, and well-designed data governance.

The contributions in this part wrestle with questions of data governance, informed by the heightened sensitivity of recording from the home. Each chapter focuses on different questions regarding data governance. In that sense, each contribution touches on "part of the elephant." By reading these chapters, the reader may be able to see the full elephant – in this case, the challenges and opportunities inherent in data governance for digital home health products. The answers to these questions can help articulate an overall vision of data governance for data coming out of digital home health products.

Barbara J. Evans opens this part with her chapter, "In the Medical Privacy of One's Own Home: Four Faces of Privacy in Digital Home Health Care." Evans's contribution challenges the reader to deeply engage with the concept of privacy, especially as it is applied to digital home health products. She argues that digital home health products are truly different in kind from other medical devices, in part because data handlers may not have fiduciary duties limiting their use of data gleaned from these products. State legislation, particularly designed to provide individual control over information, she argues, is the answer to how we should govern data from digital home health products.

Charles Duan and Christopher J. Morten focus on the patients/users of digital home health products in their chapter, "Patient Access to Health Device Data: Toward a Legal Framework." The driving question of their work is, "Should patients have access to health device data and, if so, how should we facilitate that access?" Duan and Morten argue that intellectual property laws and policies often form a barrier to patient access to their own health data, and that a robust, administrable patients' "bill of rights" is necessary. This legal framework should have incentives and requirements for device manufacturers to share data with users, more technical standards on how this data is shared and accessed, and guidelines for how data from multiple users may be aggregated.

Whereas Evans seeks to answer, "What should data governance of digital home health products look like in the coming years?" Danaja Fabcic Povse focuses on articulating what data governance structures already exist for this product category in her contribution "Challenges of Remote Patient Care Technologies under the General Data Protection Regulation: Preliminary Results of the TeNDER Project." Povse answers the question, "What challenges does the GDPR [General Data Protection Regulation] pose for designers of remote patient care technologies (RCTs), and how can those questions be addressed in practice?" through the concrete experience of the TeNDER project, a Horizon 2020 funded work to empower patients with Alzheimer's, Parkinson's, and cardiovascular diseases, by helping them to monitor their health and manage their treatments. Povse highlights the legal challenges that developers of digital home health technologies face, including how to build consent for persons suffering from cognitive decline and the ideal terms of use for service providers working with external processors.

Jodyn Platt and Sharon Kardia focus on the question, "What lessons can be learned from newborn screening for the data governance of digital home health devices?" in their chapter, "Renegotiating the Social Contract for Use of Health Information: Lessons Learned from Newborn Screening and Implications for At-Home Digital Care." Platt and Kardia argue that many of the data governance questions raised by digital home health products were also raised by the expansion of newborn screening bloodspot programs and the organizations tasked with stewarding these databases of health information. Social norms and expectations around consent, commercialization, and governance informed the evolution of the Michigan BioTrust, which holds all the newborn bloodspots for children born in Michigan. The lessons learned by BioTrust can help to answer the questions raised by digital home health developers, users, and regulations.

How should we use the data coming from digital home health products? This is, at first glance, a straightforward, simple question. But, as the authors of the chapters in this section demonstrate, this question is not so easily answered. By focusing on smaller questions – What access should patients have to their own data? Does the GDPR provide enough data governance guidance to developers? – we can begin to build a comprehensive vision of a data-governance structure that can protect users while also facilitating innovation.

1

In the Medical Privacy of One's Own Home

Four Faces of Privacy in Digital Home Health Care[*]

Barbara J. Evans

I INTRODUCTION

Digital tools to diagnose and treat patients in the home: The phrase hits several tripwires, each sounding its own privacy alarm. Invading the "castle" of a person's home is one privacy tripwire.[1] Sustained digital surveillance of the individual is another. Anything to do with personal health information is still another. Each alarm calls attention to a different strand of privacy law, each with its own account of why privacy matters and how to protect it. No overarching conception of privacy leaps out, which calls to mind Daniel Solove's remark that "the law has attempted to adhere to overarching conceptions of privacy that do not work for all problems. Not all privacy problems are the same."[2]

This chapter explores four faces of privacy: (1) Privacy of the home, which links privacy to the location where information is created or captured; (2) privacy as individual control over personal information, without regard to location, in an age of pervasive digital surveillance; (3) contextual privacy frameworks, such as medical privacy laws addressing the use and sharing of data in a specific context: clinical health care; and (4) content-based privacy, unmoored from location or context and, instead, tied to inherent data characteristics (e.g., sensitive data about health, sexual behavior, or paternity, versus nonsensitive data about food preferences). The hope here is to find a workable way to express what is special (or not) about digital tools for diagnosis and treatment in the home.

---

[*] The author thanks the Health Policy and Bioethics Consortium of Harvard Medical School and the Harvard Law School Petrie-Flom Center for the opportunity to receive feedback on an early draft of this chapter at the February 11, 2022 virtual meeting entitled, "Diagnosing Alzheimer's with Alexa?" The author has no conflicts to disclose.
[1] See Eric R. Claeys, Kelo, the Castle, and Natural Property Rights, in *Private Property, Community Development, and Eminent Domain* 35, 35–36 (Robin Paul Malloy ed., 2008) (discussing the metaphor of the home as one's castle).
[2] Daniel J. Solove, Conceptualizing Privacy, 90 Calif. L. Rev. 1087, 1147 (2002).

II THE PRIVACY OF THE HOME

An "interest in spatial privacy" feels violated as the home – the "quintessential place of privacy" – becomes a site of digital medical observation and surveillance.[3] Yet electronic home health monitoring originated decades ago, which invites the question of what has sparked sudden concern about digital home health privacy now.

Past experience with home diagnostics clarifies the privacy challenge today. In 1957, Dr. Norman J. Holter and his team developed an ambulatory electrocardiograph system, building on the 1890s string galvanometer for which Willem Einthoven won the 1924 Nobel Prize.[4] The resulting wearable device, known as a Holter monitor, records electrocardiographic signals as heart patients go about their routine activities at home and, since 1961, has been the backbone of cardiac rhythm detection and analysis outside the hospital.[5] Six decades of at-home use of this and similar devices have passed without notable privacy incidents.

There is a distinction that explains why traditional home diagnostics like Holter monitors were not controversial from a privacy standpoint, while today's digital home health tools potentially are. Jack Balkin stresses that "certain kinds of information constitute matters of private concern" not because of details like the content or location, "but because of the *social relationships* that produce them."[6] For example, an injured driver receiving care from an ambulance crew at the side of a road should not be filmed and displayed on the evening news – not because the person is in a private location (which a public highway is not), but because the person is in a medical treatment relationship at the time.[7] It is *"relationships* – relationships of trust and confidence – that governments may regulate in the interests of privacy."[8]

Traditional devices like Holter monitors are prescribed in a treatment relationship by a physician who refers the patient to a laboratory that fits the device and instructs the patient how to use it. After a set period of observation, the patient returns the device to the laboratory, which downloads and analyzes the data stored on the device and conveys the results to the ordering physician. Everyone touching the data is in a health care relationship, bound by a web of general health care laws and norms that place those who handle people's health information under duties of confidentiality.[9]

---

[3] Julie Cohen, Privacy, Visibility, Transparency, and Exposure, 75 U. Chi. L. Rev. 181, 190–91 (2008); Solove, supra note 2, at 1137.
[4] Ateeq Mubarik & Arshad Muhammad Iqbal, Holter Monitor, *StatPearls* (2022), www.ncbi.nlm.nih.gov/books/NBK538203/. See also Moises Rivera-Ruiz et al., Einthoven's String Galvanometer: The First Electrocardiograph, 35 Tex. Heart Inst. J. 174 (2008).
[5] Mubarik & Iqbal, supra note 4.
[6] Jack M. Balkin, Information Fiduciaries and the First Amendment, 49 UC Davis L. Rev. 1183, 1205 (2016).
[7] *Shulman v. Group W Prods., Inc.*, 955 P.2d 469 (Cal. 1998).
[8] Balkin, supra note 6, at 1187.
[9] Barry R. Furrow et al., *Health Law: Cases, Materials and Problems* (8th edn.) 117 (2018).

These duties flow less from privacy law than from general health care laws and norms predating modern concerns about information privacy. For example, state licensing statutes for health care professionals focus mainly on their competence but also set norms of confidentiality, enforceable through disciplinary sanctions and the potential loss of licensure.[10] Professional ethics standards, such as those of the American Medical Association, amplify the legally enforceable duties of confidentiality.[11] State medical records laws govern the collection, use, and retention of data from medical treatment encounters and specify procedures for sharing the records and disposing of or transferring them when a care relationship ends.[12] State courts enforce common law duties for health care providers to protect the confidential information they hold.[13]

Jack Balkin's first law of fair governance in an algorithmic society is that those who deploy data-dependent algorithms should be "information fiduciaries" with respect to their clients, customers, and end-users.[14] Traditional health care providers meet this requirement. The same is not always (or perhaps ever) true of the new generation of digital tools used to diagnose and treat patients at home. The purveyors of these devices include many new players – such as medical device manufacturers, software developers and vendors, and app developers – not subject to the confidentiality duties that the law imposes on health care professionals, clinics, and hospitals.

The relationships consumers will forge with providers of digital home health tools are still evolving but seem unlikely to resemble the relationships of trust seen in traditional health care settings. Responsibility for protecting the data generated and collected by digital home health devices defaults, in many instances, to vendor-drafted privacy policies and terms of service. Scott Peppet's survey of twenty popular consumer sensor devices found these privacy protections to be weak, inconsistent, and ambiguous.[15]

Nor is the privacy of the home a helpful legal concept here. As conceived in American jurisprudence, the privacy of the home is a Fourth Amendment protection against governmental intrusion to gather evidence for criminal proceedings.[16] This has little relevance to a private-sector medical device manufacturer or software

---

[10] Id.
[11] See, for example, Am. Med. Ass'n, Code of Medical Ethics Opinion 3.2.1: Confidentiality, https://code-medical-ethics.ama-assn.org/ethics-opinions/confidentiality.
[12] See P. Jon White & Jodi Daniel, *Privacy and Security Solutions for Interoperable Health Information Exchange: Report on State Medical Record Access Laws* (2009), www.healthit.gov/sites/default/files/290-05-0015-state-law-access-report-1.pdf (providing a multistate survey of various aspects of state medical records laws).
[13] Furrow et al., supra note 9, at 161.
[14] Jack M. Balkin, The Three Laws of Robotics in the Age of Big Data, 78 Ohio State L. J. 1217, 1221 (2017).
[15] Scott R. Peppet, Regulating the Internet of Things: First Steps Toward Managing Discrimination, Privacy, Security, and Consent, 93 Tex. L. Rev. 85, 145 (2014).
[16] Laura K. Donahue, The Fourth Amendment in a Digital World, 71 NYU Ann. Surv. Am. L. 553, 562–68 (2017).

vendor offering home diagnostic tools that gather personal health data that could be repurposed for research or a variety of other commercial uses that threaten users' privacy. The Fourth Amendment occasionally might be helpful – for example, if the government seeks data from a home diagnostic device to refute a user's alibi that she was at home at the time she stands accused of a crime at a different location. Unfortunately, this misses the vast majority of privacy concerns with at-home medical monitoring: Could identifiable health data leak to employers, creditors, and friends in ways that might stigmatize or embarrass the individual? Might data be diverted to unauthorized commercial uses that exploit, offend, or outrage the person the data describe? The Fourth Amendment leaves us on our own to solve such problems.

The privacy of the home enters this discussion more as a cultural expectation than as a legal reality. The home as a site of retreat and unobserved, selfhood-enhancing pursuits is a fairly recent innovation, reflecting architectural innovations such as hallways, which became common in the eighteenth century and eliminated the need for every member of the household to traverse one's bedroom to get to their own.[17] The displacement of servants by nongossiping electrical appliances bolstered domestic privacy, as did the great relocation of work from the home to offices and factories late in the nineteenth century.[18] The privacy of the home is historically contingent. It may be evolving in response to COVID-19-inspired work-from-home practices but, at least for now, the cultural expectation of privacy at home remains strong.

This strong expectation does not translate into a strong framework of legal protections. Private parties admitted to one's home are generally unbound by informational fiduciary duties and are free to divulge whatever they learn while there. As if modeled on a Fourth Amendment "consent search," the host consents at the point when observers enter the home but, once there, they are free to use and share information they collect without further consent. The privacy of the home, in practice, is protected mainly by choosing one's friends carefully and disinviting the indiscreet. The question is whether this same "let-the-host-beware" privacy scheme should extend to private actors whose digital home health tools we invite into our homes.

III PRIVACY AS INDIVIDUAL CONTROL OVER IDENTIFIABLE INFORMATION

Many privacy theorists reject spatial metaphors, such as the privacy of the home, in favor of a view that privacy is a personal right for individuals to control data about themselves.[19] After the 1970s, this "control-over-information" privacy theory became

---

[17] Solove, supra note 2, at 1140.
[18] Id.
[19] Id. at 1109–12. See also Ferdinand David Schoeman, Privacy: Philosophical Dimensions of the Literature, in *Philosophical Dimensions of Privacy: An Anthology* 1, 3 (Ferdinand David Schoeman ed., 1984).

the "leading paradigm on the Internet and in the real, or off-line world."[20] It calls for people – without regard to where they or their information happen to be located – to receive notice of potential data uses and to be granted a right to approve or decline such uses.

This view is so widely held today that it enjoys a status resembling a religious belief or time-honored principle. Few people recall its surprisingly recent origin. In 1977, a Privacy Protection Study Commission formed under the Privacy Act of 1974 found that it was quite common to use people's health data in biomedical research without consent and recommended that consent should be sought.[21] That recommendation was widely embraced by bioethicists and by the more recent *Information Privacy Law Project* on the ethics of data collection and use by retailers, lenders, and other nonmedical actors in modern "surveillance societies."[22]

Control-over-information theory has its critics. An obvious concern is that consent may be ill-informed as consumers hastily click through the privacy policies and terms of use that stand between them and a desired software tool. In a recent survey, 97 percent Americans recalled having been asked to agree to a company's privacy policy, but only 9 percent indicated that they always read the underlying policy to which they are agreeing (and, frankly, 9 percent sounds optimistic).[23] Will people who consent to bring digital health devices into their homes carefully study the privacy policies to which they are consenting? It seems implausible.

A more damning critique is that consent, even when well-informed, does not actually protect privacy. A person who freely consents to broadcast a surgery or sexual encounter live over the Internet exercises control over their information but is foregoing what most people think of as privacy.[24] Notice-and-consent privacy schemes can be likened to the "dummy thermostats" in American office skyscrapers – fake thermostats that foster workplace harmony by giving workers the illusion that they can control their office temperature, which, in fact, is set centrally, with as many as 90 percent of the installed thermostats lacking any connection to the heating and air-conditioning system.[25] Consent norms foster societal harmony by

---

[20] Paul M. Schwartz, Internet Privacy and the State, 32 Conn. L. Rev. 815, 820 (2000).
[21] 5 USC § 552(a) and (d); Priv. Prot. Study Comm'n, *Personal Privacy in an Information Society* 280 (1977), https://archive.epic.org/privacy/ppsc1977report/.
[22] See, for example, Federal Policy for the Protection of Human Subjects of Biomedical Research ("Common Rule"), 45 CFR §§ 46.101–124 (2018); see, for example, Neil Richards, The Information Privacy Law Project, 94 Geo. L.J. 1087 (2006) and David Lyon, Surveillance Society: Monitoring Everyday Life, 33–35, 114–18 (2001).
[23] Brooke Auxier et al., Americans' Attitudes and Experiences with Privacy Policies and Laws, *Pew Rsch. Ctr.* (2019), www.pewresearch.org/internet/2019/11/15/americans-attitudes-and-experiences-with-privacy-policies-and-laws/.
[24] Anita L. Allen, Privacy-as-Data Control: Conceptual, Practical, and Moral Limits of the Paradigm, 32 Conn. L. Rev., 861, 867 (2000).
[25] See Barbara J. Evans, The HIPAA Privacy Rule at Age 25: Privacy for Equitable AI, 50 Fla. State U. L. Rev., 781–82(2023) (citing investigative reports on dummy thermostats).

giving people the illusion that they can control their privacy risks, but, in reality, consent rights are disconnected from privacy and, indeed, exercising consent rights *relinquishes* privacy.

The loss of privacy is systemic in modern information economies: It is built into the way the economy and society work, and there is little an individual can do. Privacy is interdependent, and other people's autonomous decisions to share information about themselves can reveal facts about you.[26] Bioethicists recognize this interdependency in a number of specific contexts. For example, genomic data can reveal a disease-risk status that is shared with one's family members,[27] and, for Indigenous people, individual consent to research can implicate the tribal community as a whole by enabling statistical inferences affecting all members.[28]

Less well recognized is the fact that, in a world of large-scale, generalizable data analytics, privacy interdependency is not unique to genetically related families and tribal populations. It potentially affects everyone. When results are generalizable, you do not necessarily need to be reflected in the input data in order for a system to discover facts about you.[29] If people like you consent to be studied, a study can reveal facts about you, even if you opted out.

Biomedical science aims for generalizability and strives to reduce biases that cause scientific results not to be valid for everyone. These are worthy goals, but they carry a side effect: Greater generalizability boosts systemic privacy loss and weakens the power of consent as a shield against unwanted outside access to personal facts. Whether you consent or refuse to share whatever scraps of personal data you still control, others can know things about you because you live in a society that pursues large-scale data analytics and strives to make the results ever-more generalizable, including to you. Just as antibiotics cease to work over time as microbes evolve and grow smarter at eluding them, so consent inexorably loses its ability to protect privacy as algorithms grow smarter, less biased, and more clever at surmising your missing data.

There is another concern with notice-and-consent privacy schemes in biomedical contexts, where the problem of bias has been empirically studied more than in some other sectors. Selection bias occurs when the people included in a study fail to reflect the entire population that, ultimately, will rely on results from that study.[30]

---

[26] Gergely Biczók & Pern Hui Chia, Interdependent Privacy: Let Me Share Your Data, in *Financial Cryptography and Data Security* 338 (Ahmad-Reza Sadeghi ed., 2013).

[27] Marwan K. Tayeh et al., The Designated Record Set for Clinical Genetic and Genomic Testing: A Points to Consider Statement of the American College of Medical Genetics and Genomics (ACMG), 25 Genet. Med. (2022).

[28] Krystal S. Tsosie et al., Overvaluing Individual Consent Ignores Risks to Tribal Participants, 20 Nat. Revs. Genetics 497 (2019).

[29] Cynthia Dwork et al., Calibrating Noise to Sensitivity in Private Data Analysis, in *Theory of Cryptography. TCC 2006. Lecture Notes in Computer Science* vol. 3876, 265 (S. Halevi & T. Rabin eds., 2006).

[30] James J. Heckman, Selection Bias, in *Encyclopedia of Social Measurement* (2005).

Consent norms can produce selection bias if some demographic groups – for example, older white males – consent more eagerly than other groups do. People's willingness to consent to secondary data uses of their health data varies among racial, ethnic, and other demographic groups.[31] If digital home health tools are trained using data acquired with consent, those tools may be biased in ways that cause them to deliver unreliable results and health care recommendations for members of historically underrepresented population subgroups, such as women and the less affluent.[32] Consent norms can fuel health care disparities. Admittedly, this is only one of many equity concerns with digital home health tools. The more salient concern, obviously, is whether these tools will be available to nonprivileged members of society *at all*. Many of these tools are commercially sold on a self-pay basis with no safety net to ensure access by those who cannot pay.

In October 2022, the White House published its *Blueprint for an AI Bill of Rights*, recommending a notice-and-consent privacy scheme in which "designers, developers, and deployers of automated systems" must "seek your permission" to use data in an artificial intelligence (AI) system.[33] It simultaneously calls for AI tools to be "used and designed in an equitable way" that avoids disparities in how the tools perform for different population subgroups.[34] In domains where selection bias is well-documented,[35] as in health care, these two goals may clash.

IV MEDICAL PRIVACY LAW

One possibility for regulating AI/machine learning (ML) home health tools would be to place them under the same medical privacy regulations – for example, the Health Insurance Portability and Accountability Act (HIPAA) Privacy Rule,[36] a major US medical privacy framework – used for data generated in clinical health care settings. This section argues against doing so.

---

[31] Kayte Spector-Bagdady, Governing Secondary Research Use of Health Data and Specimens: The Inequitable Distribution of Regulatory Burden Between Federally Funded and Industry Research, 8 J. L. & Biosciences 1, 2–3 (2021); Reshma Jagsi et al., Perspectives of Patients with Cancer on the Ethics of Rapid-Learning Health Systems, 35 J. Clinical Oncology 2315, 2321 (2017); Christine L. M. Joseph et al., Demographic Differences in Willingness to Share Electronic Health Records in the All of Us Research Program, 29 J. Am. Med. Informatics Ass'n 1271 (2022).
[32] US Gov't Accountability Off., GAO-21-7SP, *Artificial Intelligence in Health Care: Benefits and Challenges of Technologies to Augment Patient Care* 24 (2020).
[33] The White House Off. of Sci. & Tech. Pol'y, *Blueprint for an AI Bill of Rights: Making Automated Systems Work for the American People* 5, 26–27 (2022), www.whitehouse.gov/ostp/ai-bill-of-rights/.
[34] Id.
[35] See Brian Buckley et al., Selection Bias Resulting from the Requirement for Prior Consent in Observational Research: A Community Cohort of People with Ischaemic Heart Disease, 93 Heart 1116 (2007); Sharyl J. Nass et al. (eds.), Comm. on Health Rsch. & the Priv. of Health Info.: The HIPAA Priv. Rule, *Beyond the HIPAA Privacy Rule: Enhancing Privacy, Improving Health Through Research* 209–14 (2009), www.nap.edu/catalog/12458.html (surveying studies of consent and selection bias).
[36] 45 CFR pts. 160 and 164.

Medical privacy law rejects control-over-information theory in favor of "privacy's other path" – confidentiality law,[37] a duty-based approach that places health care providers under duties to handle data carefully.[38] The HIPAA Privacy Rule does not itself impose any confidentiality duties. It does not need to do so, because it regulates one specific context – clinical health care – where most of the "covered entities"[39] it regulates have confidentiality duties under state law.[40]

The Privacy Rule is best modeled as what Helen Nissenbaum refers to as a contextual privacy scheme.[41] It states a set of "informational norms" – data-sharing practices that have been deemed permissible in and around clinical health care.[42] The Privacy Rule allows protected health information (PHI) to be disclosed after de-identification or individual authorization (HIPAA's name for consent).[43] This leads casual observers to think that it is a notice-and-consent privacy scheme, but it then goes on to state twenty-three additional rules allowing disclosure of PHI, often in identifiable formats, without consent but subject to various alternative privacy protections that, at times, are not as strong as one might wish.[44]

Where medical privacy is concerned, the European Union (EU)'s General Data Protection Regulation (GDPR) is more like the HIPAA Privacy Rule than most Americans realize. It grants leeway for the twenty-seven EU member states, when regulating data privacy in clinical health care settings, to go higher or *lower* than the GDPR's baseline consent standard.[45] A 2021 report for the European Commission

---

[37] Neil M. Richards & Daniel J. Solove, Privacy's Other Path: Recovering the Law of Confidentiality, 96 Geo. L.J. 123 (2007).
[38] See supra notes 9–13 and accompanying text.
[39] See 45 CFR § 160.102 (2018) (providing that the HIPAA regulations, including the Privacy Rule, apply to health care providers, such as physicians, clinics, hospitals, laboratories, and various other entities, such as insurers, that transmit "any health information in electronic form in connection with a transaction covered by this subchapter [the Administrative Simplification provisions of HIPAA]" and to their business associates); see also id. § 160.103 (defining the terms "covered entity" and "business associate").
[40] See Furrow et al., supra note 9.
[41] See Helen Nissenbaum, *Privacy in Context: Technology, Policy, and the Integrity of Social Life* (2010); Helen Nissenbaum, Privacy as Conceptual Integrity, 79 Wash. L. Rev. 119 (2004); Adam Barth et al., Privacy and Contextual Integrity: Framework and Applications, in *Proceedings of the 2006 IEEE Symposium on Security and Privacy* 184 (2006).
[42] See Evans, supra note 25, at 749–50, tbl. 1 (elaborating these norms). See also Letter from William W. Stead, Chair, Nat'l Comm. on Vital & Health Stat., to Hon. Sylvia M. Burwell, Secretary, U.S. Dep't of Health & Hum. Servs. app. A at 15–19 (November 9, 2016), www.ncvhs.hhs.gov/wp-content/uploads/2013/12/2016-Ltr-Privacy-Minimum-Necessary-formatted-on-ltrhead-Nov-9-FINAL-w-sig.pdf (https://perma.cc/J7DF-X9VP).
[43] 45 CFR § 164.502(d) (2013); see 45 CFR § 160.103 (defining "protected health information" (PHI, the information that the HIPAA Privacy Rule protects) as "individually identifiable health information" and defining the term "health information" for the purposes of the HIPAA Privacy Rule). See 45 CFR§ 164.502(a)(1)(iv) (allowing PHI to be released with individual authorization). See also id. at § 164.508 (describing the requirements for a valid individual authorization, which is HIPAA's term for a consent).
[44] Evans, supra note 25, at 749–50, tbl. 1.
[45] See Regulation 2016/679 of the European Parliament and of the Council of April 27, 2016 on the Protection of Natural Persons with Regard to the Processing of Personal Data and on the Free

summarized member state medical privacy laws, which replicate many of the same unconsented data flows that the HIPAA Privacy Rule allows.[46]

The bottom line is that when you enter the clinical health care setting – whether in the United States or elsewhere – you will only have limited control over your information. A certain amount of data sharing is necessary to support the contextual goals of health care: For example, saving the life of a patient whose symptoms resemble yours by sharing your data with their physician; conducting medical staff peer review to rout out bad doctors; tracking epidemics; detecting child abuse; enabling the dignified burial of the deceased; and monitoring the safety of FDA-approved medical products. Your data can be used, with or without your consent, to do these and many other things considered essential for the proper functioning of the health care system and of society.

Notably, the HIPAA Privacy Rule takes no position on individual data ownership, so state medical records laws that vest the ownership of medical records in health care providers are not "less stringent" than HIPAA and, thus, are not preempted.[47] In many states, providers legally own their medical records, subject to various patient interests (such as confidentiality and patient access rights) in the data contained in those records.[48] Some states clarify provider ownership in their state medical records acts; others reach this conclusion through case law.[49] Only New Hampshire deems the medical information in medical records to be the property of the patient,[50] and a handful of states provide for individuals to own their genetic information.[51]

Movement of Such Data and Repealing Directive 95/46/EC, OJ 2016 No. L 119, 1. See GDPR art. 6 (requiring consent for the processing of personal data, id. § 1(a), but allowing unconsented processing for various purposes such as legal compliance, "to protect the vital interests of the data subject or another natural person," for tasks "carried out in the public interest," see id. §§ 1(b)–(f), and allowing member states to specify provisions "to adapt the applications of the rules" in some of these circumstances). See GDPR art. 9 (addressing the processing of "special categories of personal data," which include health data and requiring consent, id. § 2(a), but allowing member states to establish different conditions and safeguards for data used in "preventive or occupational medicine, for the assessment of the working capacity of the employee, medical diagnosis, the provision of health or social care or treatment, or the management of health or social care systems and services," id. § 2(h), and for public health, id. § 2(i), and for public interest purposes including scientific research, id. § 2(j)). See also GDPR art. 89 (allowing member state law to derogate from the various rights provided by the GDPR when those "rights are likely to render impossible or seriously impair the achievement" of various public-interest goals including scientific research).

[46] Johan Hansen et al., *Assessment of the EU Member States' Rules on Health Data in the Light of GDPR*, Eur. Comm'n, Specific Contract No. SC 2019 70 02 (in the context of the Single Framework Contract Chafea/2018/Health/03) (2021), https://health.ec.europa.eu/system/files/2021-02/ms_rules_health-data_en_0.pdf.

[47] See 45 CFR §§ 160.202–.203 (Privacy Rule preemption provisions).

[48] See Am. Health Laws. Ass'n, *Health Law Practice Guide* § 4:11 (2022).

[49] See, for example, *Pyramid Life Ins. Co. v. Masonic Hosp. Ass'n of Payne Cty.*, 191 F. Supp. 51 (W.D. Okla., 1961).

[50] Am. Health Laws. Ass'n, supra note 54.

[51] See Jessica L. Roberts, *Progressive Data Ownership*, 93 Notre Dame L. Rev. 1105, 1128 (2018) (citing five states' genetic data ownership statutes).

What could go wrong if purveyors of digital home health devices were added to the list of covered entities governed by the HIPAA Privacy Rule? The Privacy Rule relies on an underlying framework of state laws to place its covered entities under duties of confidentiality.[52] Many sellers of home health devices are not bound by those laws. Without those laws, the Privacy Rule's liberal norms of data sharing could allow too much unauthorized data sharing.

Similar problems arose after 2013, when "business associates" were added to the list of HIPAA-covered entities.[53] Many business associates – such as software service providers offering contract data-processing services to hospitals – fall outside the scope of the state health laws that place health care providers under duties of confidentiality. The amended Privacy Rule did not address this problem adequately, leaving an ongoing privacy gap.[54]

Placing business associates – or, by analogy, digital home health care providers – under strong duties of confidentiality seemingly requires legal reforms at the state level. Federal solutions, such as HIPAA reforms or the proposed AI Bill of Rights, are not, by themselves, sufficient.

V CONTENT-BASED PRIVACY PROTECTION

A uniform scheme of content-based privacy regulations stratifies the level of privacy protection based on inherent data characteristics (e.g., data about health) without regard to where in the overall economy the data are held. The fact that Sally is pregnant receives the same protection whether it came from a home pregnancy test, a clinical diagnostic test, or a Target™ store's AI marketing algorithm.[55] This reasoning has strong superficial appeal, but there may be good reasons to distinguish health-related inferences drawn within and outside the clinical care context.

Some factors justify *stronger* privacy protections for digital home health data than for clinical health data. In clinical settings, most (not all) unconsented HIPAA data disclosures go to information fiduciaries, such as health care professionals, courts, and governmental agencies subject to the federal Privacy Act. In home care settings, the baseline assumption is that the users and recipients of people's digital health data are not information fiduciaries, which strengthens the case for strong individual control over data disclosures.

---

[52] See supra notes 9–13 and accompanying text.
[53] See US Dep't of Health & Hum. Servs., *Direct Liability of Business Associates* (July 16, 2021) www.hhs.gov/hipaa/for-professionals/privacy/guidance/business-associates/factsheet/index.html (discussing 2013 revisions to the HIPAA Privacy Rule).
[54] See Jim Hawkins et al., Non-Transparency in Electronic Health Record Systems, in *Transparency in Health and Health Care in the United States* 273, 281 (Holly Fernandez Lynch et al. eds., 2019).
[55] Charles Duhigg, How Companies Learn Your Secrets, *The New York Times Magazine* (February 16, 2012).

There can be important differences in data quality. Data generated in clinical settings is subject to regulatory and professional standards aimed at ensuring data quality and accuracy. Data generated by home health devices does not always meet these same quality standards. Digital home health data might be inaccurate, so that its release is not only stigmatizing but defamatory (false). Again, this counsels in favor of strong consent norms. Other factors might cut the other way.

The EU's GDPR and the California Consumer Privacy Act are sometimes cited as consistent, content-based privacy schemes.[56] Such schemes could offer consistency in a home care system where licensed professionals, nonmedical caregivers, and commercial device companies are all differently regulated. Yet these laws are inferior to the HIPAA Privacy Rule in various respects. An important example is the treatment of inferential knowledge. Under the GDPR, people have access to their raw personal input data but can have trouble accessing inferences drawn from those data.[57] Wachter and Mittelstadt note that "individuals are granted little control or oversight over how their personal data is used to draw inferences about them" and their "rights to know about (Articles 13–15), rectify (Article 16), delete (Article 17), object to (Article 21), or port (Article 20) personal data are significantly curtailed for inferences."[58]

The GDPR recognizes the legitimacy of competing claims to inferential knowledge. Inferences are not just a product of the input data from which they were derived, so that an inference "belongs" to the person it describes. Data handlers invest their own effort, skills, and expertise to draw inferences. They, too, have legitimate claims to control the inference. In contrast, the HIPAA Privacy Rule grants individuals a right to inspect, to obtain a copy of, and to request correction of not only their raw personal data (e.g., medical images and test results), but also the medical opinions and inferences drawn from those data.[59] This is the only informational norm in the HIPAA Privacy Rule that is mandatory: Covered entities *must* provide people with such access if they request it. The point of this example is that fact-specific analysis is needed before jumping to policy conclusions about which framework is better or worse for digital home health care.

VI CONCLUSION

This chapter ends where it began, with Solove's insight that "[n]ot all privacy problems are the same." The modern generation of digital home health devices raises novel privacy concerns. Reaching for solutions devised for other contexts – such as

---

[56] See supra note 45 (GDPR); California Consumer Privacy Act of 2018, Cal. Civ. Code § 1798.100–.199.
[57] See generally Sandra Wachter & Brent Mittelstadt, A Right to Reasonable Inferences: Re-thinking Data Protection Law in the Age of Big Data and AI, 2019 Colum. Bus. L. Rev. 494 (2018).
[58] Id. at 494–95.
[59] See 45 CFR §§ 164.524 and .526.

expanding the HIPAA Privacy Rule to cover digital home health providers or cloning the GDPR – may yield suboptimal policies. Consent norms, increasingly, are understood to afford weak data-privacy protections. That is especially true in digital home health care, where consent rights are not reliably backstopped by fiduciary duties limiting what data handlers can do with health data collected in people's homes. State legislation to set fiduciary duties for digital home health providers may, ultimately, be a better place to focus than on new federal privacy policies. Medical privacy law reminds us that achieving quality health care – in any context – requires an openness to responsible data sharing. Will those needed data flows exist in a world of privately sponsored digital home health tools whose sellers hoard data as a private commercial asset? The goal of a home health privacy framework is not merely to protect individual privacy; it also must enable the data flows needed to ensure high-quality care in the home health setting. At the same time, the "wild west" environment of digital home health might justify a greater degree of individual control over information than has been customary in traditional clinical care settings. Forging a workable consensus will require hard work, and the work has only just begun.

2

Patient Access to Health Device Data

Toward a Legal Framework

Charles Duan and Christopher J. Morten

I INTRODUCTION

The connected at-home health care device industry is booming.[1] Wearable health trackers alone constituted a $21 billion market in 2020, anticipated to grow to $195 billion by 2027.[2] At-home devices now purportedly make it possible to diagnose and monitor health conditions, such as sleep apnea, diabetes, and fertility, automatically, immediately, and discreetly. By design, these devices produce a wealth of data that can inform patients of their health status and potentially even recommend life-saving actions.[3]

But patients and their health care providers often lack access to this data.[4] Manufacturers typically design connected at-home devices to store data in cloud services run by the manufacturers themselves, requiring device owners to register accounts and accept the terms of use and limitations that the manufacturers impose. A recent survey of 222 mobile "app families" associated with wellness devices found that 64.4 percent "did not report sharing any data" with other apps or services.[5] A parent testified in Congress as to how a lack of data access impaired his daughter's ability

---

[1] See, for example, Erin Brodwin, Remote Monitoring Is Rapidly Growing – and a New Class of Patient-Consumer Is Driving the Shift, STAT (September 16, 2020), www.statnews.com/2020/09/16/remote-patient-monitoring-stat-report/; Sarah Krouse, Covid-19 Pandemic Drives Patients – and Deal Makers – to Telemedicine, *The Wall Street Journal* (August 25, 2020), www.wsj.com/articles/covid-19-pandemic-drives-patients-to-telemedicine-deal-makers-too-11598358823.

[2] Fortune Business Insights, Wearable Medical Devices Market Size Worth USD 195.57 Bn by 2027, *GlobeNewswire* (March 2, 2022), www.globenewswire.com/news-release/2022/02/03/2378221/0/en/Wearable-Medical-Devices-Market-Size-worth-USD-195-57-Bn-by-2027-With-stunning-26-4-CAGR.html.

[3] I. Glenn Cohen, Sara Gerke, & Daniel B. Kramer, Ethical and Legal Implications of Remote Monitoring of Medical Devices, 98 Milbank Q. 1257, 1259 (2020).

[4] See, for example, id. at 1266–67; John T. Wilbanks & Eric J. Topol, Stop the Privatization of Health Data, 535 Nature 345, 347 (2016); Elizabeth A. Rowe, Sharing Data, 104 Iowa L. Rev. 287 (2018).

[5] Quinn Grundy et al., Tracing the Potential Flow of Consumer Data: A Network Analysis of Prominent Health and Fitness Apps, 19 J. Med. Internet Res. e233, at 4 (2017).

to manage Type I diabetes,[6] and patients with sleep apnea have had to circumvent technological device locks to extract data on their own sleep.[7] Many medical and wellness devices that patients use for in-home diagnosis and monitoring – which we simply call "health devices" – lock patients into manufacturers' ecosystems. This limits patients', and society's, ability to tap into the full value of the data, despite the extensive individual and social benefits that access could provide.

The problem here is not solely technical; it is also legal. Existing law in the United States provides patients with no guarantee of access to their data when it is generated and stored outside the traditional health care system. The Health Insurance Portability and Accountability Act (HIPAA) provides patients a legally enforceable right of access to copies of their electronic health records (EHRs), and, in recent years, the Department of Health and Human Services (HHS) has moved to make this right enforceable and meaningful.[8] But as HHS itself has observed about health devices and other "mHealth" technologies used outside the EHR ecosystem, manufacturers "are not obligated by a statute or regulation to provide individuals with access to data about themselves," so patients with data on such devices "may not have the ability to later obtain a copy."[9]

This chapter begins by identifying the individual and societal benefits of patient access to health device data. It then addresses the arguments for restricting such access, especially those based on intellectual property laws and policies. We conclude that such arguments are ultimately doctrinally and normatively unconvincing, such that they should not dissuade legislatures and federal agencies from legislating or regulating rights of access. We then consider what can and should be done to create a robust, administrable right of patients to access health device data that protects all stakeholders' interests, and we offer a nascent framework that draws from other regimes for patient and consumer access to personal information. We hope the framework will guide legislatures and regulators as they begin to address this important issue.

II BENEFITS OF PATIENT ACCESS

There are important individual and societal benefits when patients can access their own health data. Foremost for individuals is the fulfillment of patient autonomy

---

[6] Smart Health: Empowering the Future of Mobile Applications, Hearing Before the Subcomm. on Rsch. & Tech. of the H. Comm. on Sci., Space and Tech., 114th Cong. 43–44 (2016) (testimony of Howard Look).

[7] Jason Koebler, Why Sleep Apnea Patients Rely on a CPAP Machine Hacker, Vice News (November 15, 2018), www.vice.com/en/article/xwjd4w/im-possibly-alive-because-it-exists-why-sleep-apnea-patients-rely-on-a-cpap-machine-hacker.

[8] See, for example, press release, US Dep't of Health and Human Svcs. (HHS), Five Enforcement Actions Hold Healthcare Providers Accountable for HIPAA Right of Access (November 30, 2021), www.healthit.gov/sites/default/files/non-covered_entities_report_june_17_2016.pdf (on HHS Office of Civil Rights' HIPAA Right of Access Initiative).

[9] HHS, Examining Oversight of the Privacy & Security of Health Data Collected by Entities Not Regulated by HIPAA (2020), https://perma.cc/2JZU-DQJF.

2

Patient Access to Health Device Data

Toward a Legal Framework

Charles Duan and Christopher J. Morten

I INTRODUCTION

The connected at-home health care device industry is booming.[1] Wearable health trackers alone constituted a $21 billion market in 2020, anticipated to grow to $195 billion by 2027.[2] At-home devices now purportedly make it possible to diagnose and monitor health conditions, such as sleep apnea, diabetes, and fertility, automatically, immediately, and discreetly. By design, these devices produce a wealth of data that can inform patients of their health status and potentially even recommend life-saving actions.[3]

But patients and their health care providers often lack access to this data.[4] Manufacturers typically design connected at-home devices to store data in cloud services run by the manufacturers themselves, requiring device owners to register accounts and accept the terms of use and limitations that the manufacturers impose. A recent survey of 222 mobile "app families" associated with wellness devices found that 64.4 percent "did not report sharing any data" with other apps or services.[5] A parent testified in Congress as to how a lack of data access impaired his daughter's ability

---

[1] See, for example, Erin Brodwin, Remote Monitoring Is Rapidly Growing – and a New Class of Patient-Consumer Is Driving the Shift, STAT (September 16, 2020), www.statnews.com/2020/09/16/remote-patient-monitoring-stat-report/; Sarah Krouse, Covid-19 Pandemic Drives Patients – and Deal Makers – to Telemedicine, *The Wall Street Journal* (August 25, 2020), www.wsj.com/articles/covid-19-pandemic-drives-patients-to-telemedicine-deal-makers-too-11598358823.

[2] Fortune Business Insights, Wearable Medical Devices Market Size Worth USD 195.57 Bn by 2027, *GlobeNewswire* (March 2, 2022), www.globenewswire.com/news-release/2022/02/03/2378221/0/en/Wearable-Medical-Devices-Market-Size-worth-USD-195-57-Bn-by-2027-With-stunning-26-4-CAGR.html.

[3] I. Glenn Cohen, Sara Gerke, & Daniel B. Kramer, Ethical and Legal Implications of Remote Monitoring of Medical Devices, 98 Milbank Q. 1257, 1259 (2020).

[4] See, for example, id. at 1266–67; John T. Wilbanks & Eric J. Topol, Stop the Privatization of Health Data, 535 Nature 345, 347 (2016); Elizabeth A. Rowe, Sharing Data, 104 Iowa L. Rev. 287 (2018).

[5] Quinn Grundy et al., Tracing the Potential Flow of Consumer Data: A Network Analysis of Prominent Health and Fitness Apps, 19 J. Med. Internet Res. e233, at 4 (2017).

to manage Type I diabetes,[6] and patients with sleep apnea have had to circumvent technological device locks to extract data on their own sleep.[7] Many medical and wellness devices that patients use for in-home diagnosis and monitoring – which we simply call "health devices" – lock patients into manufacturers' ecosystems. This limits patients', and society's, ability to tap into the full value of the data, despite the extensive individual and social benefits that access could provide.

The problem here is not solely technical; it is also legal. Existing law in the United States provides patients with no guarantee of access to their data when it is generated and stored outside the traditional health care system. The Health Insurance Portability and Accountability Act (HIPAA) provides patients a legally enforceable right of access to copies of their electronic health records (EHRs), and, in recent years, the Department of Health and Human Services (HHS) has moved to make this right enforceable and meaningful.[8] But as HHS itself has observed about health devices and other "mHealth" technologies used outside the EHR ecosystem, manufacturers "are not obligated by a statute or regulation to provide individuals with access to data about themselves," so patients with data on such devices "may not have the ability to later obtain a copy."[9]

This chapter begins by identifying the individual and societal benefits of patient access to health device data. It then addresses the arguments for restricting such access, especially those based on intellectual property laws and policies. We conclude that such arguments are ultimately doctrinally and normatively unconvincing, such that they should not dissuade legislatures and federal agencies from legislating or regulating rights of access. We then consider what can and should be done to create a robust, administrable right of patients to access health device data that protects all stakeholders' interests, and we offer a nascent framework that draws from other regimes for patient and consumer access to personal information. We hope the framework will guide legislatures and regulators as they begin to address this important issue.

II BENEFITS OF PATIENT ACCESS

There are important individual and societal benefits when patients can access their own health data. Foremost for individuals is the fulfillment of patient autonomy

---

[6] Smart Health: Empowering the Future of Mobile Applications, Hearing Before the Subcomm. on Rsch. & Tech. of the H. Comm. on Sci., Space and Tech., 114th Cong. 43–44 (2016) (testimony of Howard Look).

[7] Jason Koebler, Why Sleep Apnea Patients Rely on a CPAP Machine Hacker, Vice News (November 15, 2018), www.vice.com/en/article/xwjd4w/im-possibly-alive-because-it-exists-why-sleep-apnea-patients-rely-on-a-cpap-machine-hacker.

[8] See, for example, press release, US Dep't of Health and Human Svcs. (HHS), Five Enforcement Actions Hold Healthcare Providers Accountable for HIPAA Right of Access (November 30, 2021), www.healthit.gov/sites/default/files/non-covered_entities_report_june_17_2016.pdf (on HHS Office of Civil Rights' HIPAA Right of Access Initiative).

[9] HHS, Examining Oversight of the Privacy & Security of Health Data Collected by Entities Not Regulated by HIPAA (2020), https://perma.cc/2JZU-DQJF.

and dignity. Health device data informs decisions about treatment, so a patient without access can neither make fully informed decisions about a course of care nor evaluate a provider's recommendations.[10] Patients may also need access to health device data to "transport" their data to new health care providers for safekeeping,[11] or to repair their devices.[12] From a research perspective, patients can and do exploit health device data to useful ends, since their own health stands to benefit from insights and discoveries drawn from that data.[13] Many patients use health device data for "quantified self" or "n=1" research to discover how best to manage their own health.[14]

Turning to broader societal benefits, a key starting point is the research that is enabled when patient data is aggregated.[15] For example, the National Institutes of Health (NIH)-run ClinVar database receives genetic variant data authorized for inclusion by individual patients and now contains over two million records representing 36,000 different genes, which public and private enterprises have used to advance research and create consumer products and services.[16] The ClinVar model of government-supported collaborative dataset-building is one starting point for the idealistic vision of "medical information commons" – the collective, shared governance of medical knowledge (rather than proprietary or authoritarian governance of the same)[17] – that researchers and regulators alike believe would be a tremendous boon to science.[18]

---

[10] See generally Charlotte Blease, I. Glenn Cohen, & Sharon Hoffman, Sharing Clinical Notes: Potential Medical-Legal Benefits and Risks, 327(8) JAMA 717 (2022). For example, the US Copyright Office has observed that people with sleep apnea use "CPAP machine data to adjust their machines and enhance their treatment and health." US Copyright Office, Section 1201 Rulemaking: Eighth Triennial Proceeding to Determine Exemptions to the Prohibition on Circumvention 143 (October 2021) [hereinafter Eighth Triennial], https://cdn.loc.gov/copyright/1201/2021/2021_Section_1201_Registers_Recommendation.pdf. Patients cannot always "rely on the data directly provided on the machines' displays because the algorithms in CPAP machines could provide inaccurate readings." Id.

[11] See, for example, Sharona Hoffman, Access to Health Records: New Rules Another Step in the Right Direction, JURIST (February 20, 2019), www.jurist.org/commentary/2019/02/sharona-hoffman-health-records-proposal/.

[12] See Fed. Trade Comm'n, Nixing the Fix: An FTC Report to Congress on Repair Restrictions 41–42 (2021), www.ftc.gov/reports/nixing-fix-ftc-report-congress-repair-restrictions.

[13] Mary A. Majumder & Amy L. McGuire, Data Sharing in the Context of Health-Related Citizen Science, 48 J.L. Med. & Ethics 167 (2020); Sharona Hoffman, Citizen Science: The Law and Ethics of Public Access to Medical Big Data, 30 Berkeley Tech. L.J. 1741, 1755 (2015).

[14] See Melanie Swan, The Quantified Self: Fundamental Disruption in Big Data Science and Biological Discovery, 1 Big Data 85, 91–92 (2013).

[15] See Wilbanks & Topol, supra note 4.

[16] See Melissa J. Landrum & Brandi L. Kattman, ClinVar at Five Years: Delivering on the Promise, 39 Hum. Mutation 1623, 1625 (2018); ClinVar Submissions, Nat'l Lib. Med. (last visited April 19, 2022), www.ncbi.nlm.nih.gov/clinvar/submitters/.

[17] Katherine J. Strandburg, Brett M. Frischmann, & Michael J. Madison, The Knowledge Commons Framework, in Governing Medical Knowledge Commons 9 (Katherine J. Strandburg, Brett M. Frischmann, & Michael J. Madison eds., 2017).

[18] See, for example, Jorge L. Contreras, Leviathan in the Commons: Biomedical Data and the State, in Governing Medical Knowledge Commons 19 (Katherine J. Strandburg, Brett M. Frischmann, &

Research on aggregated health data also allows patient groups and civil society watchdogs to verify manufacturers' claims and ensure that health devices function as advertised – especially important given that those devices are only lightly regulated.[19] Aggregated health device data also promises to become a variety of the "real-world evidence" increasingly used to conduct public health research and validate the safety and efficacy of other products the same patients are using.[20] But these potential benefits depend on patient data aggregated at a sufficient scale.[21]

Societal spillover effects explain, at least in part, why market forces do not prompt manufacturers to satisfy patient demand for data access. Patient self-researchers tend to be consumer-innovators who share their insights and discoveries altruistically, at low or no cost, which may undercut the manufacturers.[22] And the value of aggregated patient data cannot easily be captured by a single entity. As a result, there is no straightforward way for patients and health device manufacturers to transact for data access.

Another economic disconnect arises from competition among device manufacturers. When patients can easily extract their data from one device and port it to a competing device, they avoid "lock-in," which promotes patient choice and fosters competition.[23] In an effort to avoid such competition, however, device manufacturers have incentives to limit patient data access. Indeed, some have implemented technical measures to keep even savvy patients from extracting data and asserted laws against the circumvention of those technological measures to further keep patients from their data.[24]

III LEGALITY OF PATIENT ACCESS

To be sure, there are real concerns with giving patients access to health device data.[25] Device manufacturers have pointed to these as reasons to limit such access. The main concerns fall into three categories.

Michael J. Madison eds., 2017) (on government's role in fostering public medical databases); Critical Path Inst., Rare Disease Cures Accelerator-Data and Analytics Platform, https://c-path.org/programs/rdca-dap/ (exemplary FDA-funded effort).

[19] See Rowe, supra note 4, at 313.
[20] Sanket S. Dhruva et al., Real-World Evidence: Promise and Peril for Medical Product Evaluation, 43 PT 464, 469 (2018).
[21] See, for example, Barbara J. Evans, Genomic Data Commons, in *Governing Medical Knowledge Commons* 74, 81 (Katherine J. Strandburg, Brett M. Frischmann, & Michael J. Madison eds., 2017) (on the "data access challenge").
[22] See Eric von Hippel, *Democratizing Innovation* 77–91 (2005).
[23] David Blumenthal, A Big Step Toward Giving Patients Control over Their Health Care Data, *Harvard Business Review* (March 15, 2019), https://hbr.org/2019/03/a-big-step-toward-giving-patients-control-over-their-health-care-data.
[24] See Wilbanks & Topol, supra note 4.
[25] By "access" to their own data, we mean not just patients' ability to view their own data, but also their ability to download it, to archive it, and to share it.

First, there are costs associated with authenticating users, formatting data, and otherwise providing access to records. This problem can be solved by permitting reasonable, small charges for data access.[26]

Second, device manufacturers may be better stewards of sensitive health data than patients, in terms of privacy and cybersecurity.[27] In theory, manufacturers enjoy economies of scale that enable them to protect health records from data breaches and other compromising disclosures, while individual patients may fail to secure their data or fall victim to privacy-invading scams. Yet, there are countervailing considerations: Manufacturers' vast databases are themselves an attractive and recurring target for data malfeasance,[28] and some manufacturers' shady deals with privacy-intrusive data brokers suggest that companies holding volumes of lightly regulated personal data may not be better positioned than patients to protect data security and privacy.[29]

The third concern often raised as a reason to limit patient access is that the data is somehow proprietary to the device manufacturers. This intellectual property concern requires a bit of conceptual unpacking, as it operates on two different levels. First, it is a *legal* or *doctrinal* argument, in which the manufacturers assert specific intellectual property rights over the data. Second, it is a *normative, policy-oriented* argument that exclusive control over patient data is desirable to protect incentives to develop health devices and data ecosystems.

Evaluating these arguments requires distinguishing the types of health device data. First, there is the software code that the device manufacturer writes. Second, the device takes the raw measurements of the patient and stores them. Third, the device (or external software) may perform computations on the raw data to produce values intended to approximate a natural phenomenon, such as a pulse. Fourth, the device may compute data outputs of the manufacturer's own invention. For example, a device might use pulse measurements across a night to produce a "sleep score," indicating how well, in the manufacturer's opinion, the patient slept, and offer recommendations on how to sleep better.[30]

---

[26] See 45 CFR § 164.524(c)(4) (providing for a "reasonable, cost-based fee" for patient data access under the HIPAA).

[27] See Cohen et al., supra note 3, at 1282–83.

[28] FDA Issues New Alert on Medtronic Insulin Pump Security, *Healthcare IT News* (July 1, 2019), www.healthcareitnews.com/news/fda-issues-new-alert-medtronic-insulin-pump-security; Joe Carlson, FDA Says Pacemakers, Glucose Monitors and Other Devices Could Be Vulnerable to Hackers, *Star Tribune* (March 3, 2020), www.startribune.com/fda-says-pacemakers-glucose-monitors-and-other-devices-could-be-vulnerable-to-hackers/568452772/.

[29] Joseph Cox, How the US Military Buys Location Data from Ordinary Apps, *Vice News* (November 16, 2020), www.vice.com/en/article/jgqm5x/us-military-location-data-xmode-locate-x; Alfred Ng & Jon Keegan, Who Is Policing the Location Data Industry?, *The Markup* (February 24, 2022), https://themarkup.org/ask-the-markup/2022/02/24/who-is-policing-the-location-data-industry.

[30] See, for example, Larry Magid, Devices Measure Quantity, Quality of Sleep, *Mercury News* (December 21, 2018), www.mercurynews.com/2018/12/20/magid-devices-measure-quantity-quality-of-sleep/.

Our focus is the second and third types of information – raw measurements and computed estimates of physiological properties – because they are likely to be of the most interest to patients. We therefore refer hereinafter to these two types of data together simply as "patient data." With access to this patient data, patients likely will not need to view source code on the device to put the data to use. Manufacturer-specific computations and scores are likely not useful for cross-device interoperability, and the black-box nature of the algorithms often used to compute such scores limits their usefulness for care and research alike.[31]

Two intellectual property regimes are most frequently raised to justify withholding patient data from patients: Copyright law and trade secret protection.[32] Yet neither provides a genuine doctrinal basis for "ownership" of patient data or barriers to patient access.

Copyright law, which protects creative works of authorship from unauthorized copying, almost certainly cannot justify withholding patient data. Raw physiological measurements and estimates of natural phenomena are facts, ineligible for protection under copyright.[33] Furthermore, given the immense health benefits that patients can enjoy from their own data, data access likely qualifies as fair use, exempt from copyright infringement.[34] Indeed, the US Copyright Office has consistently agreed since 2015 that patient access to medical device data is not copyright infringement, thus, permitting patients to circumvent the technological locks that interfere with their access to data on medical devices.[35]

Nor is patient data a trade secret. First, every legal definition of a trade secret requires the information in question be *secret* to qualify for protection.[36] Patient data

---

[31] To be sure, patient access to these types of information would be useful in some situations, such as testing the reliability of manufacturers' invented health "scores." The nature of proprietary rights over device source code and manufacturer-specific computed data is an important area for further research.

[32] See, for example, Timo Minssen & Justin Pierce, Big Data and Intellectual Property Rights in the Health and Life Sciences, in *Big Data, Health Law, and Bioethics* 307 (I. Glenn Cohen et al. eds., 2018); Rowe, supra note 4, at 299–301 (2018); Comments of AdvaMed and Medical Imaging and Technology Alliance opposing the 1201 exemption at 5 (2015), https://cdn.loc.gov/copyright/1201/2015/comments-032715/class%2025/AdvaMed_Class25_1201_2014.pdf [hereinafter AdvaMed-MITA 2015]. Cf. *Med. Imaging & Tech. All. v. Libr. of Cong.*, no. 1:22-cv-00499 (DDC filed February 25, 2022) (ongoing litigation alleging, *inter alia*, that the US Copyright Office violates copyright law by authorizing repair personnel to circumvent technical "locks" on health devices) [hereinafter MITA litigation].

[33] See *Feist Publ'ns, Inc. v. Rural Tel. Serv. Co.*, 499 US 340, 345 (1991); US Copyright Office, *Section 1201 Rulemaking: Sixth Triennial Proceeding to Determine Exemptions to the Prohibition on Circumvention* 393 (October 2015). See also, for example, *Midler v. Ford*, 849 F.2d 460 (9th Cir. 1988) (holding voices uncopyrightable); US Copyright Office, in *re Second Request for Reconsideration for Refusal To Register Equilibrium* (2020), www.copyright.gov/rulings-filings/review-board/docs/equilibrium.pdf, at 5 (concluding fingerprints are uncopyrightable).

[34] See Eighth Triennial, supra note 10.

[35] Id. But see MITA litigation, supra note 32 (alleging that the US Copyright Office erred in permitting repair personnel to do so).

[36] See, for example, 18 USC 1839(3)(B) (federal definition); UTSA § 1.4 (definition common in state law).

of all sorts is shared with patients, health care providers, and others and, thus, is not actually secret. Second, even if subsets of patient data are kept secret, they are not the sort of information that trade secrecy law protects. To qualify as a trade secret, information must derive "independent economic value" from its secrecy.[37] As Hrdy has explained, "secret information *whose value does not stem from secrecy* cannot be a trade secret."[38] Unlike traditionally protectable information – manufacturing processes, precise recipes, and so on – patient data derives economic value from aggregation and sharing, not secrecy.[39]

To be sure, some (nonpatient data) aspects of devices' software and mechanical designs may be deemed trade secrets.[40] The European Medicines Agency (EMA) offers helpful guidance here, in its official view of the limits of trade secrecy protection of clinical trial data.[41] (Like the patient data that is the focus of this chapter, clinical trial data describes patients' health and is enormously valuable to researchers and patients themselves.) EMA announced that a large majority of clinical trial data "should not be considered" proprietary.[42] In EMA's view, only "innovative features" of the methods *through which data is collected* can constitute trade secrets.[43] EMA expressly defines narrow categories of information it deems innovative and protectable.[44] These focus on methods for gathering data more quickly or cheaply, such as immunogenicity assays.[45] Notably, EMA's categories do *not* permit proprietary claims to the outcome data that describes patients' health (analogous to health devices' patient data); EMA instead mandates that all outcome data be publicized.[46]

---

[37] Id.
[38] Camilla Alexandra Hrdy, The Value in Secrecy, 91 Fordham L. Rev. 557, 596 (2022).
[39] Id. See also, for example, *Yield Dynamics, Inc. v. TEA Sys. Corp.*, 154 Cal. App. 4th 547, 561 n.13, 564–65, 566–67 (2007) (holding a company's software not a trade secret, despite secrecy and economic value, because the software was built on a combination of open-source and secret code and the company had not proven that economic value derived from continued secrecy).
[40] See, for example, AdvaMed-MITA 2015, supra note 32, at 5–6 (asserting trade secret rights in the source code in medical devices).
[41] Eur. Med. Agency, *External Guidance on the Implementation of the European Medicines Agency Policy on the Publication of Clinical Data for Medicinal Products for Human Use* (2018) [hereinafter EMA], https://perma.cc/28UL-6ZQK.
[42] Id. at 52.
[43] Id. at 54.
[44] Eur. Med. Agency, *Policy on Publication of Clinical Data for Medicinal Products for Human Use* Annex 3 (2019) [hereinafter EMA 2019], www.ema.europa.eu/en/documents/other/european-medicines-agency-policy-publication-clinical-data-medicinal-products-human-use_en.pdf; Regulation 536/2014, of the European Parliament and of the Council of April 16, 2014 on Clinical Trials on Medicinal Products for Human Use and Repealing Council Directive 2001/20/EC Text with EEA relevance, O.J. (L 158) 1, 1–76.
[45] EMA 2019, supra note 44, at Annex 3.
[46] EMA, supra note 41, at 58. The NIH apparently shares the EMA's view. See 81 Fed. Reg. 64,982, 64,996–97 (stating that "trial results in summary form" "can be provided without disclosing trade secret or confidential commercial information").

What remains of health device manufacturers' intellectual property claims is a normative argument that data inaccessibility gives manufacturers incentives to innovate.[47] Yet, there are serious defects to this normative argument. First, patients themselves have a countervailing incentive to innovate – their own health depends on it. Second, the "innovation" manufacturers wish to protect may not be beneficial at all: Secrecy can conceal safety problems, false claims of efficacy, racially biased outcomes, and other defects. Normatively and doctrinally, trade secrecy should not and does not protect this kind of secrecy.[48] As the Supreme Court has stated, if the disclosure of secret information reveals "harmful side effects of the [trade secret holder's] product and causes the [holder] to suffer a decline in the potential profits from sales of the product, that decline in profits stems from a decrease in the value of the [product] to consumers, rather than from the destruction of an edge the [holder] had over its competitors, and cannot constitute the taking of a trade secret."[49]

IV TOWARD A REGULATORY FRAMEWORK

Although we have argued patients should have access to health device data as a legal and policy matter, the practical fact remains that manufacturers are currently free to build devices that deny such access at a technological level. There is, thus, a need for a legal framework to secure such access. No such framework currently exists: The existing regulations are generally limited to narrow classes of medical records or apply only to traditional health care providers and some of their business associates.

To develop an effective framework, it is useful to survey existing consumer data-access regimes both within the health care system and otherwise. We arrange them into three categories, roughly ranked by the strength of their mandates.

The most powerful regimes mandate patients' right to data access. The HIPAA Privacy Rule provides patients with "a right of access to inspect and obtain a copy of protected health information" from health care providers.[50] Similarly, European law and the laws of some states provide consumers with rights to retrieve

---

[47] Manufacturers tend to emphasize the policy argument that innovation could suffer without strengthened intellectual property protection of some sort – perhaps acknowledging that existing doctrine does not prohibit patients from accessing patient data. See, for example, 2015 comments of AdvaMed opposing the 1201 exemption, https://cdn.loc.gov/copyright/1201/2015/comments-032715/class%2027/AdvaMed_Class27_1201_2014.pdf, at 7 (asserting vaguely that patient access "poses trade secrecy concerns" while insisting "trade secrets may be the only viable form of protection for companies conducting research and development in this area").

[48] See Hrdy, supra note 38, at 7–8 (discussing "type failures"); Sharon Sandeen, Out of Thin Air: Trade Secrets, Cybersecurity, and the Wrongful Acquisition Tort, 19 Minn. J.L. Sci. & Tech. 373 (2018); Amy Kapczynski, The Public History of Trade Secrets, U.C. Davis L. Rev. 1367, 1429–36 (2022).

[49] *Ruckelshaus v. Monsanto Co.*, 467 U.S. 986, 1011 n.15 (1984). See also *Pub. Citizen Health Rsch. Grp. v. FDA*, 704 F.2d 1280, 1291 n.30 (D.C. Cir. 1983).

[50] 45 CFR § 164.524.

data about themselves.[51] These laws employ a range of enforcement mechanisms, including civil actions by consumers, state attorney general investigations, and administrative monetary penalties. For example, the HHS's Office for Civil Rights recently began penalizing HIPAA-covered health care providers that fail to supply patients' protected health information upon request or charge excessive fees for them,[52] prompting improvement after years of subpar compliance.[53]

A second approach is softer financial incentives and disincentives – "carrots" and "sticks" – to encourage data holders to offer access. This was the primary approach used for the adoption of EHRs: The HITECH Act of 2004 both offered providers incentive payments for adopting certified EHR systems in their practices, and imposed a modest penalty on Medicare reimbursements for providers who did not.[54] Today, after billions of dollars of investment by HHS, the vast majority of providers have adopted EHRs,[55] and those systems largely comply with HHS's voluntary certification standards because the financial benefits created sufficient demand.[56] HHS's ongoing ability to set certification standards has enabled the agency to require EHR systems to export data in standardized interoperability formats, to expose application programming interfaces for data access, and to stop companies' "information blocking" practices that hamper patients' ability to access their own health records.[57]

A third possibility is to build public infrastructure or subsidize private infrastructure that coordinates patient data access. With ClinVar, for example, genetic testing laboratories voluntarily submit annotated reports of genetic variants to an NIH-run database, with patient consent. They make these voluntary submissions because, among other reasons, foundations and publishers often require them as a condition of grants or publication.[58] The presence of established, stable, government-supported infrastructure for data sharing makes such data submission requirements more common and more effective. In this way, legislatures and regulators can incentivize data sharing even without direct regulation.

---

[51] See, for example, Cal. Civ. Code § 1798.100(a); GDPR art. 15.
[52] Jennifer J. Hennessy et al., HIPAA Right of Access Initiative: 2020 Year in Review, *The National Law Review* (December 11, 2020), www.natlawreview.com/article/hipaa-right-access-initiative-2020-year-review.
[53] Carolyn T. Lye et al., Assessment of US Hospital Compliance with Regulations for Patients' Requests for Medical Records, 1 JAMA Netw. Open e183014 (2018).
[54] Centers for Medicare and Medicaid Services, Medicare and Medicaid Programs, Electronic Health Record Incentive Program Final Rule, 75 Fed. Reg. 44,314 (July 28, 2010).
[55] HHS Office of the Nat'l Coordinator for Health Info. Tech. (ONC), *HealthIT Quick Stat #61: National Trends in Hospital and Physician Adoption of Electronic Health Records*, www.healthit.gov/data/quickstats/national-trends-hospital-and-physician-adoption-electronic-health-records. ("As of 2019, about three-quarters of office-based physicians (72%) and nearly all non-federal acute care hospitals (96%) had adopted a certified EHR.")
[56] Id.
[57] 21st Century Cures Act Final Rule, 85 Fed. Reg. 25642 (May 1, 2020) (codified at 45 CFR pts. 170, 171).
[58] See Karen E. Wain et al., The Value of Genomic Variant ClinVar Submissions from Clinical Providers: Beyond the Addition of Novel Variants, 39 Hum. Mutation 1660, 1661 (2018).

We integrate aspects from these regimes into a nascent framework for patient access to at-home health care device data. Our framework-in-progress has three elements: A legal hook to induce device manufacturers to make patient data accessible to patients, a technical standard for data storage and access, and infrastructure for patients to deposit and use their data.

As to the first element, legislation or regulation to compel access, akin to HIPAA, would be most forceful and effective. For example, in 2019, Senators Klobuchar and Murkowski proposed creating a HIPAA-like statutory right of patients "to access, amend, and delete a copy of the personal health data that companies collect or use,"[59] including data from all "cloud-based or mobile technologies that are designed to collect individuals' personal health data."[60]

US states also have substantial authority to legislate around HIPAA and could themselves create statutory patient-data access rights. Texas, for example, subjects some HIPAA-exempt entities, such as schools and public health researchers, to some of the obligations that HIPAA imposes.[61] The California Consumer Privacy Act (CCPA) arguably creates a right of access to health device data not covered by HIPAA, though this theory is so far untested.[62]

Federal regulators could also explore their existing legal authority to require device manufacturers to share data. For example, the Federal Trade Commission could apply its authority to police unfair and deceptive practices to health device makers that market patient access to data as a feature of their products and require that these companies meet their claims.[63]

Alternatively, following the example of the HITECH Act, Congress could provide financial incentives for health devices that meet data access standards, for example, making such devices reimbursable under Flexible Spending Account (FSA) plans or Medicare. A different, intriguing possibility could leverage the status quo of minimal regulation to create new financial incentives and disincentives. Current Food and Drug Administration (FDA) guidance exempts health devices from clearance and approval requirements only if they "present a low risk to the safety of users and other persons."[64] As noted above, patients' data access can enable researchers to

---

[59] Protecting Personal Health Data Act, S. 24, 117th Cong. (2021); press release, *Klobuchar, Murkowski Introduce Legislation to Protect Consumers' Private Health Data* (February 2, 2021), www.klobuchar.senate.gov/public/index.cfm/2021/2/klobuchar-murkowski-introduce-legislation-to-protect-consumers-private-health-data.
[60] S. 24, supra note 59.
[61] See Tex. Health & Safety Code Ann. §§ 181.001(b)(2)(A) (defining a "covered entity" under Texas law).
[62] Jonathan Deitch, Protecting Unprotected Data in Mhealth, 18 Nw. J. Tech & Intell. Prop. 107 (2020); see also Cohen et al., supra note 3, at 1276.
[63] HHS ONC, *Conceptualizing a Data Infrastructure for the Capture, Use, and Sharing of Patient-Generated Health Data in Care Delivery and Research Through 2024* 23 (January 2018), www.healthit.gov/sites/default/files/onc_pghd_final_white_paper.pdf.
[64] US Food and Drug Admin., *General Wellness: Policy for Low-Risk Devices* 2 (September 26, 2019), www.fda.gov/media/90652/download.

study the safety risks of devices, so it could be reasonable for the FDA to change its policies and extend a presumption of safety (and thus of exemption from regulation) only to those devices that make data accessible to patients – and perhaps to qualified researchers, too. Manufacturers that choose to withhold data would not be, per se, prohibited from marketing their products, but would be subject to stricter FDA oversight, which would come with new costs.

The second element of the framework is a technical standard to govern how data is to be stored and accessed. Since health devices typically store data in manufacturers' cloud servers, there is little sense in requiring less than electronic access via a network-connected application programming interface, akin to the requirements for EHR systems. Furthermore, both research and interoperability would benefit from greater standardization of data formats, in light of the profusion of health devices and manufacturers.[65] HHS and its Office of the National Coordinator for Health Information Technology could play an important role here, as it did in the standardization of EHRs.

The third element is an institutional infrastructure for aggregating and sharing data. We propose a public, ClinVar-like repository of patient-authorized submissions of appropriately anonymized device data. Without such a repository, patient access and data interoperability will likely still enable new research and other benefits for patients, but they also could augment the power of firms that amass data and broker access. A government-run repository of patient data arguably has several benefits. As a focal point for data aggregation, it empowers all researchers, not just the largest firms. Also, firms that contribute to this central repository share a relationship with the government that could be leveraged to ensure data privacy and security. And a public repository enables the government and outside experts to think through and develop privacy practices that best protect patients, rather than leaving these questions, in the first instance, to profit-driven firms.

V CONCLUSION

In this chapter, we have argued for a legal right of patients to access their own health device data. We have begun to trace a legal framework for access, one that includes three key elements: A legal "hook" to coax or compel device manufacturers to share data with patients, a technical standard to govern how data is stored and accessed, and an institutional infrastructure for aggregating and sharing data. We intend to expand on this framework in future work.

---

[65] See Dov Greenbaum, Avoiding Overregulation in the Medical Internet of Things, in *Big Data, Health Law, and Bioethics* 129, 138 (I. Glenn Cohen et al. eds., 2018).

3

Challenges of Remote Patient Care Technologies under the General Data Protection Regulation

Preliminary Results of the TeNDER Project

Danaja Fabcic Povse

I INTRODUCTION

Patients with complex diseases like Alzheimer's or Parkinson's often require round-the-clock care. Since caregivers may not always be able to be present, remote care technologies (RCTs) can supplement human caregiver intervention and provide the patient with better care. In the TeNDER project,[1] we are building technology that will create an alert system for caregivers: For example, if the person falls, their relative or nurse receives a phone alert and can go and check up on them. Such technology relies on remote patient monitoring to detect anomalies in the person's environment and combines data sources, including electronic health records (EHRs) and data from connected devices (e.g., wearables). The use of these technologies raises questions of data protection since especially sensitive data are involved.[2]

Legal frameworks that govern the use of RCTs are, by their nature, abstract and high-level, meaning that their application might not take into account the specific type of technology or its use in a particular care situation, leaving developers and users in an unclear legal situation.[3]

This chapter aims to bridge the gap between the high-level data protection framework and practical, micro-level application of RCTs by providing an overview of the challenges under European Union (EU) law when developing and using RCTs, exploring how initial results from the TeNDER project on resolving those challenges can help with the practical implementation of similar solutions, as well as examining gaps in the regulation itself. Using these technologies as a starting point, the chapter analyzes the obligations the General Data Protection Regulation

---

[1] See generally TeNDER Health – TeNDER Project, www.tender-health.eu/. Disclaimer: This research has been funded by the European Commission under the Horizon 2020 mechanism – grant no. 875325 (TeNDER, affecTive basEd iNtegrateD carE for betteR Quality of Life).

[2] Eur. Parliamentary Rsch. Serv., *The Rise of Digital Health Technologies During the Pandemic* (2021), www.europarl.europa.eu/RegData/etudes/BRIE/2021/690548/EPRS_BRI(2021)690548_EN.pdf.

[3] Craig E. Kuziemsky et al., Ethics in Telehealth: Comparison between Guidelines and Practice-based Experience – The Case for Learning Health Systems, 29 Y.B. Med. Informatics 44 (2020).

(GDPR) lays upon developers in order to address the following research question: "What challenges does the GDPR pose for designers of remote patient care technologies (RCTs), and how can those questions be addressed in practice?"

To answer the research question, the chapter first introduces key legal concerns that data protection poses regarding the use of RCTs, focusing on their field of application and the key principles and obligations relevant to developers. At the same time, the work draws upon the preliminary results of the TeNDER project (2019–2023) to discuss any potential shortcomings in the regulation.

The RCTs discussed in this chapter are in-house, as they are specifically developed to be used remotely, and digital, including digital technologies such as wearables, smart devices, microphones etc. However, TeNDER is not designed to be a medical device and, thus, performs no diagnostics.

II REMOTE CARE TECHNOLOGIES AND THE GDPR

RCTs are a type of technology that can help patients manage their illnesses better, as well as help elderly people live more independently. They can be used institutionally (e.g., in a care home or hospital) or in the home, where they can contribute to a better quality of life for the user. A variety of different technologies can be used – monitoring devices, smartphones, apps, social media, videoconferencing tools, etc.[4] RCT is distinct from telehealth or eHealth, which refer to the phenomenon of digital health care in general, while remote monitoring or remote care describes the technology (or technologies) being used. RCT is, thus, a specific technology that is used by health care providers, either in a telehealth or a classical health care setting.[5]

The advent of 5G and the Internet of things, combined with the two years of pandemic, has led to a heightened uptake of telehealth solutions, including remote monitoring applications and wearables that help people age better.[6] The use of RCTs is especially beneficial for older adults with chronic conditions, for whom monitoring devices, communication tools, and follow-up phone calls enable the 24-hour availability of health management tools.[7]

RCTs, like many other eHealth technologies, rely on advanced data processing techniques and different devices, both medical and general-purpose ones, to provide functionalities. The devices and technologies must, at the same time, meet the goals they were designed for and ensure patients' privacy and safety.[8] In terms

---

[4] Alexandra Queirós et al., Remote Care Technology: A Systematic Review of Reviews and Meta-Analyses, 6 *Technologies* 22 (2018).
[5] Caregility Team, *The Difference Between Remote Patient Monitoring and Telehealth*, https://caregility.com/blog/the-difference-between-remote-patient-monitoring-and-telehealth/.
[6] Eur. Parliamentary Rsch. Serv., supra note 2.
[7] Queirós et al., supra note 4.
[8] Ana Isabel Martins et al., Ambient Assisted Living: Introduction and Overview, in *Usability, Accessibility and Ambient Assisted Living* 1 (Alexandra Queirós & Nelson Pacheco da Rocha eds., 2018).

of data privacy, patients risk losing control over their health data – especially when it comes to their EHRs[9] – when remote monitoring devices, such as wearables, are used.[10] Elderly users may not have consented to the processing of their health data; they may consider monitoring devices as a form of spying upon their private lives.[11]

The GDPR,[12] adopted in 2016, binds controllers and processors involved in the processing of health data to put in place appropriate technical and organizational mechanisms to ensure patients' data protection and the confidentiality of medical information.

The first issue is determining the GDPR's scope of application to RCTs. The regulation applies when personal data, defined as "any information relating to an identified or identifiable natural person ('data subject')" (art. 4(1) of the GDPR), are being processed, meaning "any operation or set of operations which is performed on personal data or on sets of personal data, whether or not by automated means, such as collection, recording, organization, structuring," and so on (art. 4(2) of the GDPR). Data concerning health (also referred to as health data) are defined as "personal data related to the physical or mental health of a natural person, including the provision of health care services, which reveal information about his or her health status" (art. 4(15) of the GDPR).

How can we determine what constitutes personal data in a remote care scenario? As per the definition of art. 4(1), as long as information can be linked to a data subject, it is considered personal data. Since the scenario deals with a health care setting, health data are very likely going to be processed. More specifically, the 2007 opinion of the Article 29 Working Party states that "all data contained in medical documentation, in electronic health records and in EHR systems should be considered to be 'sensitive personal data.'"[13] However, data that cannot be linked to a data subject is not considered personal data, for example because it has been irreversibly anonymized.[14]

The regime under the GDPR is centered on a data controller, a central entity in charge of the processing activity, which determines the purposes and means of the processing (art. 4(7) of the GDPR). In order to process data, a controller must

---

[9] Benedict Stanberry, Telemedicine: Barriers and Opportunities in the 21st Century, 247 J. of Internal Med. 615 (2000).

[10] I. Glenn Cohen et al., Ethical and Legal Implications of Remote Monitoring of Medical Devices, 98 Milbank Q. 1257 (2020).

[11] S. Stowe & S. Harding, Telecare, Telehealth and Telemedicine, 1 Eur. Geriatric Med. 193 (2010).

[12] Regulation (EU) 2016/679 of the European Parliament and of the Council of April 27, 2016 on the Protection of Natural Persons with regard to the Processing of Personal Data and on the Free Movement of Such Data, and Repealing Directive 95/46/EC (GDPR) (text with EEA relevance), 2016 O.J. (L 119) 1, http://data.europa.eu/eli/reg/2016/679/oj/eng.

[13] Article 29 Working Party, Eur. Commn', *Working Document on the Processing of Personal Data Relating to Health in Electronic Health Records (EHR)* (2007), https://ec.europa.eu/justice/article-29/documentation/opinion-recommendation/files/2007/wp131_en.pdf.

[14] Article 29 Working Party, Eur. Commn', *Opinion 05/2014 on Anonymisation Techniques* (2014), https://ec.europa.eu/justice/article-29/documentation/opinion-recommendation/index_en.htm.

comply with data quality principles, such as data minimization and accuracy (art. 5(3) and 5(4) of the GDPR, respectively), and ensure the existence of valid legal grounds, as per art. 6 of the GDPR. Controllers can engage processors to help them carry out the processing operation – art. 4(8) of the GDPR defines a processor as a natural or legal person, public authority, agency, or other body which processes personal data on behalf of the controller.

Since RCT relies on different technologies and different service providers, defining the controller and the processor may be difficult. Recent decisions of the Court of Justice of the EU, such as *Wirtschaftsakademie*[15] and *Fashion ID*,[16] as well as advisory opinions,[17] point to an "essential means" test. Essential means are key elements which are closely linked to the purpose and the scope of the data processing, such as whose data will be processed, which data types, for how long, and who will have access to them. The entity that determines the essential means of processing is, therefore, the data controller.

Determining the controller is important for ensuring that the right party can demonstrate compliance with the applicable principles and obligations ("accountability" – art. 5(2) of the GDPR). Among them are the data quality principles of art. 5(1): Lawfulness, fairness, and transparency; purpose limitation, data minimization, accuracy, storage limitation, integrity, and confidentiality. The controller is further responsible for implementing appropriate technical and organizational measures ensuring compliant processing (art. 24(1) of the GDPR) and for building privacy into the system by design and by default (art. 25(1)–(2) of the GDPR). Moreover, proactively implementing data protection during the development process helps eventual adopters in ensuring compliance, especially with the data protection by design approach.[18]

III THE TENDER APPROACH

The TeNDER project, funded by the Horizon 2020 mechanism, seeks to empower patients with Alzheimer's, Parkinson's, and cardiovascular diseases, by helping them to monitor their health and manage their social environments, prescribed

---

[15] Case C-210/16, *Unabhängiges Landeszentrum für Datenschutz Schleswig-Holstein v. Wirtschaftsakademie Schleswig-Holstein GmbH*, interveners: Facebook Ireland Ltd, Vertreter des Bundesinteresses beim Bundesverwaltungsgericht, ECLI:EU:C:2018:388 (June 5, 2018).
[16] Case C-40/17, *Fashion ID GmbH & Co. KG v. Verbraucherzentrale NRW eV*, interveners: Facebook Ireland Ltd, Landesbeauftragte für Datenschutz und Informationsfreiheit Nordrhein-Westfalen, ECLI:EU:C:2019:629 (July 29, 2019).
[17] Eur. Data Prot. Bd., *Guidelines 07/2020 on the Concepts of Controller and Processor in the GDPR* (2020), https://edpb.europa.eu/our-work-tools/our-documents/guidelines/guidelines-072020-concepts-controller-and-processor-gdpr_en.
[18] Ann Cavoukian, International Council on Global Privacy and Security, By Design, 35 IEEE Potentials 43 (2016).

treatments, and medical appointments. It follows an integrated care model, linking both medical and social aspects, such as (mis)communication and the fragmentation of care. The development process combines existing technologies, such as smartphones, wearables, and sensors, in order to monitor vital signals or alert a caregiver in case of an accident or fall, always consulting with patients to account for their preferences.[19]

As a research project, TeNDER crosses a number of different legal frameworks. Concerning the development process, we have focused on the requirements found in the GDPR, such as the legal basis for processing health data, privacy by design, and pseudonymization measures, and addressed the potential applicability of the Medical Devices Regulation. Once the results are finalized and marketed to health care organizations and caregivers, the preliminary legal findings, contained in several reports conducted through the lifecycle of the project, can serve as guidance to adopters.

In the project, we have adopted a three-step methodology to address the gaps in the regulation of eHealth technologies and to establish good practices for lawful and ethical implementation. First, a benchmark report identified applicable laws and ethical principles in abstracto and analyzed the initial concerns of the nexus between technology and applicable frameworks.[20] Building upon its findings, the three follow-up impact assessments take into consideration privacy, data protection, ethical-societal aspects, and the regulation of medical devices.[21] The final legal report, released in April 2023, provided an evaluation from legal and ethical perspectives of the technologies developed during the project, as well as recommendations for future adopters.[22]

Since the development of eHealth products necessarily takes place in a controlled environment, with a limited number of participants and the roles of different providers known in advance, the legal requirements in a post-project, real-life setting may vary slightly. For example, if the pilots in the project are based on small patient groups, a data protection impact assessment (DPIA) is not always necessary as per art. 35 of the GDPR, while in a larger organizational context it may well be obligatory.[23]

---

[19] TeNDER Health – How TeNDER Works, www.tender-health.eu/project/how-tender-works/.
[20] TeNDER, D1.1 "*First Version of Fundamental Rights, Ethical and Legal Implications and Assessment*" (2020), www.tender-health.eu/project/.here-you-can-find-a-selection-of-the-projects-public-deliverables-as-they-become-available/.
[21] TeNDER, D1.4, "*First version Legal/Ethical Monitoring and Review*" (2021), www.tender-health.eu/project/here-you-can-find-a-selection-of-the-projects-public-deliverables-as-they-become-available/.
[22] TeNDER, D1.6, "*Final Version of Fundamental Rights, Ethical and Legal Implications and Assessment*" (2023), www.tender-health.eu/project/here-you-can-find-a-selection-of-the-projects-public-deliverables-as-they-become-available/.
[23] Danaja Fabcic Povse, Fragmented eHealth Regulation in the EU TeNDER (2022), www.tender-health.eu/fragmented-ehealth-regulation-in-the-eu/.

IV ADDRESSING DATA PROTECTION CHALLENGES: LESSONS LEARNED IN TENDER

A *Roles and Obligations*

In a remote care scenario, the controller will be processing patients' health data, which are considered particularly sensitive due to the data's intimate character. Therefore, a stricter regime applies: Under art. 9, the processing of health data (and other special categories of data) is not permitted, unless one of the criteria in art. 9(2) is met. In this kind of scenario, that could be the explicit consent of the data subject unless prohibited under EU or national law (art. 9(2)(a)). Alternatively, the processing of health data is permitted if the processing is necessary for protecting the vital interests of the data subject, or another person when the data subject is incapable of giving consent (art. 9(2)(c)), such as when the patient is unconscious following an accident. Finally, processing is also permitted if the personal data have been made manifestly public by the data subject (art. 9(2)(d)), which happens when the data are already available to the caregiver or have been published on a social media platform.

In the TeNDER project, we identified legal grounds for consent from art. 6, with the explicit consent from art. 9(b) as an exemption from the art. 9(a) prohibition of processing. However, as many patients with Alzheimer's and Parkinson's diseases experience a decrease in cognitive function, ensuring the informed-ness of their consent can be a challenge. While the GDPR contains special rules for *children's consent* (art. 8 of the GDPR), there is no similar rule for obtaining informed consent from *incapable adults*, nor is this gap addressed in the relevant guidelines of the European Data Protection Board (EDPB).[24]

To resolve this legal gap and ensure that patients were fully briefed, they were provided with both lengthy and simplified information sheets, following bioethical recommendations contained in several (nonbinding) international documents, such as the Declaration of Helsinki and the Council of Europe Recommendation No. R(99)4 on Principles Concerning the Legal Protection of Incapable Adults.[25] While these are not requirements for consent under binding law, they contribute to better involvement of patients with Alzheimer's in research projects.[26]

---

[24] Eur. Data Protection Bd., *Guidelines 05/2020 on Consent under Regulation 2016/679* version 1.1 (2020), https://edpb.europa.eu/sites/edpb/files/files/file1/edpb_guidelines_202005_consent_en.pdf.

[25] World Med. Ass'n, WMA *Declaration of Helsinki – Ethical Principles for Medical Research Involving Human Subjects* (1964), www.wma.net/policies-post/wma-declaration-of-helsinki-ethical-principles-for-medical-research-involving-human-subjects/; Council of Eur., *Recommendation No. R(99)4 of the Committee of Ministers to Member States on Principles Concerning the Legal Protection of Incapable Adults* (1999), www.coe.int/t/dg3/healthbioethic/texts_and_documents/Rec(99)4E.pdf.

[26] Alzheimer Eur., *Understanding Dementia Research*, www.alzheimer-europe.org/research/understanding-dementia-research.

In order to address data protection requirements, we must first identify the controllers and processors involved. In the TeNDER project, we employed fitness wearables in combination with RGB skeleton cameras and microphones, which were placed in different care settings – a retirement home, rehabilitation room in the hospital, day care center, etc. This meant that the user partners, such as health care organizations, were acting as data controllers, since they had determined which tools they would use (*the means*) and what kind of care or therapeutic outcomes (*the purposes*) would be achieved using those means. Technology providers, both external and part of a consortium, acted as data processors, carrying out the instructions given by the controllers. The patients enrolled in the evaluation pilots were recruited by the health care providers and represent the data subjects in this scenario.

To ensure an appropriate techno-legal conversation, the user partners and technology providers (i.e., the controllers and processors) were asked to provide feedback by means of impact assessment questionnaires. Their feedback has informed our approach to solving the specific challenges described below.

B *Specific Challenges of the TeNDER Remote Care Technology*

i Data Sharing with a Third-Party Service Provider

The responsibility of the controller for ensuring compliance with the data protection requirements is complicated by the fact that many RCTs are provided by external providers. To a certain extent, the privacy risks can be mitigated by measures taken by developers and users, including patients, caregivers, and organizations. These counter-measures can help minimize the amount of data processed by external parties when opting out of data sharing is not possible. Normally, the controller and the processor will adopt relevant agreements, such as the controller-processor agreement (art. 28(3)) of the GDPR; however, with external service providers that is sometimes not feasible, and the terms of use/terms of service apply instead.

Data protection in the wearables market calls for special attention as the functionalities of wearables become even more sophisticated and provide for wide-ranging data collection. Personal data of the most intimate nature – activity, moods, emotions, and bodily functions – can be combined with other sources of data, raising such potential harms as discriminatory profiling, manipulative marketing, and data breaches.[27] The lack of data privacy protections could be addressed by a greater adoption of the data protection by design principle and more transparency, especially regarding privacy policies.[28]

---

[27] Kathryn C. Montgomery et al., Ctr. for Digit. Democracy, *Health Wearable Devices in the Big Data Era: Ensuring Privacy, Security, and Consumer Protection* (2016), www.democraticmedia.org/sites/default/files/field/public/2016/aucdd_wearablesreport_final121516.pdf.

[28] Id.; T. Mulder & M. Tudorica, Privacy Policies, Cross-Border Health Data and the GDPR, 28 Info. & Commc'n Tech. L. 261 (2019).

At TeNDER pilot sites, we used fitness wearables, such as the Fitbit, to follow up on patients' rehabilitation and daily routines by tracking events such as energy expenditure, sleep, and activity. The wearables were connected to smartphones and tablets, and the data from the wearables was extracted to paint a comprehensive picture of a patient's movement.[29]

The potential access of Fitbit to the data on the device and the wearable, as the service provider, has been identified as a potential challenge. The Fitbit blog provides some tips on enhancing privacy and data protection while using their services, including going incognito, editing the profile and display name, making personal stats (such as birthday, height, and weight) private, hiding badges, and adjusting for different location settings.[30] However, generally opting out of data sharing with the service provider is not possible. Considering the TeNDER project involves very vulnerable populations, additional safeguards were adopted in the process: Setting up dedicated accounts and email addresses, using devices specifically for the project purposes, and avoiding real names or specific dates of birth as much as possible. These safeguards contribute to the implementation of the principle of data minimization, set in art. 5(1)(c) of the GDPR, which is one of the keystones of privacy and data protection by design.[31]

ii Infrared Cameras and Accidental Capture

In the pilots, we plan to use infrared cameras to keep track of patients' rehabilitation processes and to alert the caregiver should the patient fall. However, cameras can accidentally capture other people aside from the patient.

Our approach was based on the GDPR and the opinion of the EDPB.[32] A video system used to process special categories of data must be based on valid legal grounds as well as a derogation under art. 9. Since TeNDER is a research project, informed explicit consent was collected from the patients prior to the data processing. Adopters in a research setting could rely on the derogation of "scientific research purposes" under art. 9(2)(j), where obtaining explicit consent could not be feasibly done. In this regard, it is noteworthy that the GDPR provides that the term research setting

---

[29] TeNDER, supra note 21.
[30] Danielle Kosecki, 13 Fitbit Community Features You Can Customize for More (or Less!) Privacy, *Fitbit News* (2017), https://blog.fitbit.com/fitbit-privacy-settings/; Danielle Kosecki, Ask Fitbit: How Can I Keep My Stats Private?, *Fitbit News* (2017), https://blog.fitbit.com/go-incognito/.
[31] Nor. Consumer Council, *Consumer Protection in Fitness Wearables* (2016), https://fil.forbrukerradet.no/wp-content/uploads/2016/11/2016-10-26-vedlegg-2-consumer-protection-in-fitness-wearables-forbrukerradet-final-version.pdf; Eur. Data Protection Bd., *Guidelines 4/2019 on Article 25: Data Protection by Design and by Default* version 2.0 (2020), https://edpb.europa.eu/sites/default/files/files/file1/edpb_guidelines_201904_dataprotection_by_design_and_by_default_v2.0_en.pdf.
[32] Eur. Data Protection Bd., *Guidelines 3/2019 on Processing of Personal Data Through Video Devices* version 2.0 (2020), https://edpb.europa.eu/sites/default/files/files/file1/edpb_guidelines_201903_video_devices_en_0.pdf.

"should be interpreted in a broad manner, including for example technological development and demonstration." However, since accidental capture can happen to an undefined audience, relying on their consent is not realistic. In the EDPB's opinion,[33] the legitimate interests of the controller are suggested as an alternative legal basis. However, this basis cannot be relied on if the data subject's rights and interests outweigh the legitimate interest. Considering that RCTs involve health data, it is difficult to see how that would meet the legitimate interests balance test.[34]

To avoid accidental capture in the pilot, the infrared cameras, which process skeleton outlines without biometric data or identifying facial characteristics, will only be used in physiotherapy sessions as part of the rehabilitation room pilot.

iii Integration with EHRs

In order to ensure a more comprehensive overview of a patient's medical history, the development phase includes integrating electronic health records (EHRs) into the system. Clinical history will, later in the project, be matched with data from other devices to ensure an integrated care service. In data protection terms, this contributes to the data accuracy principle. This principle requires that personal data must be accurate and, where necessary, kept up to date, and that inaccurate personal data must be erased or rectified without delay (art. 5(1)(d) of the GDPR). Where patient data is concerned, this principle is very important to ensure the appropriate treatment of the patient, especially if data are going to be fed into artificial intelligence (AI) systems.[35]

One of the challenges in the EU is the diversity of EHR data formats in different member states. To this end, the Commission has adopted a "Recommendation on a European Electronic Health Record" (REHR) exchange format.[36] According to its Recital 10, the goal of the REHR is the interoperability of different EHRs and to allow for processing information in a consistent manner between those health information systems, so that the provision of cross-border health care services (including remote care) becomes easier for the patient. REHR is a voluntary interoperability system – member states that sign up should ensure that at least the following data points should be interoperable: Patient summaries, e-prescriptions and e-dispensations, laboratory results, medical imaging and records, and hospital discharge reports (point 11 of the REHR).

---

[33] Id.
[34] Article 29 Working Party, Eur. Commn', *Opinion 06/2014 on the Notion of Legitimate Interests of the Data Controller Under Article 7 of Directive 95/46/EC* (2014), https://ec.europa.eu/justice/article-29/documentation/opinion-recommendation/files/2014/wp217_en.pdf.
[35] Studio Legale Stefanelli & Stefanelli, Artificial Intelligence, Medical Devices and GDPR in Healthcare: Everything You Need to Know About the Current Legal Frame, *Lexology* (2022) www.lexology.com/library/detail.aspx?g=8cba1347-0323-4951-b9b5-69015f6e169f.
[36] Eur. Comm'n, *Commission Recommendation of 6.2.2019 on a European Electronic Health Record exchange format* C (2019) 800 final.

Since EHRs involve patient data, the link to the GDPR is clear. To set up the system in accordance with the data protection framework, the development follows the Article 29 Working Party's guidelines on EHR.[37] Even though this document was released on the basis of the Directive 95/46, many of its principles are still relevant under the new regime. Among the recommendations of the document are strong access controls and authentication measures for the patient and the health care professional; further use of information contained in the EHR only for legitimate purposes, such as providing better treatment; and data security and data minimization measures, such as separate storage of especially sensitive data.[38]

The integration of electronic health care records is still in progress, and its legal aspects will be evaluated at the end of the project. The techno-legal collaboration on EHR integration has, so far, focused on two aspects: The mapping of applicable legal frameworks, as described in the above paragraphs, and their take-up by developers in order to build the products.[39]

iv Preliminary Results: Essential Data Protection Requirements for Developing Remote Care Technologies

The main takeaway from our work in the TeNDER project so far can be summarized as a set of essential requirements for potential future developers and users of similar technologies. This is by no means an exhaustive list – as explained above, unlike real-life health care settings, research projects are a controlled environment with highly formalized procedures aimed at developing and testing technologies. In contrast, organizations who adopt RCTs for their own patients may be required to comply with additional obligations, including carrying out a data protection impact assessment as required by art. 35 of the GDPR or adopting processing agreements under art. 28(3), enabling data subject rights requests (especially the right to access) and the portability of health care records, and so on. While the system is being developed in line with the GDPR, future end-users will play a major role in complying with data protection and other sectoral or national laws. An expanded list of the requirements summarized below in Table 3.1 is available in the last legal report of the project, published in April 2023.[40]

---

[37] Article 29 Working Party, supra note 13.
[38] Id.
[39] TeNDER, D5.3, *First Report on the Health Record and Pathway Gathering* (2021), www.tender-health.eu/project/here-you-can-find-a-selection-of-the-projects-public-deliverables-as-they-become-available/.
[40] TeNDER, D1.6, *"Final Version of Fundamental Rights, Ethical and Legal Implications and Assessment"* (2023), www.tender-health.eu/project/here-you-can-find-a-selection-of-the-projects-public-deliverables-as-they-become-available/.

TABLE 3.1 *Essential data protection requirements for RCTs: Preliminary results of TeNDER*

Role in RCT	Potential data protection role	Essential requirements
Developers and technology providers	Potential processors	Design RCTs according to the principles of data protection by design and by default (art. 25 of the GDPR), especially when different devices and tools are being used, such as in the case of EHR integration. This will also operationalize the principle of data minimization: no other personal data than that which is adequate and relevant to the specific purpose will be processed. If EHR are fed into the system, ensure the data contained in the records are accurate and kept up to date, as per art. 5(1)(d) of the GDPR. Assess whether they are a processor under art. 4(8) of the GDPR (the entity that carries out the processing on behalf of the controller) and take the required measures, such as notifying the controller (the health care organization) about the involvement of other processors (third parties such as external providers of RCTs or other technologies).
Users (health organizations)	Potential controllers	Apply technical and organizational measures to ensure general compliance with data protection rules (art. 5(2) and 24 of the GDPR). Ensure valid consent is given. Since many of the patients enrolled in the pilots are experiencing cognitive decline, the information given must be appropriate to the patients' level of understanding. Preferably, a trusted person should be involved in the process of obtaining consent (e.g., a family member or other caregiver). If using cameras or other especially intrusive technologies, consult the patients on their placement within the room, and inform them of the option to turn the device off. Keep data in the EHR accurate and up to date; respond to patient requests for rectification of their medical information.
Users (patients)	Data subjects	The onus to maintain data protection and security measures is on the developers and health care organizations, not on the user (the principle of data protection by default). When using third-party devices and opting out of data sharing is desired but not possible (e.g., in the case of wearables), use mitigation measures, such as using pseudonyms instead of names, inputting approximate date of birth, not connecting the device to social media presence, etc.

V CONCLUSION

What do the findings of this chapter mean for the development of RCTs? I have taken a two-pronged approach and discussed the application of selected legal provisions to RCTs in general, against the application of the same provisions to specific technology developed as part of the TeNDER project. While it may not be possible to fully resolve the tension between particular technologies and abstract legal frameworks, in general, knowing how to interpret the law can bring us closer to bridging the gap.

Responding to the data protection challenges of developing RCTs involves both a technological and organizational angle, such as using different tools in appropriate contexts (e.g., cameras in the rehabilitation room rather than in patients' homes), as well as legal solutions (e.g., applying additional safeguards to ensure the informed-ness of the patients' consent). What is acceptable to patients who are receiving remote care in the privacy of their own home, rather than in health care organizations, as well as what kind of technological development is feasible, should be further explored by interdisciplinary, socio-technological-legal research. Nor are all the legal questions resolved, such as the lack of legal provisions under the GDPR that safeguard the consent of persons with cognitive decline. The same problem applies regarding the role of the terms of use of service providers in ensuring that the external processors will comply with the data protection rules.

The scope of this chapter is likewise limited by the scope of the project itself. Since the latter is largely concerned with development, this chapter explores the development process as well, rather than the eventual use of the products in health care organizations after the end of the project. Further, the project will be running for another year, and the results reported in this chapter are preliminary as of the spring of 2022. Legal findings will mature together with the technology, and some of the legal aspects concerning the future use of the TeNDER technologies will be clearer at the end of the development and testing phases.

4

Renegotiating the Social Contract for Use of Health Information

Lessons Learned from Newborn Screening and Implications for At-Home Digital Care

Jodyn Platt and Sharon Kardia

I INTRODUCTION

At-home digital and diagnostic care has expanded in the wake of the COVID-19 pandemic. This change has set off a cascade of secondary effects including new pathways for information flows with an array of direct-to-consumer companies and products, alternative uses of information for health, and a renegotiation of space by shifting when, where, and how we interact with the health care system. This new landscape requires a reexamination of the implicit and explicit social contract between patients, clinicians, and the health delivery system. At-home digital care involves monitoring patients outside of the clinic walls and increased data sharing between traditional care providers and the private companies that build devices. For example, Cue Health offers testing for COVID-19, with the results sent to an app on a personal smartphone and to providers who can provide follow-up treatment.[1] The expansion of at-home digital care raises a number of ethical and policy questions: How is health information shared and with whom? What is the appropriate role of commercial companies? Are people who continue to receive care in clinical settings subject to the new norms of at-home care with respect to remote patient monitoring or data sharing?

Many of these questions have been raised before. Technology and circumstance have often driven change in health care, with policy playing a formative role. The electronic medical record, for example, was rapidly adopted as the American Recovery and Reinvestment Act of 2009 and the Health Information Technology for Economic and Clinical Health Act (HITECH) were passed in response to the 2009 financial crisis in the USA. These acts of legislation led to the investment of billions of dollars in health information infrastructure, and the widespread adoption of the electronic medical record meant that data could be collected, stored, and (ideally)

---

[1] Cue, *What Is the Cue Health Monitoring System?* (November 20, 2022), https://cuehealth.com/products/.

readily shared to support learning, health care systems,[2] precision health,[3] and comparative effectiveness research.[4] Subsequent policies in the 21st Century Cures Act have continued this investment and commitment to incentivizing interoperability and data sharing.

In clinical research, the Human Genome Project similarly sparked innovation in research information infrastructure that enabled shared data and biospecimens, often in the context of biobanks. The number of large population biobanks housing millions of biological samples linked to individuals' health data has increased over the past decades in response to demand for the scientific and economic efficiencies that multi-use biobanks offer.[5] Technological advances have made it simpler, safer, and more inexpensive to measure vast arrays of molecular data (e.g., genome-wide chips for DNA, RNA, and methylation), as well as to catalogue and store sensitive health information (e.g., barcoding, robotic retrieval, encryption, and firewalls). In the United States, biobank repositories have emerged primarily from large health systems (e.g., Kaiser Permanente, Marshfield Clinic, Veterans Administration) and research institutions (e.g., Vanderbilt University) as natural extensions of the data collection and research already underway therein.[6]

The rapid adoption of new technologies impacts health care culture, care delivery pathways, payment, patient engagement, and, ultimately, the social contract between patients and the systems that care for them. In this chapter, we examine the emergence of the Michigan BioTrust for Health in 2009 as an instance of renegotiation of the social contract between stakeholders in response to new technologies and evolutionary changes in the scientific and health enterprises. Based on prior research on the ethical and policy implications for patients that were part of the legacy system (i.e., those being asked to make the change from old to new systems of care), we review the key findings on attitudes about informed consent, notification, and partnerships with commercial companies, and consider the implications for the governance of at-home digital health care.

II FROM NEWBORN SCREENING TO THE MICHIGAN BIOTRUST FOR HEALTH

With a century-long history of collecting, storing, and analyzing information for surveillance and monitoring community health, public health departments are

---

[2] Lynn M. Ethredge, A Rapid-Learning Health System, 26 *Health Affairs* W107–18 (2007).
[3] Francis S. Collins et al., A Vision for the Future of Genomics Research, 6934 Nature 422, 835–47 (2003).
[4] Jeremy Sugarman, Ethics and Regulatory Challenges and Opportunities in Patient-Centered Comparative Effectiveness Research, 4 Acad. Med.: J. Ass'n American Med. Colls. 91, 455–57 (2016).
[5] David Altshuler, Mark J. Daly, & Eric S. Lander, Genetic Mapping in Human Disease, 5903 Science 322, 881–88 (2008).
[6] Helen Swede, Carol L. Stone, and Alyssa R. Norwood, National Population-Based Biobanks for Genetic Research, 3 Genetics in Med. 9, 141–49 (2007).

potentially major contributors to the growing number of large population biobanks. For example, the residual newborn screening bloodspots that health departments collect and store are almost fully representative of a population, as they contain blood samples from ~99.9 percent of children born in a particular state. From an epidemiological perspective, this resource is the gold standard for population health assessment and research, given its completeness and lack of ascertainment bias. If made available or even marketed as public health biobanks, these repositories could contribute to robust population health studies when linked to a wide range of public health surveillance databases. And yet, the repurposing of newborn screening bloodspots to include research use challenges the expectations under which they were collected.

In 2009, the state of Michigan endeavored to pursue expanded uses of newborn screening bloodspots by opening the Michigan BioTrust for Health as a steward organization, tasked with navigating the data governance challenges inherent to the large-scale aggregation of medical information. Michigan's BioTrust for Health holds bloodspot cards for over four million children born in the state of Michigan and is one of the largest biobanks in the USA. The BioTrust is run through a nonprofit organization, the Michigan Neonatal Biobank, providing health researchers with access to de-identified samples and information, contingent on scientific review, institutional review board (IRB) approval, and payment. The biobank comprises a retrospective ("legacy") collection of approximately four million bloodspot cards stored from babies born in Michigan between July 1984 and April 2010 – before consent mechanisms were put in place – along with a prospective collection of dried bloodspots added to the biobank since its formal inception in Fall 2010, and included in the research pool only with a written consent.[7]

III CONSUMER PREFERENCES FOR THE USE OF NEWBORN SCREENING BLOODSPOTS AND HEALTH INFORMATION: IMPLICATIONS FOR DIGITAL HEALTH AT HOME

Over the course of approximately five years (2009–2015), we conducted several empirical studies assessing consumer perspectives on the uses of newborn screening bloodspots, including preferences for consent and notification to understand. This work focused on the so-called "legacy collection" of bloodspots held by the Michigan Department of Community Health (MDCH) and collected prior to policies being put in place for obtaining consent for research uses. There were approximately four million people with bloodspots in the BioTrust who fell into this group. We held ten community meetings across the state of Michigan ($n = 393$),[8] met with

---

[7] Daniel B. Thiel et al., Community Perspectives on Public Health Biobanking: An Analysis of Community Meetings on the Michigan BioTrust for Health, 2 J. Cmty. Genetics 5, 125–38 (2014).
[8] Id.

college students at 20 campuses (n = 2,010),[9] and conducted an online deliberative jury (n = 67).[10] We also conducted surveys, including three cohorts of the State of the State Survey (n = 2,618) and a simulated dynamic consent process (n = 187).[11] To try to reach a greater proportion of people in Michigan, we conducted a Facebook campaign that reached over 1.8 million people.[12] In this section of the chapter, we draw on the published work in this area, as well as our own reflections on it nearly ten years later, to describe what we learned about three key issues that are likely to shape ethical and policy assessments for at-home digital care: (1) Preferences for consent and notification, (2) relationships with commercial companies, and (3) trust and governance.

A *Consent and Notification*

Our findings with respect to expectations for consent and notification were consistent throughout our work on the BioTrust.[13] We found that a clear majority of people would like some form of notification. With respect to consent, preferences were divided. When offered a choice between providing a one-time "broad consent" that allows for unspecified future uses versus providing consent for each use of bloodspots, we found that about half of the people we interviewed or surveyed prefer a one-time notification and about half want to provide informed consent for specific uses of their information. These findings were consistent with other research on preferences for consent in similar activities, such as large-scale, longitudinal cohort studies.[14] We also found that feelings of respect and trust predicted preferences for broad versus specific consent. Specifically, those who see specific informed consent as important also see consent as an important sign of respect and may have less trust in the health system, while those who do not need to provide consent every time are more trusting of the health system.

---

[9] J.E. Platt et al., "Born in Michigan? You're in the Biobank": Engaging Population Biobank Participants through Facebook Advertisements, 4 Pub. Health Genomics 16, 145–58 (2013).

[10] Ann Mongoven et al., Negotiating Deliberative Ideals in Theory and Practice: A Case Study in "Hybrid Design," 1 J. Deliberative Democracy 12 (2016).

[11] Michigan State University Institute for Public Policy and Social Research, *State of the State Survey 63 (Fall 2012)* (2012), http://ippsr.msu.edu/soss/; Michigan State University Institute for Public Policy and Social Research, *State of the State Survey 66 (Fall 2013)* (2013), http://ippsr.msu.edu/soss/; Michigan State University Institute for Public Policy and Social Research, *State of the State Survey 67 (Winter 2014)* (2014), http://ippsr.msu.edu/soss/; Daniel B. Thiel et al., Testing an Online, Dynamic Consent Portal for Large Population Biobank Research, 1 Pub. Health Genomics 18, 26–39 (2015).

[12] Platt et al., supra note 9.

[13] Id.; Thiel et al., supra note 12; Tevah Platt et al., Engaging a State: Facebook Comments on a Large Population Biobank, 3 J. Cmty. Genetics 8, 183–97 (2017).

[14] Jodyn Platt et al., Public Preferences Regarding Informed Consent Models for Participation in Population-Based Genomic Research, 16 Genetics in Med. 1, 11–18 (2014).

Expectations for informed consent for the collection of data for research are well-established, while there are none for data used in the context of public health or quality improvement. Notification of data sharing is addressed in the Health Insurance Portability and Accountability Act (HIPAA) regulations, but, in practice, it is a blackbox for consumers. Developing, implementing, and maintaining consent for research is one of the greatest practical barriers in creating public health biobanks or repurposing the use of public health data and biological samples. Operationalizing consent depends on whether proposed research uses already-existing samples and databases, or if the research requires samples and data to be collected prospectively. For newborn screening, it would be impracticable for many states to obtain individual consent given the age of the data or the number of samples. In Michigan, the federal Office of Human Research Protections advised the MDCH that its storage and use of newborn screening bloodspots constituted human subjects research necessitating IRB review. The MDCH IRB stated that new samples would need documentation of consent. The existing four million samples could be issued a waiver of consent based on the impracticability of contacting subjects individually, contingent upon a good-faith effort to inform the public that the repository exists and that there are clear processes for those who choose to withdraw.

Digital health at home faces a similar quagmire of ethical and pragmatic challenges to implementing consent or notification. There are complex contingencies to the social license that purveyors of digital health face; trust in their services depends on the service being provided, their consumer base, the quality of the product, and the risk associated with faulty products.[15] At present, informed consent in digital applications is reduced to the notification of privacy policies. Cue Health, for example, which rapidly specialized in at-home COVID-19 testing and services, addresses the collection, use, sharing, and privacy of data gathered from patients participating in their website, app, and testing services.[16] Updates are posted on the website, meaning consumers need to check for updates rather than being notified directly. Consent is further complicated by the complex set of relationships required to deliver care and the limited responsibilities of any one actor. The Cue Health privacy policy (typical of this type of service and application) notes that they may link to outside websites and services for which they are not responsible. This leaves the responsibility for notification, in essence, up to consumers themselves to follow from one use and user to the next. Our experience with the BioTrust suggests this is not sufficient and that the future of digital health at home would benefit from greater levels of specificity and higher standards for quality of informed consent and notification that account for the full spectrum and scope of data sharing.

---

[15] Camille Nebeker, John Torous, & Rebecca J. Bartlett Ellis, Building the Case for Actionable Ethics in Digital Health Research Supported by Artificial Intelligence, 17 BMC Med. 1, 137 (2019).

[16] Cue, *Cue® Health Privacy Policy* (November 20, 2022), https://cuehealth.com/about/data-and-privacy/us/privacy-policy/.

B Comfort with Commercial Companies

One factor that drove the expanded use of newborn screening bloodspots for research is the potential use of the resource by commercial companies. The use of newborn screening bloodspots for research was hailed as a goldmine.[17] Our research has revealed the desire for greater transparency about partnerships with commercial companies, calling for policies of "disclosure plus" that take extra measures to communicate about the commercial aspects of research.[18] In our qualitative work, we have found that many people are acutely aware of commercial partnerships as a reality of health systems in the United States. Beyond this common recognition, there were two attitudes about this aspect of the biomedical enterprise that often lay in tension with one another. First, there were those who already had a mistrust of the system and considered profit-seeking as evidence that the government and/or the medical community could not be trusted. Second, there were those who saw commercial partnerships as a benefit to society that should be an object of investment. For both groups, demonstrating the benefits of sharing health information, and to whom they accrue, is a way of being accountable to the trust given to the public health system as being good stewards of information. Our experience was consistent with the findings in contemporary literature on the issue of the commercialization of biobanks.[19]

For biobanks and, more recently, health care systems, the consequence of mingling the business aspects of information with expectations of responsible stewardship has been volatile. In managing public health information as a marketable biobank, the relationship of a health department to the public becomes a critical consideration. Accusations of the Texas Department of Health bartering with newborn screening bloodspots still resonate today.[20] The University of Chicago faced litigation after it partnered with Google to analyze health records to develop digital diagnostics.[21] Memorial Sloan Kettering entered a deal with Paige.AI to hold an exclusive license to tissue slides and pathology reports for twenty-five million

---

[17] Jennifer Couzin-Frankel, Science Gold Mine, Ethical Minefield, 5924 Science 324, 166–68 (2009).
[18] Kayte Spector-Bagdady et al., Encouraging Participation and Transparency in Biobank Research, 8 Health Affairs 37, 1313–20 (2018).
[19] Timothy Caulfield et al., A Review of the Key Issues Associated with the Commercialization of Biobanks, 1 J. Law Biosciences 1, 94–110 (2014); Christine Critchley, Dianne Nicol, & Margaret Otlowski, The Impact of Commercialisation and Genetic Data Sharing Arrangements on Public Trust and the Intention to Participate in Biobank Research, 3 Pub. Health Genomics 18, 160–72 (2015).
[20] Ellen Matloff, Your Baby's Newborn Screening Blood Sample Could Be Used To Convict You Of A Crime. It Just Happened In New Jersey, Forbes (November 21, 2022), www.forbes.com/sites/ellenmatloff/2022/09/22/your-babys-newborn-screening-blood-sample-could-be-used-to-convict-you-of-a-crime-it-just-happened-in-new-jersey/.
[21] Daisuke Wakabayashi, Google and the University of Chicago Are Sued Over Data Sharing, The New York Times (June 26, 2019), www.nytimes.com/2019/06/26/technology/google-university-chicago-data-sharing-lawsuit.html.

patients, causing an "uproar": Concerns over the commercialization of patient data – even if it is anonymized – renewed interest in the scope and significance of conflicts of interest.[22] Rational people could argue for both sides of each of these cases. The case against the University of Chicago, for example, was eventually dismissed, and Sloan Kettering issued a statement clarifying the relationship between the institution and Paige.AI.[23]

Each of these cases suggests that the risk of navigating in the "gray zone" is, at the minimum, a betrayal of trust as a harbinger of what may come for the companies and health systems moving out of the clinic and laboratory and into the home. Commercial companies are an integral part of the expansion of at-home care that is digital and diagnostic, but a policy of "disclosure plus" for at-home digital health is complicated given the nature of the digital health ecosystem and the lack of clear chains of accountability. Regulatory modernization will need to be a priority as partnerships become more ubiquitous. Novel strategies for licensing data, for example, might be pursued to give consumers greater control over how their health information is used and how profits are shared to promote the use of data as a public good. Novel policy regimes such as this can address the lack of transparency about commercial data use. They can also promote autonomy and respect for persons – the goal of informed consent – in an environment in which informed consent is not feasible or practicable.

C Trust and Governance

The use of newborn screening bloodspots for research demanded a shift in the terms of use. Such renegotiations have happened before – and will continue. Experience suggests that such shifts are motivated by a promise to improve public health and health care delivery systems, but they also raise questions of equity and challenge the public's trust in the biomedical enterprise. The seminal case settled by Arizona State University and the Havasupai Indian Tribe underscores the importance of communicating the scope and nature of the use of samples and data to research participants.[24] At issue was the secondary use of data and samples without the permission or knowledge of the participants, a fact that deeply offended tribal leaders, leading not only to a lawsuit, but also to an effective moratorium on medical research in that community and a rift in a partnership that had taken decades to build.[25] A distrust of

---

[22] Charles Ornstein & Katie Thomas, Sloan Kettering's Cozy Deal with Start-Up Ignites a New Uproar, *The New York Times* (September 20, 2018), www.nytimes.com/2018/09/20/health/memorial-sloan-kettering-cancer-paige-ai.html.

[23] Memorial Sloan Kettering Cancer Center, *Memorial Sloan Kettering and Paige.AI* (November 20, 2022), www.mskcc.org/news-releases/msk-and-paige-ai.

[24] Amy Harmon, Indian Tribe Wins Fight to Limit Research of Its DNA, *The New York Times* (April 21, 2010), www.nytimes.com/2010/04/22/us/22dna.html.

[25] Rex Dalton, When Two Tribes Go to War, 6999 Nature 430, 500–502 (2004).

research and public health continues for many in African American communities, where past public health programs, such as sickle cell screening in the 1970s, were implemented unjustly. A failure to invest in appropriate education about sickle cell anemia resulted in genetic discrimination in the form of discriminating and stigmatizing marriage laws.[26] In our work with communities in Michigan, we often heard skepticism that key stakeholders would be included: For example, "Can I truly trust you? African American people are always last to know. I want involvement and information." We also heard a concern about a slippery slope of hidden data collection and use: "What other lab specimens are being taken without the knowledge of the person being tested? This will end as a trust issue...."[27]

Public health biobanks that use newborn screening information and biospecimens are unique in their inclusivity, and yet the policies and practices that stem from the use of health information may be discriminatory and inequitable. At the same time, the collection of data when it is used for health often faces fewer barriers and is treated as exceptional when compared to other types of information. Public health data is often collected without consent, but as an activity of a public institution makes it accountable as such, expanding the use of data to include research and research institutions demands a new layer of accountability and a demonstration of the trustworthiness of both the stewards (i.e., public health bodies) and the users of health information.

The risk associated with the collection of information without ongoing governance to ensure fair use of the information longitudinally is exemplified by the 2009 *Beleno v. Texas Department of State Health Services* case, in which the Department of Health settled by agreeing to destroy their repository of five million bloodspots collected as a part of their newborn screening program.[28] Reporters reviewing nine years-worth of emails at the health department found evidence that the department suffered from a lack of guidance or policies to handle novel requests for biobanked data.[29]

Digital health operates as a market that lacks clear governance and ethical guidelines. Trustworthiness of the enterprise as a whole is a goal, but it is unclear who should be involved in oversight. The limitations to accountability for any one actor leaves consumers with the responsibility of tracking privacy policies from one user to the next. Innovation of traditional governance mechanisms is

---

[26] Neil A. Holtzman & Michael S. Watson (eds.) Promoting Safe and Effective Genetic Testing in the United States. Task Force on Genetic Testing. National Institutes of Health-Department of Energy (1997), www.genome.gov/10001733/genetic-testing-report.

[27] Daniel B. Thiel et al., Community Perspectives on Public Health Biobanking: An Analysis of Community Meetings on the Michigan BioTrust for Health, 2 J. Cmty. Genetics 5, 125–38 (2014).

[28] Richard Hughes IV, Spreeha Choudhury, & Alaap Shah, Newborn Screening Blood Spot Retention And Reuse: A Clash Of Public Health And Privacy Interests, *Health Affairs Forefront* (November 20, 2022), https://doi.org/10.1377/forefront.20221004.177058.

[29] Emily Ramshaw, DNA Deception, *The Texas Tribune* (February 22, 2010), www.texastribune.org/2010/02/22/dshs-turned-over-hundreds-of-dna-samples-to-feds/.

needed to temper special interests and meaningfully manage conflicts of interest. Obtaining meaningful community awareness would require an investment in outreach and education for large, diverse populations through novel governance structures that engage the range of stakeholders and actors in the digital health ecosystem. This provides an opportunity to apply principles that emphasize equity and inclusion such as "centering at the margins,"[30] that is, including minoritized people and interests.

IV CONCLUSION

The experience of biobanking residual newborn screening bloodspots matters not only because these repositories are vast, valuable, and politically volatile, but also because they are harbingers of the ethical and policy issues that will continue to arise in this new era of integrated health information technology and digital health at home. Learning from the public about data and biospecimen use in the context of the BioTrust suggests that the future of digital health at home would benefit from clear expectations and mechanisms for consent and notification. Those who prefer greater involvement in informed consent also see consent as an important sign of respect and may have less trust in the health system. Furthermore, demonstrating the benefits of sharing health information, and to whom they accrue, is a way of being accountable to the trust given to information systems – be they public or private – as being good stewards of information. Novel strategies for licensing data, for example, might be pursued to give consumers greater control over how their health information is used and how profits are shared to promote the use of data as a public good.

Both newborn screening and at-home digital health care are examples of data-generating activities that create information that is of potential value beyond its original intended use. For newborn screening, public health interests justified the original data collection, while research benefits justified the expanded use of those bloodspots. In the case of at-home digital health care, launching digital modalities involves a wider range of entities, including commercial consumer technology companies and a broad scope for data sharing. Public health biobanking has raised issues for consumers with respect to consent and notification, the role of commercial companies, and sustainable governance. Underlying these issues are questions of how to sufficiently notify consumers about the use of their data, how to negotiate the commercial interests in their data, and how to engage and empower the public as a key stakeholder. The issues raised around newborn screening biobanks presented in this chapter suggest that governance should include policies for access, conflicts of interest, and equity, while investing in outreach and education so that

---

[30] Chandra L. Ford & Collins O. Airhihenbuwa, The Public Health Critical Race Methodology: Praxis for Antiracism Research, 8 Social Science & Med. 71, 1390–98 (2010).

patients are informed and transparency is both meaningful and maintained. As a rapidly expanding area of health care, digital health at home has, an opportunity to create new avenues for access and equity that may be honored first by assessing its guiding principles, and then by creating systems of governance and engagement that improve upon the current system of care.

PART II

Digital Home Diagnostics for Specific Conditions

Daniel B. Kramer

INTRODUCTION

Part I of this volume explored the novel concerns about privacy and data raised by home-based digital diagnostics. These arguments surrounding data access, rights, and regulation were framed primarily in abstract terms applicable to the very broad category of digital diagnostics. Part II carries these themes forward into three specific disease areas of profound public health, policy, and bioethical importance. The rise of new technology and telemedicine-based diagnostic pathways for these conditions – cardiovascular disease, reproductive health, and neurodegenerative disease – builds on accelerating advances in sensors, data transmission, artificial intelligence (AI), and data science. The COVID-19 pandemic amplified the opportunity and imperative to provide diagnostic and potentially therapeutic services outside of traditional clinical settings. New devices and systems may not only replace traditional care, but also expand the reach of critical screening and diagnosis to patients otherwise unable to access or navigate health systems. The three chapters in this part thus present real-world case studies of the hopes and hazards of applying digital diagnostics with a disease-specific focus at population-wide scale.

Patrik Bächtiger and colleagues introduce this part with their chapter, "Patient Self-Administered Screening for Cardiovascular Disease Using Artificial Intelligence in the Home." The authors outline a novel attempt in the United Kingdom to address late or missed diagnoses of congestive heart failure, valvular heart disease, and atrial fibrillation – all conditions with high morbidity and mortality that can be substantially mitigated with early treatment. Using electronic health records from general practitioners, patients at high risk for these conditions are invited to use (in their own homes) an electronic stethoscope with the ability to record electrocardiograms (ECGs) as well as heart sounds, which then feed into AI algorithms for near-immediate diagnoses. While the theoretical clinical, public health, and economic benefits of this new pathway may be well-grounded, the authors consider several ethical features of the program to be in need of greater scrutiny. Equity may be both advanced or hindered by AI-enabled cardiovascular screening, which may reduce barriers to accessing traditional clinical evaluation and mitigate cognitive bias, at the cost of exposing patients to the biases of the algorithms themselves. Relatedly, decentralizing clinical screening into the home necessarily creates new roles and responsibilities for patients and families, and establishes new data structures with distinct potential risks and benefits. The authors propose programmatic metrics that might capture empirical evidence to adjudicate these ethical questions.

Equity, agency, and control of data extend into Donley and Rebouché's contribution, "The Promise of Telehealth for Abortion," which evaluates the growing but tremulous landscape for abortion services supported by telehealth and related advances. The authors trace the legal and regulatory arc of medical abortion services provided without direct in-person care, and the more recent conflicts raised by new state laws in the wake of the epochal *Dobbs* decision. In many states, the possibility of digital surveillance supporting abortion-related prosecutions raises the stakes for data rights and digital privacy just as new options expand for consumer- and clinically driven diagnostic devices or wearables capturing physiologic signals consistent with pregnancy. In theory and practice, it may already be the case that a smartwatch might "know" someone is pregnant before its wearer, and that knowledge necessarily lives in a digital health ecosystem potentially accessible to law enforcement and other parties. Donley and Rebouché nimbly forecast the challenges and future conflict in balancing access and safe provision of abortion services, while posing difficult questions about the legal risks borne by both patients and providers.

This part concludes by moving from the beginning of life toward its twilight, with Erickson and Largent's exploration of the intersection between digital diagnostics and neurodegenerative diseases, "Monitoring (on) Your Mind: Digital Biomarkers for Alzheimer's Disease." Alzheimer's disease and its related disorders retain their status as classical "clinical diagnoses" – those that cannot be made based on a physical exam, imaging, symptoms, or traditional blood tests alone, but only by an expert amalgamation of individual findings. While Alzheimer's currently lacks the disease-modifying treatments available for many cardiovascular conditions, facilitating diagnoses through digital means may offer other benefits to patients and their families, and could potentially provide a bridgehead toward studying treatments in the future. The authors outline several novel avenues for leveraging digital diagnostics to identify cognitive impairment, many of which draw insights from everyday activities not usually considered as inputs for health measurement. Increasingly, digitized and wirelessly-connected features of daily life, including driving, appliances, phones, and smart speakers, will enable the algorithmic identification of early cognitive or functional limitations. Erickson and Largent ask how these advances complicate questions of consent and communication outside of traditional clinics, and revisit concerns about equity and either improved or exacerbated disparities in access to care.

Uniquely within this part, however, Erickson and Largent confront a more fundamental question posed by increasingly powerful digital diagnostics: *How much do we really want to know about our own health?* While fraught in other ways, diagnoses of heart failure or pregnancy generally cannot be ignored or dismissed, and (legal risks aside) patient care can generally be improved with earlier and more precise diagnosis. Identifying early (in particular, very early) cognitive impairment, however, offers more complex trade-offs among patients and their current or future caregivers, particularly in the absence of effective therapies. While genetics can offer similar pre-diagnosis or risk prediction, a critical distinction raised by digital diagnostics is their ubiquity: Anyone who drives, uses a smartphone, or types on a keyboard creates potential inputs to their eventual digital phenotyping, with all the attendant burdens. Digital diagnostics, used in our own homes, applied to more and more disease areas, will require a deeper reconciliation between relentless innovation and the boundaries of individuals' desire to understand their own health.

5

Patient Self-Administered Screening for Cardiovascular Disease Using Artificial Intelligence in the Home

Patrik Bächtiger, Mihir A. Kelshiker, Marie E. G. Moe, Daniel B. Kramer, and Nicholas S. Peters

I INTRODUCTION

The United Kingdom (UK) National Health Service (NHS) is funding technologies for home-based diagnosis that draw on artificial intelligence (AI).[1] Broadly defined, AI is the ability of computer algorithms to interpret data at human or super-human levels of performance.[2] One compelling use case involves patient-recorded cardiac waveforms that are interpreted in real time by AI to predict the presence of common, clinically actionable cardiovascular diseases. In this case, both electrocardiograms (ECGs) and phonocardiograms (heart sounds) are recorded by a handheld device applied by the patient in a self-administered smart stethoscope examination, communicating waveforms to the cloud via smartphone for subsequent AI interpretation – principally known as AI-ECG. Validation studies suggest the accuracy of this technology approaches or exceeds many established national screening programs for other diseases.[3] More broadly, the combination of a new device (a modified handheld stethoscope), novel AI algorithms, and communication via smartphone coalesce into a distinct clinical care pathway that may become increasingly prevalent across multiple disease areas.

However, the deployment of a home-based screening program combining hardware, AI, and a cloud-based digital platform for administration – all anchored in patient self-administration – raises distinct ethical challenges for safe, effective, and trustworthy implementation. This chapter approaches these concerns in five parts. First, we briefly outline the organizational structure of the NHS and associated regulatory bodies responsible for evaluating the safety of medical technology. Second,

---

[1] United Kingdom Government Department of Health and Social Care, *Health Secretary Announces £250 Million Investment in Artificial Intelligence*, Gov.UK (August 8, 2019), www.gov.uk/government/news/health-secretary-announces-250-million-investment-in-artificial-intelligence.
[2] Patrik Bächtiger, et al., Artificial Intelligence, Data Sensors and Interconnectivity: Future Opportunities for Heart Failure, Cardiac Failure Rev. 6 (2020).
[3] Patrik Bächtiger, et al., Point-of-Care Screening for Heart Failure with Reduced Ejection Fraction Using Artificial Intelligence during ECG-Enabled Stethoscope Examination in London, UK: A Prospective, Observational, Multicentre Study, 4 Lancet Digit. Health 117, 117–25 (2022).

we highlight NHS plans to prioritize digital health and the specific role of AI in advancing this goal with a focus on cardiovascular disease. Third, we review the clinical imperative for early diagnosis of heart failure in community settings, and the established clinical evidence supporting the use of a novel AI-ECG-based tool to do so. Fourth, we examine the ethical concerns with the AI-ECG diagnostic pathway according to considerations of equity, agency, and data rights across key stakeholders. Finally, we propose a multi-agency strategy anchored in a purposefully centralized view of this novel diagnostic pathway – with the goal of preserving and promoting trust, patient engagement, and public health.

II THE UK NATIONAL HEALTH SERVICE AND RESPONSIBLE AGENCIES

For the purposes of this chapter, we focus on England, where NHS England is the responsible central government entity for the delivery of health care (Scotland, Wales, and Northern Ireland run devolved versions of the NHS). The increasing societal and political pressure to modernize the NHS has led to the formation of agencies tasked with this specific mandate, each of which plays a key role in evaluating and deploying the technology at issue in this chapter. Within NHS England, the NHSX was established with the aim of setting national NHS policy and developing best practices across technology, digital innovation, and data, including data sharing and transparency. Closely related, NHS Digital is the national provider of information, data, and IT systems for commissioners, analysts, and clinicians in health and social care in England. From a regulatory perspective, the Medicines and Healthcare products Regulatory Agency (MHRA) is responsible for ensuring that medicines and medical devices (including software) work and are acceptably safe for market entry within the scope of their labelled indications. Post Brexit, the UK's underlying risk-based classification system remains similar to that of its international counterparts, categorizing risk into three incremental classes determined by the intended use of the product. In practice, most diagnostic technology (including ECG machines, stethoscopes, and similar) would be considered relatively low-risk devices (class I/II) compared with invasive, implantable, or explicitly life-sustaining technologies (class III). One implication of this risk tiering is that, unlike a new implanted cardiac device, such as a novel pacemaker or coronary stent, the market entry of diagnostic technology (including AI-ECGs) would not be predicated on having demonstrated their safety and effectiveness through, for example, a large trial with hard clinical endpoints.

Once a medical device receives regulatory authorization from the MHRA, the UK takes additional steps to determine whether and what the NHS should pay for it. The National Institute for Health and Clinical Excellence (NICE) evaluates the clinical efficacy and cost-effectiveness of drugs, health technologies, and clinical practices for the NHS. Rather than negotiating prices, NICE makes recommendations for system-wide funding and, therefore, deployment, principally based on using tools such as quality-adjusted life years. In response to the increasing number and complexity of digital health technologies, NICE partnered with NHS England to develop standards that aim to ensure that new digital health technologies are clinically effective and offer economic value. The subsequent evidence standards framework for digital health technologies aims to inform stakeholders by exacting appropriate evidence, and to be dynamic and value-driven, with a focus on offering maximal value to patients.[4]

Considering the role of the regulatory bodies above, as applied to a novel AI-ECG device, we observe the following: Manufacturers seeking marketing authority for new digital health tools primarily focused on the diagnosis rather than treatment of a specific condition (like heart failure), must meet the safety and effectiveness standards of the MHRA – but those standards do not necessarily (or likely) require a dedicated clinical trial illustrating real-world clinical value. By contrast, convincing the NHS to pay for the new technology may require more comprehensive evidence sufficient to sway NICE, which is empowered to take a more holistic view of the costs and potential benefits of novel health tools. The advancement of this evidence generation for digital health tools is increasingly tasked to NHS sub-agencies. All of this aims to align with the NHS Long Term Plan, which defines the key challenges and sets an ambitious vision for the next ten years of health care in the UK.[5] AI is singled-out as a key driver for digital transformation. Specifically, the "use of decision support and AI to help clinicians in applying best practice, eliminate unwarranted variation across the whole pathway of care, and support patients in managing their health and condition." Here we already note implicit ethical principles: Reducing unjustified variability in care (as a consideration of justice) and promoting patient autonomy by disseminating diagnostic capabilities that otherwise may be accessible only behind layers of clinical or administrative gatekeeping. Focusing on the specific imperative of heart failure, this chapter discusses whether either of these or other ethical targets are, on balance, advanced by AI-ECG. To do this, we first outline the relevant clinical and technological background below.

III SCREENING FOR HEART FAILURE WITH AI-ECG

The symptomatic burden and mortality risks of heart failure – where the heart is no longer able to effectively pump blood to meet the body's needs under normal pressures – remain worse than those of many common, serious cancers. Among all chronic conditions, heart failure has the greatest impact on quality of life and costs the NHS over £625 million per year – 4 percent of its annual budget.[6] The NHS

---

[4] National Institute for Health and Care Excellence, *Evidence Standards Framework for Digital Health Technologies* (2018), www.nice.org.uk/corporate/ecd7.
[5] NHS England, *The NHS Long Term Plan* (2019), www.longtermplan.nhs.uk/.
[6] Nathalie Conrad, et al., Temporal Trends and Patterns in Heart Failure Incidence: A Population-Based Study of 4 Million Individuals, 391 The Lancet 572, 572–80 (2018).

Long Term Plan emphasizes that "80% of heart failure is currently diagnosed in hospital, despite 40% of patients having symptoms that should have triggered an earlier assessment." Subsequently, the Plan advocates for "using a proactive population health approach focused on ... earlier detection and intervention to treat undiagnosed disorders."[7] While the exact combination of data will vary by context, a clinical diagnosis of heart failure may include the integration of patients' symptoms, physical exams (including traditional stethoscope auscultation of the heart and lungs), and various cardiac investigations, including blood tests and imaging. Individually, compared with a clinical diagnosis gold standard, the test characteristics of each modality vary widely, with sensitivity generally higher than specificity.

Similar to most chronic diseases in high-income countries, the burden of heart failure is greatest in those who are most deprived and tends to have an earlier age of onset in minority ethnic groups, who experience worse outcomes.[8] Therefore, heart failure presents a particularly attractive target for disseminated technology with the potential to speed up diagnosis and direct patients toward proven therapies, particularly if this mitigates the social determinants of health driving observed disparities in care. Given the epidemiology of the problem and the imperative for practical screening, a tool supporting the community-based diagnosis of heart failure has the potential to be both clinically impactful and economically attractive. The myriad diagnostics applicable to heart failure described, however, variously require phlebotomy, specialty imaging, and clinical interpretation to tie together signs and symptoms into a clinical syndrome. AI-supported diagnosis may overcome these limitations.

The near ubiquity of ECGs in well-phenotyped cardiology cohorts supports the training and testing of AI algorithms among tens of thousands of patients. This has resulted in both clinical and, increasingly, consumer-facing applications where AI can interrogate ECGs and accurately identify the presence, for example, of heart rhythm disturbances. Building on an established background suggesting that the ECG can serve as an accurate digital biomarker for the stages of heart failure, a recent advance in AI has unlocked the super-human capability to detect heart failure from a single-lead ECG alone.[9]

The emergence of ECG-enabled stethoscopes, capable of recording single-lead ECGs during contact for routine auscultation (listening), highlighted an opportunity to apply AI-ECG to point-of-care screening. The Eko DUO (Eko Health, Oakland, CA, US) is one example of such an ECG-enabled stethoscope (see Figure 5.1). Detaching the tubing leaves a small cell phone-sized device embedded with sensors (electrodes and microphone) for recording both ECGs

---

[7] NHS England, supra note 5.
[8] Claire A Lawson, et al., Risk Factors for Heart Failure: 20-year Population-Based Trends by Sex, Socioeconomic Status, and Ethnicity, 13 Circulation: Heart Failure (2020).
[9] Patrik Bächtiger, et al., supra note 3.

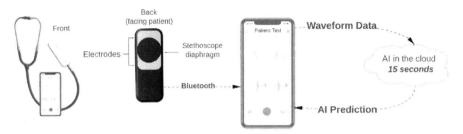

FIGURE 5.1 Left to right: Eko DUO smart stethoscope; patient-facing "bell" of stethoscope labelled with sensors; data flow between Eko DUO, user's smartphone, and cloud for the application of AI

and phonocardiograms (heart sounds). Connectivity via Bluetooth allows the subsequent live streaming of both ECG and phonocardiographic waveforms to a user's smartphone and the corresponding Eko app. Waveforms can be recorded and transmitted to cloud-based infrastructure, allowing them to be analyzed by cloud-based AI algorithms, such as AI-ECG.

While the current programmatic focus is on identifying community heart failure diagnoses, AI can, in theory, also be applied to ECG and phonocardiographic waveforms to identify the presence of two additional public health priorities: Atrial fibrillation, a common irregular heart rhythm, and valvular heart disease, typified by the presence of heart murmurs. Therefore, taken in combination, a fifteen-second examination with an ECG-enabled smart stethoscope may offer a three-in-one screening test for substantial drivers of cardiovascular morbidity and mortality, and systemically important health care costs.

The authors are currently embarking on the first stage of deploying such a screening pathway, anchored in primary care, given the high rates of undiagnosed heart failure and further cardiovascular disease, including atrial fibrillation and valvular disease, in communities across England.[10] The early stages of this pathway involve using NHS general practitioner electronic health records and applying search logic to identify those at risk for heart failure (e.g., risk factors such as hypertension, diabetes, previous myocardial infarction). Patients who consent are mailed a small parcel containing an ECG-enabled stethoscope (Eko DUO) and a simple instruction leaflet on how to perform and transmit a self-recording. Patients are encouraged to download the corresponding Eko App to their own phones (those who are unable to are sent a phone with the app preinstalled as part of the package). Patients whose data, as interpreted by AI, suggests the presence of heart failure, atrial fibrillation, or valvular heart disease are invited for further investigation in line with established NICE clinical pathways.

[10] Michael Soljak, et al., Variations in Cardiovascular Disease Under-Diagnosis in England: National Cross-Sectional Spatial Analysis, 11 BMC Cardiovascular Disorders 1, 1–12 (2011).

This sets the scene for a novel population health intervention that draws on a technology-driven screening test, initiated in the patient's home, by the patient themselves. The current, hospital-centric approach to common and costly cardiovascular conditions combines clinical expertise and the available technologies to screen and unlock substantial clinical and health economic benefits through early diagnosis. Opportunities for more decentralized (outside of hospital), patient-activated screening with digital diagnostics will surely follow if AI-ECG proves tractable. Notably, here we have described what we believe to be among the earliest applications of "super-human" AI – accurately inferring the presence of heart failure from a single-lead ECG was previously thought impossible – with the potential for meeting a major unmet need through a clinical pathway that scales access to this potentially transformative diagnostic.

IV ETHICAL CONSIDERATIONS FOR SELF-ADMINISTERED CARDIOVASCULAR DISEASE SCREENING AT HOME

Having outlined the health policy and stakeholder landscape and specified how this relates to heart failure and AI-ECG, we can progress to discussing the unique ethical challenges posed by patient self-administration of this test in their own homes. Enthusiasm for such an approach to community, patient-driven cardiovascular screening is founded in not only clinical expediency, but also a recognition of the way in which this pathway may support normative public health goals, particularly around equity and patient empowerment. Despite these good-faith expectations, the deployment of such a home-based screening program combining hardware, AI, and a cloud-based digital platform for administration – all hinging on patient self-administration – raises distinct ethical challenges. In this section, we explore the ethical arguments in favor of the AI-ECG program, as well its potential pitfalls.

A Equity

One durable and compelling argument supporting AI-ECG arises from well-known disparities in cardiovascular disease and treatment. Cardiovascular disease follows a social gradient; this is particularly pronounced for heart failure diagnoses, where under-diagnosis in England is most frequent in the lowest-income areas. This tracks with language skills, a key social determinant of health related to a lower uptake of preventative health care and subsequently worse health outcomes. In England, nearly one million people (2 percent of the total population) lack basic English language skills. AI-ECG attenuates these disparities in several ways.

First, targeted screening based on risk factors (such as high blood pressure and diabetes) will, based on epidemiologic trends, necessarily and fruitfully support vulnerable patient groups for whom these conditions are more prevalent. These same patients will also be less able to access traditional facility-based cardiac testing. AI-ECG overcomes these concerns for the patients most in need.

Second, AI-ECG explicitly transfers a key gatekeeping diagnostic screen away from clinicians: The cognitive biases of traditional bedside medicine. Cross-cultural challenges in subjective diagnosis and treatment escalation are well documented, including in heart failure across a spectrum of disease severity, ranging from outpatient symptoms ascertainment to referral for advanced cardiac therapies and even transplant.[11] AI-ECG overcomes the biases embedded in traditional heart failure screenings by simplifying a complex syndromic diagnosis into a positive or negative result that is programmatically entwined with subsequent specialist referral.

These supporting arguments grounded in reducing the disparities in access to cardiac care may be balanced by equally salient concerns. Even a charitable interpretation of the AI-ECG pathway assumes a relatively savvy, engaged, and motivated patient. The ability to mail the AI-ECG screening package widely to homes is just the first step in a series of necessary steps: Opening and setting up the screening kit, including the phone and ECG-enabled stethoscope, successfully activating the device, and recording a high-quality tracing that is then processed centrally without data loss. While the authors' early experience using this technology in various settings has been reassuring, it remains uncertain whether the established "digital divide" will complicate the equitable application of AI-ECG screening. Assuming equal (or even favorably targeted) access to the technology, are patients able to use it, and *do they want to*? The last point is critical: In the UK as well as the United States, trust in health care varies considerably and, (broadly speaking) in cardiovascular disease, tracks unfortunately and inversely with clinical need.

Indeed, one well-grounded reason for suspicion recalls another problem for the equity-driven enthusiasm for AI-ECG, which is the training and validation of the AI algorithms themselves. The "black box" nature of some forms of AI, where the reasons for model prediction cannot easily be inferred, has appropriately led to concerns over insidious algorithmic bias and subsequent reservations around deploying these tools for patient care.[12] Even low-tech heart failure screening confronts this same problem, as (for example) the most widely used biomarker for heart failure diagnosis has well-known performance variability according to age, sex, ethnicity, patient weight, renal function, and clinical comorbidities.[13] Conversely, studies to date have suggested that AI-ECG for heart failure detection does not exhibit these

---

[11] Fouad Chouairi, et al., Evaluation of Racial and Ethnic Disparities in Cardiac Transplantation, 10 J. of the Am. Heart Ass'n (2021).

[12] Matthew DeCamp & Jon C. Tilburt, Why We Cannot Trust Artificial Intelligence in Medicine, 1 Lancet Digit. Health 390 (2019).

[13] Theresa A. McDonagh, et al., 2021 ESC Guidelines for the Diagnosis and Treatment of Acute and Chronic Heart Failure: Developed by the Task Force for the Diagnosis and Treatment of Acute and Chronic Heart Failure of the European Society of Cardiology (ESC) With the Special Contribution of the Heart Failure Association (HFA) of the ESC, 42 European Heart J. 3599, 3618 (2021).

biases. It may still be the case that biases do exist, but that they require further large-scale deployment to manifest themselves.

To address these concerns, we propose several programmatic features as essential and intentional for reinforcing the potential of wide-scale screening to promote equity. First, it is imperative for program managers to prominently collect self-identified race, ethnicity, and other socioeconomic data (e.g., language, education) from all participants at each level of outreach – screened, invited, agreed, successfully tested, identified as "positive," referred for specialist evaluation, and downstream clinical results. Disproportionate representation at each level, and differential drop-out at each step, must be explored, but that can only begin with high-quality patient-level data to inform analyses and program refinement. This is an aspiration dependent on first resolving the outlined issues with trust. Trust in AI-ECG may be further buttressed in several ways, recognizing the resource limitations available for screening programs generally. One option may be providing accommodations for skeptical patients in a way that still provides suitable opportunities to participate through alternative means. This could simply involve having patients attend an in-person appointment during which the AI-ECG examination is performed on them by a health care professional.

The patient end-user needs to feel trust and confidence in using the technology. This can be achieved through user-centric design that prioritizes a simple protocol, to maximize uptake, with the requisite level of technical detail to ensure adequate recording quality (e.g., getting the right position). The accuracy of AI-ECG depends on these factors, in contrast with other point-of-care technologies where the acquisition of the "input" is less subject to variability (e.g., finger-prick blood drop tests).

The centralized administration of NHS screening programs by NHS England paired with NHS Digital's repository data on the uptake of screening offers granular insights to anticipate and plan for regions and groups at risk of low uptake. We propose enshrining a dedicated data monitoring plan into the AI-ECG screening protocol, with prespecified targets for uptake and defined mitigation strategies – monitored in near real-time. This is made possible through the unique connectivity (for a screening technology) of the platform driving AI-ECG, with readily available up-to-date data flows for highlighting disparities in access. However, a more proactive approach to targeting individuals within a population with certain characteristics needs to be balanced against the risk of stigmatization, and, ultimately, potential loss of trust that may further worsen the cardiovascular outcomes seeking to be improved.

Lastly, equity concerns around algorithmic performance are necessarily empirical questions that will also benefit from patient-level data collection. We acknowledge that moving from research in the form of prospective validation studies to deployment for patient care requires judgment in the absence of consensus, within the NHS or more globally, around the minimum scrutiny for an acceptable level (if any) of differential performance across – for starters – age, sex, and ethnicity. To avoid these potentially impactful innovations remaining in the domain of research, and to anticipate the wide-reaching implications of a deployment found to exhibit bias retrospectively, one possible solution would be to, by design, prospectively monitor for inconsistent test performance. Specifically, in the context of AI-ECG offering a binary yes or no screening test result for heart failure, it is important to measure the rate of false positive and false negative results. False positives can be measured through the AI-ECG technology platform linking directly into primary care EHR data. This allows positive AI-ECG results to be correlated with the outcomes of downstream gold-standard, definitive investigations for heart failure (e.g., echocardiography ultrasound scans). Such a prospective approach is less feasible for false negatives due to both the potentially longer time horizon for the disease to manifest and the uncertainty around whether AI-ECG truly missed the diagnosis. Instead, measuring the rate of false negatives may require a more expansive approach in the form of inviting a small sample of patients with negative AI screening tests for "quality control" next-step investigations. All of this risks adding complexity and, therefore, cost to a pathway seeking to simplify and save money. However, given this program's position at the vanguard of AI deployments for health, a permissive approach balanced with checkpoints for sustained accuracy may help to blueprint best practices and build confidence for similar AI applications in additional disease areas.

B Agency

Another positive argument for AI-ECG screening aligns with trends in promoting agency, understood here as patient empowerment, particularly around the use of digital devices to measure, monitor, and manage one's own health care – particularly in terms of cardiovascular disease. The enthusiastic commercial uptake of fitness wearables, for example, moved quickly past counting steps to incorporate heart rhythm monitoring.[14] Testing of these distributed technologies has shown mixed results, with the yield of positive cases necessarily depending on the population at issue.[15] Recalling the equity concerns above, the devices themselves may be more popular among younger and healthier patients, among whom true positive diagnoses may be uncommon. However, targeted and invited screening with AI-ECG may balance these concerns through enriching the population at risk by invitation.

---

[14] David Duncker, et al., Smart Wearables for Cardiac Monitoring – Real-World Use beyond Atrial Fibrillation, 21 Sensors (2021).
[15] Steven A Lubitz, et al., Screening for Atrial Fibrillation in Older Adults at Primary Care Visits: VITAL-AF Randomized Controlled Trial, 145 Circulation 946–54 (2022); Marco V Perez, et al., Large-Scale Assessment of a Smartwatch to Identify Atrial Fibrillation, 381 New England Journal of Medicine 1909–17 (2019).

Realistic concerns about agency extend beyond the previous warnings about digital literacy, access to reliable internet, and language barriers to ask more fundamental questions about whether patients actually *want* to assume this central role in their own health care. A key parallel here is the advent of mandates for shared decision-making in cardiovascular disease, particularly in the United States where federal law now requires selected Medicare beneficiaries considering certain cardiovascular procedures to incorporate "evidence based shared decision-making tools" in their treatment choices.[16] However, patients may reasonably ask if screening with AI-ECG should necessarily shift the key role of test administration (literally) into their hands. Unlike the only other at-home national screening test in the UK – simply taking a stool sample for bowel cancer screening – self-application of AI-ECG requires the successful execution of several codependent steps. Here, even a relatively low failure rate may prove untenable for population-wide scaling, risking that this technology may remain in the physician's office.

Putting such responsibility on patients could be argued to not only directly shift this responsibility away from clinicians, but also dilute learning opportunities. While subtle, shifting the cognitive work of integrating complex signs and symptoms into a syndromic diagnosis like heart failure may have unwelcome implications for clinicians' diagnostic skills. We emphasize that this is not just whimsical nostalgia for a more paternalistic time in medicine, but a genuine worry about reductionism in algorithmic diagnosis that oversimplifies complex constellations of findings into simple yes or no diagnoses (AI-ECG, strictly speaking, only flags a risk of heart failure, which is not clinically equivalent to a diagnosis). Resolving these tensions may be possible through seeing the educational opportunity and wider clinical application of the hardware enabling AI-ECG.

Careful metrics, as described previously, will allow concerns about agency to be considered empirically, at least within the categories of patient data collected. If, for example, the utilization of AI-ECG varies sharply according to age, race, ethnicity, or language fluency, this would merit investigation specifically interrogating whether this variability rests in part on patient preferences for taking on this task rather than an inability to do so. At the same time, early patient experiences with AI-ECG in real-world settings may provide opportunities for patient feedback regarding whether this specific device, or the larger role being asked of them in their own care, is perceived as an appropriate assignation of responsibility or an imposition. If, for example, patients experience this shifting of cardiovascular screening out of the office as an inappropriate deferral of care out of traditional settings, this may suggest the need for either refining the pathway (still using the device, but perhaps keeping it in a clinical setting) or more extensive community engagement and education to ensure stakeholder agreement on roles, rights, and responsibilities.

---

[16] Christopher E Knoepke, et al., Medicare Mandates for Shared Decision Making in Cardiovascular Device Placement, 12 Circulation: Cardiovascular Quality and Outcomes (2019).

C Data Rights

A central government, NHS-funded public screening program making use of patients' own smartphones necessarily raises important questions about data rights. Beyond the expected guardrails required by the General Data Protection Regulation (GDPR) and UK-specific health data legislation, AI-ECG introduces additional concerns. One is whether patient participants should be obligated to contribute their health data toward the continuous refinement of the AI-ECG algorithms themselves or instead be given opt-in or opt-out mechanisms of enrollment. We note that while employed in this context by a public agency, the intellectual property for AI-ECG is held by the device manufacturer. Thus, while patients may carry some expectation of potential future benefit from algorithmic refinement, the more obvious rewards accrue to private entities. Another potential opportunity, not lost on the authors as overseers for the nascent AI-ECG program, is the possibility that AI-ECG data linked to patients' EHR records might support entirely new diagnostic discovery beyond the core cardiovascular conditions at issue. Other conditions may similarly have subtle manifestations in ECG waveforms, phonocardiography, or their combination – invisible to humans but not AI – that could plausibly emerge from widespread use. Beyond just opt-in or opt-out permissions – known to be problematic for meaningful engagement with patient consent[17] – what control should patients have around the use of their health data in this context? For example, the NHS now holds a rich variety of health data for each patient – including free text, imaging, and blood test results. Patients may be happy to offer some but not all of this data for application to their own health, with different decisions on stratifying what can be used for AI product development.

Lastly, AI-ECG will need to consider data security carefully, including the possibility, however remote, of malicious intent or motivated intruders entering the system. Health data can be monetized by cyber criminals. Cyber threat modelling should be performed by the device manufacturer early in the design phase to identify possible threats and their mitigants.[18] Documentation provided about embedded data security features adds valuable information for patients that may have concerns about the protection of their personal data, and can help them to make informed decisions on using AI-ECG. Beyond privacy, threat modelling should also account for patient safety, such as from an intruder with access that allows the manipulation of code or data. For example, it could be possible to manipulate results to deprive selected populations of appropriate referrals for care. Sabotaging results or causing a denial-of-service situation by flooding the system with incorrect data might also

---

[17] Susan A Speer & Elizabeth Stokoe, Ethics in Action: Consent-Gaining Interactions and Implications for Research Practice, 53 British J. of Soc. Psych. 54–73 (2014).
[18] Medical Device Innovation Consortium, The MITRE Corporation, *Playbook for Threat Modelling Med. Devices* (2021), www.mitre.org/news-insights/publication/playbook-threat-modeling-medical-devices.

cause damage to the reputation of the system in such a way that patients and clinicians become wary of using it. Overall, anticipating these security and other data rights considerations beyond the relatively superficial means of user agreements remains an unmet challenge for AI-ECG.

V FINAL RECOMMENDATIONS

This chapter has outlined a novel clinical pathway to screen for cardiovascular disease using an at-home, patient self-administered AI technology that can provide a screening capability beyond human expertise. We set this against a backdrop of: (1) A diverse ecosystem of stakeholders impacted by and responsible for AI-ECG, spanning patients, NHS clinicians, NHS agencies, and the responsible regulatory and health economic bodies and (2) a health-policy landscape eager to progress the "use of decision support and AI" as part of a wider push to decentralize (i.e., modernize) care. To underscore the outlined considerations of equity, agency, and data rights, we propose two principal recommendations, framed against but generalizable beyond the pathway example of AI-ECG.

First, we advocate for a multi-agency approach that balances permissive regulation and deployment – to align with the speed of AI innovation – against ethical and statutory obligations to safeguard public health. Bodies such as NHS England, the MHRA, and NICE each have unique responsibilities, but with cross-cutting implications. The clinical and health economic case for urgent innovation for unmet needs, such as AI-ECG for heart failure, is obvious and compelling. Agencies working sequentially delays translating such innovations into clinical practice, missing opportunities to avert substantial cardiovascular morbidity and mortality. Instead, the identification of a potentially transformative technology should trigger a multi-agency approach that works together and in parallel to support timely deployment within clinical pathways to positively impact patient care. This approach holds not only during initial deployment, but also as technology progresses. Here, we could consider the challenge of AI algorithms continually iterating (i.e., improving): For a given version of AI-ECG, the MHRA grants regulatory approval, NICE endorses procurement, and NHS England guides implementation. After evaluating a medical AI technology and deeming it safe and effective, should these agencies limit its authorization to market only the version of the algorithm that was submitted, or permit the marketing of an algorithm that can learn and adapt to new conditions?[19] AI-ECG could continually iterate by learning from the ECG data accumulated during deployment, and also through continuing improvements in machine learning methodology and computational power. Cardiovascular data, including waveforms, imaging, blood, and physiological parameters, is generally high volume and repeatedly measured. This, therefore, offers a rich seam for taking advantage of

[19] Boris Babic, et al., Algorithms on Regulatory Lockdown in Medicine, 6 Science 1202 (2019).

AI's defining strength to continually improve, unlike ordinary "medical devices." Parodying the ship of Theseus, at what point is the algorithm substantially different to the original, and what prospective validation, if any, is needed if the claims remain the same? Multi-agency collaboration can reach a consensus on such questions that avoids unfamiliarity with the lifecycle of AI disrupting delivery of care by reactively resetting when new (i.e., improved) versions arrive. For AI-ECG, this could involve the expensive and time-consuming repetition of high-volume patient recruitment to validation research studies. Encouragingly, in a potential move toward multi-agency collaboration, in 2022, NHS England commissioned NICE to lead a consultation for a digital health evidence standards framework that aims to better align with regulators.[20]

Second, both to account for the ethical considerations outlined in this chapter and to balance any faster implementation of promising AI technologies, we recommend a centralized responsibility for NHS England to deploy and thoroughly evaluate programs such as AI-ECG. This chapter has covered some of the critical variables to measure that will be unique to using an AI technology for patient self-administered screening at home. Forming a comprehensive list would, again, be amenable to a multi-agency approach, where NHS England can draw on the playbook for already-monitoring existing national screening programs. An evaluation framework addressing the outlined considerations around equity, agency, and data rights should be considered not only an intrinsic but a mandatory part of the design, deployment, and ongoing surveillance of AI-ECG. The inherent connectivity and instant data flow of such technology offers, unlike screening programs to date, the opportunity for real-time monitoring and, therefore, prompt intervention, not only for clinical indications, but also for any disparities in uptake, execution, algorithm performance, or cybersecurity. Ultimately, this will not only bolster the NHS's position as a world leader in standards for patient safety, but also as an exemplar system for realizing effective AI-driven health care interventions.

Looking to the future for AI-ECG, translating the momentum for technological innovation in the NHS into patient benefit will require careful consideration of the outlined ethical pitfalls. This may, in the short term, establish best practices that build confidence for further applications. In the longer term, we see a convergence of commoditized AI algorithms for cardiovascular and wider disease, where increasingly sophisticated sensor technology may make future home-based screening a completely passive act. While moving toward such a reality could unlock major public health benefits, doing so will depend on bold early use cases, such as AI-ECG, that reveal unanticipated ethical challenges and allow them to be resolved. For

---

[20] National Institute for Health and Care Excellence, *Evidence Standards Framework (ESF) for Digital Health Technologies Update – Consultation* (2022), www.nice.org.uk/about/what-we-do/our-programmes/evidence-standards-framework-for-digital-health-technologies/esf-consultation.

now, the outlined policy recommendations can serve to underpin the stewardship of such novel diagnostic pathways in a way that preserves and promotes trust, patient engagement, and public health.

VI CONCLUSION

Patient self-administered screening for cardiovascular disease at home using an AI-powered technology offers substantial potential public health benefits, but also poses unique ethical challenges. We recommend a multi-agency approach to the lifecycle of implementing such AI technology, combined with a centrally overseen, mandatory prospective evaluation framework that monitors for equity, agency, and data rights. Assuming the responsibility to proactively address any observed neglect of these considerations instills trust as the foundation for the sustainable and impactful implementation of AI technologies for clinical application within patients' own homes.

6

The Promise of Telehealth for Abortion

Greer Donley and Rachel Rebouché

I INTRODUCTION

The COVID-19 pandemic catalyzed a transformation of abortion care. For most of the last half century, abortion was provided in clinics outside of the traditional health care setting.[1] Though a medication regimen was approved in 2000 to terminate a pregnancy without a surgical procedure, the Food and Drug Administration (FDA) required, among other things, that the drug be dispensed in person at a health care facility (the "in-person dispensing requirement").[2] This requirement dramatically limited the medication's promise to revolutionize abortion because it subjected medication abortion to the same physical barriers as procedural care.[3]

Over the course of the COVID-19 pandemic, however, that changed. The pandemic's early days exposed how the FDA's in-person dispensing requirement facilitated virus transmission and hampered access to abortion without any medical benefits.[4] This realization created a fresh urgency to lift the FDA's unnecessary restrictions. Researchers and advocates worked in concert to highlight evidence undermining the need for the in-person dispensing requirement,[5] which culminated in the FDA permanently removing the requirement in December 2021.[6]

The result is an emerging new normal for abortion through ten weeks of pregnancy – telehealth – at least in the states that allow it.[7] Abortion by telehealth (what an early study dubbed "TelAbortion") generally involves a pregnant person meeting online with a health care professional, who evaluates whether the patient is a candidate for medication abortion, and, if so, whether the patient satisfies informed

---

[1] Greer Donley, Medication Abortion Exceptionalism, 107 Cornell L. Rev. 627, 647 (2022).
[2] Id. at 643–51.
[3] Id.
[4] Id. at 648–51; Rachel Rebouché, The Public Health Turn in Reproductive Rights, 78 Wash & Lee L. Rev. 1355, 1383–86 (2021).
[5] Rebouché, supra note 4, at 1383–86.
[6] Donley, supra note 1, at 648–51.
[7] Id. at 689–73.

consent requirements.[8] Pills are then mailed directly to the patient, who can take them and complete an abortion at home. This innovation has made earlier-stage abortions cheaper, less burdensome, and more private, reducing some of the barriers that delay abortion and compromise access.[9]

In this chapter, we start with a historical account of how telehealth for abortion emerged as a national phenomenon. We then offer our predictions for the future: A future in which the digital transformation of abortion care is threatened by the demise of constitutional abortion rights. We argue, however, that the de-linking of medication abortion from in-person care has triggered a zeitgeist that will create new avenues to access safe abortion, even in states that ban it. As a result, the same states that are banning almost all abortions after the Supreme Court overturned *Roe v. Wade* will find it difficult to stop their residents from accessing abortion online. Abortion that is decentralized and independent of in-state physicians will undermine traditional state efforts to police abortion as well as create new challenges of access and risks of criminalization.

II THE EARLY ABORTION CARE REVOLUTION

Although research on medication abortion facilitated by telehealth began nearly a decade ago, developments in legal doctrine, agency regulation, and online availability over the last few years have ushered in remote abortion care and cemented its impact. This part reviews this recent history and describes the current model for providing telehealth for abortion services.

A *The Regulation of Medication Abortion*

In 2020, medication abortions comprised 54 percent of the nation's total abortions, which is a statistic that has steadily increased over the past two decades.[10] A medication abortion in the United States typically has involved taking two types of drugs, mifepristone and misoprostol, often 24 to 48 hours apart.[11] The first medication detaches the embryo from the uterus and the second induces uterine contractions to expel the tissue.[12] Medication abortion is approved by the FDA to end pregnancies through ten weeks of gestation, although some providers will prescribe its use off-label through twelve or thirteen weeks.[13]

---

[8] David Cohen, Greer Donley & Rachel Rebouché, The New Abortion Battleground, 123 Colum. L. Rev. 1, 9–13 (2023).
[9] Id.
[10] Rachel Jones et al., Abortion Incidence and Service Availability in the United States, Guttmacher Inst. (2022), www.guttmacher.org/article/2022/11/abortion-incidence-and-service-availability-united-states-2020.
[11] Donley, supra note 1, at 633.
[12] Id.
[13] Id.

The FDA restricts mifepristone under a system intended to ensure the safety of particularly risky drugs – a Risk Evaluation and Mitigation Strategy (REMS).[14] The FDA can also issue a REMS with Elements to Assure Safe Use (ETASU), which can circumscribe distribution and limit who can prescribe a drug and under what conditions.[15] The FDA instituted a REMS with ETASU for mifepristone, the first drug in the medication abortion regimen, which historically mandated, among other requirements, that patients collect mifepristone in-person at a health care facility, such as a clinic or physician's office.[16] Thus, under the ETASU, certified providers could not dispense mifepristone through the mail or a pharmacy. Several states' laws impose their own restrictions on abortion medication in addition to the FDA's regulations, including mandating in-person pick-up, prohibiting telehealth for abortion, or banning the mailing of medication abortion; at the time of writing in 2023, most of those same states, save eight, ban almost all abortion, including medication abortion, from the earliest stages of pregnancy.[17]

In July 2020, a federal district court in *American College of Obstetricians & Gynecologists (ACOG) v. FDA* temporarily suspended the in-person dispensing requirement and opened the door to the broader adoption of telehealth for abortion during the course of the pandemic.[18] Well before this case, in 2016, the non-profit organization, Gynuity, received an Investigational New Drug Approval to study the efficacy of providing medication abortion care by videoconference and mail.[19] In the study, "TelAbortion," providers counselled patients online, and patients confirmed the gestational age with blood tests and ultrasounds at a location of their choosing.[20] As the pandemic took hold, patients who were not at risk for medical complications, were less than eight weeks pregnant, and had regular menstrual cycles could forgo ultrasounds and blood tests, and rely on home pregnancy tests and a self-report of the first day of their last menstrual period. The results of the study indicated that a "direct-to-patient telemedicine abortion service was safe, effective, efficient, and satisfactory."[21] Since Gynuity's study, additional research has

---

[14] Id. at 637–43.
[15] Id.
[16] Id.
[17] Nineteen states mandate that the prescribing physician be physically present during an abortion or require patient-physician contact, such as mandatory pre-termination ultrasounds and in-person counseling. Five of these states also explicitly prohibit the mailing of abortion-inducing drugs (Arizona, Arkansas, Montana, Oklahoma, and Texas). Nine states have banned telehealth for abortion. Medication Abortion, *Abortion Law Project*, Ctr. for Pub. Health L. Rsch. (December 2021), http://lawatlas.org/datasets/medication-abortion-requirements. Of these states, currently only Alabama, Arizona, Indiana, Kansas, Montana, Nebraska, North Carolina, and Wisconsin have laws that preclude telehealth for abortion, but otherwise have not banned abortion before ten weeks.
[18] Order for Preliminary Injunction, ACOG v. FDA, No. 8:20-cv-01320-TDC 80 (D. Md. July 13, 2020).
[19] See Elizabeth Raymond et al., TelAbortion: Evaluation of a Direct to Patient Telemedicine Abortion Service in the United States, 100 Contraception 173, 174 (2019).
[20] Id.
[21] Id.

demonstrated that abortion medication can be taken safely and effectively without in-person oversight.[22]

The ACOG court's temporary suspension of the in-person dispensing requirement in 2020 relied on this research. The district court held that the FDA's requirement contradicted substantial evidence of the drug's safety and singled out mifepristone without providing any corresponding health benefit.[23] The district court detailed how the in-person requirement exacerbated the burdens already shouldered by those disproportionately affected by the pandemic, emphasizing that low-income patients and people of color, who are the majority of abortion patients, are more likely to contract and suffer the effects of COVID-19.[24] While the district court's injunction lasted, virtual clinics began operating, providing abortion care without satisfying any in-person requirements.[25]

The FDA appealed the district court's decision to the US Court of Appeals for the Fourth Circuit and petitioned the Supreme Court for a stay of the injunction in October and again in December 2020. The briefs filed by the Trump Administration's solicitor general and ten states contested that the in-person dispensing requirement presented heightened COVID-19 risks for patients.[26] Indeed, some of the same states that had suspended abortion as a purported means to protect people from COVID-19 now argued that the pandemic posed little threat for people seeking abortion care.[27] ACOG highlighted the absurdity of the government's position. The FDA could not produce evidence that any patient had been harmed by the removal of the in-person dispensing requirement, whereas, in terms of COVID-19 risk, "the day Defendants filed their motion, approximately 100,000 people in the United States were diagnosed with COVID-19 – a new global record – and nearly 1,000 people died from it."[28]

The Supreme Court was not persuaded by ACOG's arguments. In January 2021, the Court stayed the district court's injunction pending appeal with scant analysis.[29] Chief Justice Roberts, in a concurrence, argued that the Court must defer to "politically accountable entities with the background, competence, and expertise to assess

---

[22] Hillary Bracken, Alternatives to Routine Ultrasound for Eligibility Assessment Prior to Early Termination of Pregnancy with Mifepristone-Misoprostol, 118 BJOG 17–23 (2011).
[23] Am. Coll. of Obstetricians and Gynecologists v. US Food and Drug Admin., No. TDC-20-1320, 2020 WL 8167535 at 210–11 (D. Md. August 19, 2020).
[24] Id.
[25] Donley, supra note 1, at 631.
[26] Solicitor General Brief to US District Court for the District of Maryland, Case 8:20-cv-01320-TDC, November 11, 2020.
[27] Rebouché, supra note 4, at 1383–89; Greer Donley, Beatrice A. Chen & Sonya Borrero, The Legal and Medical Necessity of Abortion Care Amid the COVID-19 Pandemic, 7 J.L. & Biosciences 1, 13 (2020).
[28] Plaintiff Brief in Opposition to Defendants' Renewed Motion to Stay the Preliminary Injunction, at 1, No. 20-1320-Tdc, November 13, 2020.
[29] Food and Drug Admin. v. Am. Coll. of Obstetricians and Gynecologists, 141 S.Ct. 578 (2021).

public health."[30] Justice Sotomayor dissented, citing the district court's findings and characterizing the reimposition of the in-person dispensing requirement as "unnecessary, unjustifiable, irrational" and "callous."[31]

The impact of the Supreme Court's order, however, was short-lived. In April 2021, the FDA suspended the enforcement of the requirement throughout the course of the pandemic and announced that it would reconsider aspects of the REMS.[32] In December 2021, the FDA announced that it would permanently lift the in-person dispensing requirement.

Other aspects of the mifepristone REMS, however, have not changed. The FDA still mandates that only certified providers who have registered with the drug manufacturer may prescribe the drug (the "certified provider requirement"), which imposes an unnecessary administrative burden that reduces the number of abortion providers.[33] An additional informed consent requirement – the FDA-required Patient Agreement Form, which patients sign before beginning a medication abortion – also remains in place despite repeating what providers already communicate to patients.[34] The FDA also added a new ETASU requiring that only certified pharmacies can dispense mifepristone.[35] The details of pharmacy certification were announced in January 2023; among other requirements, a pharmacy must agree to particular record-keeping, reporting, and medication tracking efforts, as well as designate a representative to ensure compliance.[36] This requirement, as it is implemented, could mirror the burdens associated with the certified provider requirement, perpetuating the FDA's unusual treatment of this safe and effective drug.[37]

Despite these restrictions, permission for providers and, at present, two online pharmacies to mail medication abortion has allowed virtual abortion clinics to proliferate in states that permit telehealth for abortion.[38] As explored below, this change has the potential to dramatically increase access to early abortion care, but there are obstacles that can limit such growth.

---

[30] Id. (Roberts, J., concurring); Rebouché, supra note 4, at 1389.
[31] FDA v. ACOG, 141 S.Ct. at 583 (Sotomayor, J, dissenting).
[32] Joint Motion to Stay Case Pending Agency Review at 2, *Chelius v. Wright*, no. 17-cv-493 (D. Haw. May 7, 2021), ECF no. 148.
[33] Donley, supra note 1, at 643–48.
[34] Id.
[35] Id.
[36] Mifepristone REMS, US Food and Drug Admin., www.accessdata.fda.gov/drugsatfda_docs/rems/Mifepristone_2023_01_03_REMS_Full.pdf.
[37] Donley, supra note 1, at 643–48.
[38] Rachel Rebouché, Remote Reproductive Rights, 48 Am. J. L. & Med. __(in press, 2023). The FDA granted permission to two online pharmacies to dispense abortion medication while it determined the process for certification. Abagail Abrams, Meet the Pharmacist Expanding Access to Abortion Pills Across the US, *Time* (June 13, 2022), https://time.com/6183395/abortion-pills-honeybee-health-online-pharmacy/.

B Telehealth for Abortion

A new model for distributing medication abortion is quickly gaining traction across the country: Certified providers partnering with online pharmacies to mail abortion medication to patients after online intake and counseling.[39] For example, the virtual clinic, Choix, prescribes medication abortion to patients up to ten weeks of pregnancy in Maine, New Mexico, Colorado, Illinois, and California.[40] The founders describe how Choix's asynchronous telehealth platform works:

> Patients first sign up on our website and fill out an initial questionnaire, then we review their history and follow up via text with any questions. Once patients are approved to proceed, they're able to complete the consent online. We send our video and educational handouts electronically and make them available via our patient portal. We're always accessible via phone for patients.[41]

The entire process, from intake to receipt of pills, takes between two to five days and the cost is $289, which is significantly cheaper than medication abortions offered by brick-and-mortar clinics.[42] Advice on taking the medication abortion and possible complications is available through a provider-supported hotline.[43] Choix is just one of many virtual clinics. Another virtual clinic, Abortion on Demand, provides medication abortion services to twenty-two states.[44] Many virtual clinics translate their webpages into Spanish but do not offer services in Spanish or other languages, although a few are planning to incorporate non-English services.[45]

As compared to brick-and-mortar clinics, virtual clinics and online pharmacies provide care that costs less, offers more privacy, increases convenience, and reduces delays without compromising the efficacy or quality of care.[46] Patients no longer need to drive long distances to pick up safe and effective medications before driving back home to take them. In short, mailed pills can untether early-stage abortion from a physical place.[47]

---

[39] Carrie N. Baker, How Telemedicine Startups Are Revolutionizing Abortion Health Care in the US, Ms. Mag., November 16, 2020.
[40] Id.
[41] Carrie Baker, Online Abortion Providers Cindy Adam and Lauren Dubey of Choix: "We're Really Excited about the Future of Abortion Care," Ms. Mag. (April 14, 2022).
[42] Id. Choix also offers a sliding scale of cost, starting at $175, for patients with financial need. Choix, Learn, FAQ, https://choixhealth.com/faq/.
[43] Choix, Learn, FAQ, https://choixhealth.com/faq/.
[44] Carrie Baker, Abortion on Demand Offers Telemedicine Abortion in 20+ States and Counting: "I Didn't Know I Could Do This!," Ms. Mag. (June 7, 2021), https://msmagazine.com/2021/06/07/abortion-on-demand-telemedicine-abortion-fda-rems-abortion-at-home/.
[45] Ushma Upadhyay, Provision of Medication Abortion via Telehealth after Dobbs (draft presentation on file with the authors).
[46] Donley, supra note 1, at 690–92.
[47] Id.

Telehealth for abortion, however, has clear and significant limitations. As noted above, laws in about half of the country prohibit, explicitly or indirectly, telemedicine for abortion. And telemedicine depends on people having internet connections and computers or smartphones, which is a barrier for low-income communities.[48] Even with a telehealth-compliant device, "[patients] may live in communities that lack access to technological infrastructure, like high-speed internet, necessary to use many dominant tele-health services, such as virtual video visits."[49] Finally, the FDA has approved medication abortion only through ten weeks of gestation.

These barriers, imposed by law and in practice, will test how far telehealth for abortion can reach. As discussed below, the portability of medication abortion opens avenues that strain the bounds of legality, facilitated in no small part by the networks of advocates that have mobilized to make pills available to people across the country.[50] But extralegal strategies could have serious costs, particularly for those already vulnerable to state surveillance and punishment.[51] And attempts to bypass state laws could have serious consequences for providers, who are subject to professional, civil, and criminal penalties, as well as those who assist providers and patients.[52]

III THE FUTURE OF ABORTION CARE

The COVID-19 pandemic transformed abortion care, but the benefits were limited to those living in states that did not have laws requiring in-person care or prohibiting the mailing of abortion medication.[53] This widened a disparity in abortion access that has been growing for years between red and blue states.[54]

On June 24, 2022, the Supreme Court issued its decision in *Dobbs v. Jackson Women's Health Organization*, upholding Mississippi's fifteen-week abortion ban and overturning *Roe v. Wade*.[55] Twenty-four states have attempted to ban almost all abortions, although ten of those bans have been halted by courts.[56] At the time of writing, pregnant people in the remaining fourteen states face limited options: Continue a pregnancy against their will, travel out of state to obtain a legal abortion,

---

[48] David Simon & Carmel Shachar, Telehealth to Address Health Disparities: Potential, Pitfalls, and Paths, 49 J. L. Med. & Ethics 415 (2022).
[49] Id.
[50] Jareb A. Gleckel & Sheryl L. Wulkan, Abortion and Telemedicine: Looking Beyond COVID-19 and the Shadow Docket, 54 U.C. Davis L. Rev. Online 105, 112, 119–20 (2021).
[51] Carrie N. Baker, Texas Woman Lizelle Herrera's Arrest Foreshadows Post-Roe Future, *Ms. Mag* (April 16, 2022), https://msmagazine.com/2022/04/16/texas-woman-lizelle-herrera-arrest-murder-roe-v-wade-abortion/.
[52] Cohen, Donley & Rebouché, supra note 8, at 12.
[53] See Section II.
[54] Donley, supra note 1, at 694.
[55] *Dobbs v. Jackson Women's Health Organization*, 142 S. Ct. 2228, 2242 (2022).
[56] Tracking States Where Abortion is Now Banned, *The New York Times* (November 8, 2022), www.nytimes.com/interactive/2022/us/abortion-laws-roe-v-wade.html.

or self-manage their abortion in their home state.[57] Data from Texas, where the SB8 legislation[58] effectively banned abortion after roughly six weeks of pregnancy months before *Dobbs*, suggests that only a small percentage of people will choose the first option – the number of abortions Texans received dropped by only 10–15 percent as a result of travel and self-management.[59] Evidence from other countries and the United States's own pre-*Roe* history also demonstrate that abortion bans do not stop abortions from happening.[60]

Traveling to a state where abortion is legal, however, is not an option for many people.[61] Yet unlike the pre-*Roe* era, there is another means to safely end a pregnancy – one that threatens the antiabortion movement's ultimate goal of ending abortion nationwide:[62] Self-managed abortion with medication. Self-managed abortion generally refers to abortion obtained outside of the formal health care system.[63] Thus, self-managed abortion can include a pregnant person buying medication abortion online directly from an international pharmacy (sometimes called self-sourced abortion) and a pregnant person interacting with an international or out-of-state provider via telemedicine, who ships them abortion medication or calls a prescription into an international pharmacy on their behalf.[64]

Because many states have heavily restricted abortion for years, self-managed abortion is not new. The non-profit organization Aid Access started providing medication abortion to patients in the United States in 2017.[65] Each year, the number of

---

[57] Thirteen states ban abortion from the earliest stages of pregnancy and Georgia bans abortion after six weeks. In addition to those fourteen states, Utah, Arizona and Florida ban abortion after fifteen weeks, Utah after eighteen and North Carolina after twenty. Id.

[58] S.B. 8, 87th Gen. Assemb., Reg. Sess. (Tex. 2021) (codified as amended at Tex. Health & Safety Code Ann. §§ 171.201–.212 (West 2023)).

[59] See Margot Sanger-Katz, Claire Cain Miller & Quoctrung Bui, Most Women Denied Abortions by Texas Law Got Them Another Way, *The New York Times* (March 6, 2022), www.nytimes.com/2022/03/06/upshot/texas-abortion-women-data.html.

[60] Yvonne Lindgren, When Patients Are Their Own Doctors: Roe v. Wade in An Era of Self-Managed Care, 107 Cornell L. Rev. 151, 169 (2022).

[61] Three quarters of abortion patients are of low income, Abortion Patients are Disproportionately Poor and Low Income, *Guttmacher Inst.* (May 19, 2016), www.guttmacher.org/infographic/2016/abortion-patients-are-disproportionately-poor-and-low-income and the cost and time associated with in-person abortion care delayed and thwarted abortion access when a ban on pre-viability abortion was constitutionally prohibited under *Roe v. Wade*, Ushma D. Upadhyay, et al., Denial of Abortion Because of Provider Gestational Age Limits in the United States, 104 Am. J. Public Health 1687, 1689–91 (2014).

[62] Interview by Terry Gross with Mary Ziegler, Fresh Air, *Nat'l Pub. Radio* (June 23, 2022), www.npr.org/2022/06/23/1106922050/why-overturning-roe-isnt-the-final-goal-of-the-anti-abortion-movement.

[63] Rachel K. Jones & Megan K. Donovan, Self-Managed Abortion May Be on the Rise, But Probably Not a Significant Driver of The Overall Decline in Abortion, *Guttmacher Inst.* (November 2019), www.guttmacher.org/article/2019/11/self-managed-abortion-may-be-rise-probably-not-significant-driver-overall-decline.

[64] See Donley, supra note 1, at 697; Jennifer Conti, The Complicated Reality of Buying Abortion Pills Online, *Self Mag.* (April 9, 2019), www.self.com/story/buying-abortion-pills-online.

[65] Jones & Donovan, supra note 62. When this chapter was drafted, Aid Access was serviced by international providers, but as this chapter was going to press, Aid Access began working with U.S.-based

US patients they have served has grown.[66] Once Texas's SB8 became effective, Aid Access saw demand for their services increase 1,180 percent, levelling out to 245 percent of the pre-SB8 demand a month later.[67] Similarly, after *Dobbs*, the demand for Aid Access doubled, tripled, or even quadrupled in states with abortion bans.[68] There are advantages to self-managed abortion: The price is affordable (roughly only $105 for use of foreign providers and pharmacy) and the pregnant person can have an abortion at home.[69] The disadvantage is that receiving the pills can take one to three weeks (when shipped internationally) and comes with the legal risks explored below.

The portability of abortion medication, combined with the uptake of telehealth, poses an existential crisis for the antiabortion movement. Just as it achieved its decades-long goal of overturning *Roe*, the nature of abortion care has shifted and decentralized, making it difficult to police and control.[70] Before the advent of abortion medication, pregnant people depended on the help of a provider to end their pregnancies.[71] They could not do it alone. As a result, states would threaten providers' livelihood and freedom, driving providers out of business and leaving patients with few options.[72] Many turned to unqualified providers who offered unsafe abortions that lead to illness, infertility, and death.[73] But abortion medication created *safe* alternatives for patients that their predecessors lacked. Because abortion medication makes the involvement of providers no longer necessary to terminate early pregnancies, the classic abortion ban, which targets providers, will not have the same effect.[74] And out-of-country providers who help patients self-manage abortions remain outside of a state's reach.[75]

The antiabortion movement is aware of this shifting reality. Indeed, antiabortion state legislators are introducing and enacting laws specifically targeting abortion medication – laws that would ban it entirely, ban its shipment through

providers to prescribe and to mail medication abortion across the country. For additional information, see David S. Cohen, Greer Donley & Rachel Rebouché, Abortion Pills, 76 Stan. L. Rev. (forthcoming 2024), https://papers.ssrn.com/sol3/papers.cfm?abstract_id=4335735.

[66] Donley, supra note 1, at 660.
[67] Abigail R. A. Aiken et al, Association of Texas Senate Bill 8 With Requests for Self-managed Medication Abortion, 5 JAMA Netw. Open e221122 (2022).
[68] Abigail R. A. Aiken et al, Requests for Self-managed Medication Abortion Provided Using Online Telemedicine in 30 US States Before and After the Dobbs v Jackson Women's Health Organization Decision, 328 J. Am. Med. Assn. 1768 (2022).
[69] Cohen, Donley & Rebouché, supra note 8, n.98.
[70] See id.
[71] Lindgren, supra note 59, at 5–6.
[72] See Meghan K. Donovan, Self-Managed Medication Abortion: Expanding the Available Options for U.S. Abortion Care, Guttmacher Inst. (October 17, 2018), www.guttmacher.org/gpr/2018/10/self-managed-medication-abortion-expanding-available-options-us-abortion-care.
[73] Rachel Benson Gold, Lessons from Before Roe: Will Past be Prologue?, Guttmacher Inst. (March 1, 2003), www.guttmacher.org/gpr/2003/03/lessons-roe-will-past-be-prologue.
[74] Greer Donley & Jill Wieber Lens, Subjective Fetal Personhood, 75 Vand. L. Rev. 1649, 1705–06 (2022).
[75] Id.

the mail, or otherwise burden its dispensation.[76] Nevertheless, it is unclear how states will enforce these laws. Most mail goes in and out of states without inspection.[77]

This is not to suggest that self-management will solve the post-*Roe* abortion crisis. For one, self-managed abortion medication is generally not recommended beyond the first trimester, meaning later-stage abortion patients, who comprise less than 10 percent of the patient population, will either need to travel to obtain an abortion or face the higher medical risks associated with self-management.[78] Moreover, pregnant patients may face legal risks in self-managing an abortion in an antiabortion state.[79] Historically, legislators were unwilling to target abortion patients themselves, but patients and their in-state helpers may become more vulnerable as legislatures and prosecutors reckon with the inability to target in-state providers. These types of prosecutions may occur in a few ways.

First, even if shipments of abortion medication largely go undetected, a small percentage of patients will experience side effects or complications that lead them to seek treatment in a hospital.[80] Self-managed abortions mimic miscarriage, which will aid some people in evading abortion laws, although some patients may reveal to a health care professional that their miscarriage was induced with abortion medication.[81] And even with federal protection for patient health information,[82] hospital employees could report those they *suspect* of abortion-related crimes.[83] This will lead to an increase in the investigation and criminalization of both pregnancy loss and abortion.[84]

---

[76] Caroline Kitchener, Kevin Schaul & Daniela Santamariña, Tracking New Action on Abortion Legislation Across the States, *Washington Post* (last updated April 14, 2022), www.washingtonpost.com/nation/interactive/2022/abortion-rights-protections-restrictions-tracker/.

[77] The Justice Department issued an opinion in December 2022 reaffirming the mailability of abortion medication in accordance with a general prohibition on postal agency inspections of packages containing prescription drugs. Application of the Comstock Act to the Mailing of Prescription Drugs That Can Be Used for Abortions, 46 Op. O.L.C. 1, 2 (2022).

[78] The FDA has approved abortion medication through the first ten weeks, but the protocol is the same through twelve weeks. Later Abortion Initiative, *Can Misoprostol and Mifepristone be Used for Medical Management of Abortion after the First Trimester?* (2019), www.ibisreproductivehealth.org/sites/default/files/files/publications/lai_medication_abortion_0.pdf. After that, patients typically need a higher dose for an effective abortion, which takes place in a clinical facility. In a post-Dobbs world, however, some patients will attempt to self-manage second trimester abortions. Id.

[79] Donley & Lens, supra note 73, at 39–43.

[80] Id. Or people might seek after-abortion care if they are unfamiliar with how misoprostol works and believe they are experiencing complications when they likely are not.

[81] Id.

[82] Cohen, Donley & Rebouché, supra note 8, at 77 (discussing how the Health Insurance Portability and Accountability Act (HIPAA) prohibits covered health care employees from reporting health information to law enforcement unless an exception is met). The HIPAA's protections might not be a sufficient deterrent for motivated individuals who want to report suspected abortion crimes, especially if the Biden Administration is not aggressive in enforcing the statute.

[83] Donley & Lens, supra note 73, at 39–43.

[84] Id.

This is how many people have become targets of criminal prosecution in other countries that ban abortion.[85]

Second, the new terrain of digital surveillance will play an important role. Any time the state is notified of someone who could be charged for an abortion-related crime, the police will be able to obtain a warrant to search their digital life if they have sufficient probable cause. Anya Prince has explained the breadth of the reproductive health data ecosystem, in which advertisers and period tracking apps can easily capture when a person is pregnant.[86] The proliferation of "digital diagnostics" (for instance, wearables that track and assess health data) could become capable of diagnosing a possible pregnancy based on physiologic signals, such as temperature and heart rate, perhaps without the user's knowledge. As Prince notes, this type of information is largely unprotected by privacy laws and companies may sell it to state entities.[87] Technology that indicates that a person went from "possibly pregnant" to "not pregnant" without a documented birth could signal an abortion worthy of investigation. Alternatively, pregnancy data combined with search histories regarding abortion options, geofencing data of out-of-state trips, and text histories with friends could be used to support abortion prosecutions.[88] Antiabortion organizations could also set up fake virtual clinics – crisis pregnancy centers for the digital age – to identify potential abortion patients and leak their information to the police.[89]

These technologies will test conceptions of privacy as people voluntarily offer health data that can be used against them.[90] Law enforcement will, as they have with search engine requests and electronic receipts, use this digital information against people self-managing abortions.[91] And, almost certainly, low-income people and women of color will be targets of pregnancy surveillance and criminalization.[92] This is already true – even though drug use in pregnancy is the same in white and populations of color – Black women are ten times more likely to be reported to

[85] Id.; Michelle Oberman, Abortion Bans, Doctors, and the Criminalization of Patients, 48 Hastings Ctr. Rep. 5 (2018).
[86] Anya E.R. Prince, Reproductive Health Surveillance, B.C. L. Rev. (in press, 2023), https://papers.ssrn.com/sol3/papers.cfm?abstract_id=4176557.
[87] Id.
[88] Id.
[89] See Leslie Reagan, Abortion Access in Post-Roe America vs. Pre-Roe America, The New York Times (December 10, 2021), www.nytimes.com/2021/12/10/opinion/supreme-court-abortion-roe.html.
[90] David Cohen, Greer Donley & Rachel Rebouché, Abortion Pills, 59–65 (on file with the authors), https://papers.ssrn.com/sol3/papers.cfm?abstract_id=4335735 (describing impending efforts to surveil pregnancies).
[91] Data collected on people's iPads and Google searches have been used in criminal prosecutions. See Laura Huss, Farah Diaz-Tello, & Goleen Samari, Self-Care, Criminalized: August 2022 Preliminary Findings, If/When/How (2022), www.ifwhenhow.org/resources/self-care-criminalized-preliminary-findings/.
[92] In her book, Policing the Womb, Michelle Goodwin explains in great detail how the state particularly targets Black women and women of color during pregnancy. Michele Goodwin, Policing the Womb: Invisible Women and the Criminalization of Motherhood 21 (2020).

authorities.[93] And because low-income women and women of color are more likely to seek abortion and less likely to have early prenatal care, any pregnancy complications may be viewed suspiciously.[94]

State legislatures and the federal government can help to protect providers and patients in the coming era of abortion care, although their actions may have a limited reach.[95] At the federal level, the FDA could assert that its regulation of medication abortion preempts contradictory state laws, potentially creating a nationwide, abortion-medication exception to state abortion bans.[96] The federal government could also use federal laws and regulations that govern emergency care, medical privacy, and Medicare and Medicaid reimbursement to preempt state abortion laws and reduce hospital-based investigations, though the impact of such laws and regulations would be more limited.[97] As this chapter goes to press in 2023, the Biden Administration is undertaking some of these actions.[98]

State policies in jurisdictions supportive of abortion rights can also improve access for patients traveling to them. States can invest in telehealth generally to continue to loosen restrictions on telemedicine, as many states have done in response to the pandemic, reducing demand at brick-and-mortar abortion clinics and disparities in technology access.[99] They can also join interstate licensure compacts, which could extend the reach of telehealth for abortion in the states that permit the practice and allow providers to pool resources and provide care across state lines.[100] States can also pass abortion shield laws to insulate their providers who care for out-of-state residents by refusing to cooperate in out-of-state investigations, lawsuits, prosecutions, or extradition requests for abortion-related lawsuits.[101] All of these efforts will help reduce, but by no means stop, the sea change to abortion law and access moving forward. And none of these efforts protect the patients or those that assist them in states that ban abortion.

IV CONCLUSION

A post-*Dobbs* country will be messy. A right that generations took for granted – even though for some, abortion was inaccessible – disappeared in half of the country. The present landscape, however, is not like the pre-*Roe* era. Innovations in

---

[93] Id.
[94] Donley & Lens, supra note 73, at 41.
[95] Id.
[96] Cohen, Donley & Rebouché, supra note 8, at 52–79.
[97] Greer Donley, Rachel Rebouché & David Cohen, Existing Federal Laws Could Protect Abortion Rights Even if Roe Is Overturned, *Time* (January 24, 2023), https://time.com/6141517/abortion-federal-law-preemption-roe-v-wade/.
[98] Cohen, Donley & Rebouché, supra note 8, at 71–79.
[99] Id. at 65–74.
[100] Id.
[101] Id. at 31.

medical care and telehealth have changed abortion care, thwarting the antiabortion movement's ability to control abortion, just as it gained the ability to ban it. Unlike patients in past generations, patients now will be able to access safe abortions, even in states in which it is illegal. But they will also face legal risks that were uncommon previously, given the new ways for the state to investigate and criminalize them.

As courts and lawmakers tackle the changing reality of abortion rights, we should not be surprised by surprises – unlikely allies and opponents may coalesce on both sides of the abortion debate. Laws that seek to punish abortion will become harder to enforce as mailed abortion pills proliferate. This will create urgency for some antiabortion states to find creative ways to chill abortion, while other states will be content to ban abortion in law, understanding that it continues in practice. Who states seek to punish will shift, with authorities targeting not only providers, but also patients, and with the most marginalized patients being the most vulnerable.[102]

---

[102] See Goodwin, supra note 91, at 12–26.

7

Monitoring (on) Your Mind

Digital Biomarkers for Alzheimer's Disease

Claire Erickson and Emily A. Largent

I INTRODUCTION

What first comes to mind when you hear the words "Alzheimer's disease?"

For many, those words evoke images of an older adult who exhibits troubling changes in memory and thinking. Perhaps the older adult has gotten lost driving to church, although it's a familiar route. Perhaps they have bounced a check, which is out of character for them. Perhaps they have repeatedly left the stove on while cooking, worrying their spouse or adult children. Perhaps they have trouble finding words or are confused by devices like iPhones and, as a result, have lost touch with longtime friends.

Alzheimer's disease (AD) has traditionally been understood as a clinical diagnosis, requiring the presence of symptoms to be detected. The older adult we just envisioned might make an appointment with their physician. The physician would likely listen to the patient's medical history – noting the characteristic onset and pattern of impairments – and determine that the patient has *dementia*, a loss of cognitive and functional abilities severe enough to interfere with daily life. Dementia can have numerous causes, and so the physician would also conduct a comprehensive physical and cognitive examination, perhaps ordering lab tests or brain imaging scans, as well as neuropsychological testing. After excluding other causes, the clinician would diagnose the patient with "probable" AD, a diagnosis that can only be confirmed postmortem via autopsy. This approach to diagnosis interweaves the patient's experience of disabling cognitive and functional impairments (i.e., dementia) with the label of AD.[1]

Yet, our ability to measure the neuropathology of AD is rapidly evolving, as is our understanding of the preclinical and prodromal stages of disease. Thus, it is

---

[1] The utility of an AD diagnosis has been debated. Presently, there is no cure for dementia caused by AD; however, clinicians may prescribe a disease-modifying therapy or medications to temporarily improve or delay dementia symptoms or address other symptoms or conditions, such as depression or agitation. A diagnosis of AD can also be useful for informing lifestyle changes, providing clarity about what is happening, facilitating future planning, and accessing systems and support for the patient and caregiver.

now possible to identify individuals who are *at risk* for developing dementia caused by AD years or even decades before the onset of cognitive decline through clinical but also digital monitoring. A key premise of this article is that, in the future, the identification of at-risk individuals will continue to occur in clinical settings using traditional biomarker testing; but, the identification of at-risk individuals will also increasingly occur closer to – or even in – one's home, potentially using digital biomarkers.

When you hear "Alzheimer's disease," in-home monitoring should come to mind.

Here, we argue that because AD affects the mind, the challenges associated with monitoring aimed at understanding the risk for disabling cognitive impairments are heightened as compared to the challenges of monitoring for physical ailments. In Section II, we discuss the biomarker transformation of AD, which is allowing us to see AD neuropathology in living persons and to identify individuals at increased risk for developing dementia caused by AD. In Section III, we outline empirical evidence regarding five different digital biomarkers; these digital biomarkers offer further insights into an individual's risk for cognitive impairment and could soon be used for in-home monitoring. Finally, in Section IV, we identify six challenges that are particularly pronounced when monitoring for AD.

II THE EVOLVING UNDERSTANDING OF AD

The field of AD research is rapidly moving from a syndromal definition of AD (see, e.g., the diagnostic process described in Section I) to a biological one. This shift reflects a growing understanding of the mechanisms underlying the clinical expression of AD.[2]

Biomarkers can now be used to identify AD neuropathology in vivo. A biomarker is a "defined characteristic that is measured as an indicator of normal biological processes, pathogenic processes or responses to an exposure or intervention."[3] Individuals are understood to have a biomarker profile, which (as we're using it here) describes the presence or absence in their brain of three AD biomarkers: Beta-amyloid, pathologic tau, or neurodegeneration. These biomarkers can be measured using various modalities, including positron emission tomography (PET), cerebrospinal fluid (CSF) sampling, or magnetic resonance imaging (MRI); moreover, that blood-based biomarker tests are now available.[4]

---

[2] Clifford R. Jack et al., A/T/N: An Unbiased Descriptive Classification Scheme for Alzheimer Disease Biomarkers, 87 Neurology 539 (2016); Clifford R. Jack et al., NIA-AA Research Framework: Toward a Biological Definition of Alzheimer's Disease, 14 Alzheimer's & Dementia: J. Alzheimer's Ass'n 535 (2018).

[3] FDA-NIH Biomarker Working Group, *BEST (Biomarkers, EndpointS, and other Tools) Resource* (2016).

[4] Suzanne E. Schindler & Randall J. Bateman, Combining Blood-based Biomarkers to Predict Risk for Alzheimer's Disease Dementia, 1 Nat. Aging 26 (2021).

In addition to the biomarker profile, a second, independent source of information is the individual's cognitive stage. An individual may be cognitively unimpaired – within the expected range of cognitive testing scores and functioning in daily life, have mild cognitive impairment (MCI) – a slight but noticeable decline in cognitive skills, or have dementia. The patient's biomarker profile can then be used in combination with the patient's cognitive stage to characterize the patient's place – and likely progression – along the Alzheimer's continuum. The continuum spans the preclinical (i.e., clinically asymptomatic with evidence of AD neuropathology) and clinical (i.e., symptomatic) phases of AD.[5]

Individuals in the preclinical stage have AD biomarkers but do not have clinically measurable cognitive impairment. They may be truly cognitively unimpaired, or they may have subjective cognitive decline – a self-experienced decline in cognitive capacity as compared to baseline.[6] Those with preclinical AD are understood to be at an increased risk of short-term cognitive decline.[7] An estimated 46.7 million Americans have preclinical AD (defined by amyloidosis, neurodegeneration, or both), though it's important to emphasize that not all of them will progress to a dementia-level of impairment.[8]

At present, preclinical AD remains a research construct. It is not yet diagnosed clinically. Researchers hope, however, that intervening earlier rather than later in the course of the disease will allow them to delay or prevent the onset of cognitive and functional impairment. Therefore, they are conducting secondary prevention trials, which recruit individuals who are asymptomatic but biomarker-positive for AD – that is, who have preclinical AD – to test new drugs or novel interventions. It is reasonable to assume that if the preclinical AD construct is validated and if a disease-modifying therapy for AD is found, preclinical AD will move from the research to the clinical context.

In the future, people who receive a preclinical AD diagnosis will have insight into their risk of developing MCI or dementia years or even decades before the onset of impairments.[9] Monitoring digital biomarkers in the home, the focus of Section III, will likely be complementary to clinical assessment. For instance, monitoring may be used to watch for incipient changes in cognition after a preclinical AD diagnosis. Or, conversely, data generated by in-home monitoring may suggest that it is time to see a clinician for an AD workup.

---

[5] Paul S. Aisen et al., On the Path to 2025: Understanding the Alzheimer's Disease Continuum, 9 Alzheimer's Rsch. & Therapy 60 (2017).

[6] Frank Jessen et al., The Characterisation of Subjective Cognitive Decline, 19 Lancet Neurol. 271 (2020).

[7] Jack et al., supra note 2.

[8] Ron Brookmeyer & Nada Abdalla, Estimation of Lifetime Risks of Alzheimer's Disease Dementia using Biomarkers for Preclinical Disease, 14 Alzheimer's & Dementia 981 (2018); Ron Brookmeyer et al., Forecasting the Prevalence of Preclinical and Clinical Alzheimer's Disease in the United States, 14 Alzheimer's & Dementia 121 (2018).

[9] Jack et al., supra note 2.

III DIGITAL BIOMARKERS OF AD

In parallel with our evolving understanding of beta-amyloid, pathologic tau, and neurodegeneration as "traditional" biomarkers of AD, there have been advances in our understanding of digital biomarkers for AD. Efforts to concretely and comprehensively define digital biomarkers are ongoing.[10] For the purposes of this chapter, we use the following definition: "Objective, quantifiable, physiological, and behavioral data that are collected and measured by means of digital devices, such as embedded environmental sensors, portables, wearables, implantables, or digestibles."[11]

Digital biomarkers have the potential to flag uncharacteristic behaviors or minor mistakes that offer insights into an older adult's risk of cognitive and functional decline or to indicate early cognitive decline. As noted above, the preclinical stage of AD is characterized by the presence of biomarkers in the absence of measurable cognitive impairment. Despite going undetected on standard cognitive tests, subtle cognitive changes may be present. There is, in fact, a growing body of evidence that subjective cognitive decline in individuals with an unimpaired performance on cognitive tests may represent the first symptomatic manifestation of AD.[12] These small changes from the individual's baseline may have downstream effects on complex cognitive and functional behaviors. Digital biomarkers offer a means of capturing these effects.

Here, we discuss five digital biomarkers for AD, highlighting both promising opportunities for monitoring the minds of older adults and limitations in our current knowledge and monitoring abilities. Crucially, these opportunities primarily reside outside of routine clinical settings. These examples are not meant to be exhaustive, but rather have been selected to highlight a range of monitoring modalities involving diverse actors. Moreover, they reveal a variety of potential challenges, which are the focus of Section IV.

A *Driving Patterns*

Due to the complex processes involved in spatial navigation and vehicle operation, an assessment of driving patterns offers an avenue for detecting changes in thinking and behavior. Indeed, prior studies demonstrate that those with symptomatic AD drive shorter distances and visit fewer unique destinations.[13] Research also

---

[10] Christian Montag, Jon D. Elhai & Paul Dagum, On Blurry Boundaries When Defining Digital Biomarkers: How Much Biology Needs to Be in a Digital Biomarker?, 12 Front. Psychiatry 740292 (2021).
[11] Antoine Piau et al., Current State of Digital Biomarker Technologies for Real-Life, Home-Based Monitoring of Cognitive Function for Mild Cognitive Impairment to Mild Alzheimer Disease and Implications for Clinical Care: Systematic Review, 21 J. Med. Internet Rsch. e12785 (2019).
[12] Frank Jessen et al., A Conceptual Framework for Research on Subjective Cognitive Decline in Preclinical Alzheimer's Disease, 10 Alzheimer's & Dementia 844 (2014).
[13] Lidia P. Kostyniuk & Lisa J. Molnar, Self-regulatory Driving Practices among Older Adults: Health, Age and Sex Effects, 40 Accid. Anal. Prev. 1576 (2008); Jennifer D. Davis et al., Road

suggests that detectable spatial navigation deficits may precede AD symptom development in cognitively normal individuals with AD biomarkers.[14] A limitation of this work is that it was conducted using simulators, which only measure performance in very controlled settings and so are limited in their generalizability.[15] Studies have, therefore, shifted to a naturalistic approach to data collection to characterize daily driving patterns. Researchers can passively collect data using global positioning system (GPS) devices installed in participant vehicles. The resulting information includes average trip distance, number of unique destinations, number of trips with a speed of six miles per hour or more below the posted limit (i.e., underspeed), and a variety of other measures to quantify driving performance.[16] These studies have found differing behavior and driving patterns between cognitively unimpaired participants with and without AD biomarkers, including a greater decline in the number of days driving per month for those with AD biomarkers.[17]

These findings suggest that assessing driving patterns – as some insurers already do through standalone devices or apps[18] – may help identify individuals at risk for cognitive decline due to AD.

B Banking and Finances

Instrumental activities of daily living (IADLs) are complex activities necessary for individuals to live independently, such as managing one's finances. As AD progresses, IADLs become increasingly impaired. A 2021 study examined longitudinal credit report information for over 80,000 Medicare beneficiaries.[19] The researchers found that those with an AD or related dementia diagnosis were more likely to have missed bill payments over the six years prior to their dementia diagnosis. They also found that individuals with a dementia diagnosis developed subprime credit scores two-and-a-half years before their diagnosis. In a prospective study of cognitively

---

Test and Naturalistic Driving Performance in Healthy and Cognitively Impaired Older Adults: Does Environment Matter?, 60 J. Am. Geriatric Soc'y 2056 (2012).

[14] Samantha L. Allison et al., Spatial Navigation in Preclinical Alzheimer's Disease, 52 J. Alzheimers Dis. 77 (2016); Gillian Coughlan et al., Spatial navigation Deficits – Overlooked Cognitive Marker for Preclinical Alzheimer Disease?, 14 Nat'l Rev. Neurol. 496 (2018).

[15] Megan A. Hird et al., A Systematic Review and Meta-Analysis of On-Road Simulator and Cognitive Driving Assessment in Alzheimer's Disease and Mild Cognitive Impairment, 53 J. Alzheimers Dis. 713 (2016).

[16] Catherine M. Roe et al., A 2.5-Year Longitudinal Assessment of Naturalistic Driving in Preclinical Alzheimer's Disease, 68 J. Alzheimers Dis. 1625 (2019); Sayeh Bayat et al., GPS Driving: A Digital Biomarker for Preclinical Alzheimer Disease, 13 Alzheimers Rsch. & Therapy 115 (2021).

[17] Roe et al., supra note 16; Bayat et al., supra note 16.

[18] Kristen Hall-Geisler & Jennifer Lobb, How Do Those Car Insurance Tracking Devices Work?, US News & World Rep. (March 9, 2022), www.usnews.com/insurance/auto/how-do-those-car-insurance-tracking-devices-work.

[19] Lauren Hersch Nicholas et al., Financial Presentation of Alzheimer Disease and Related Dementias, 181 JAMA Internal Med. 220 (2021).

unimpaired older adults, researchers found that a low awareness of financial and other types of scams was associated with an increased risk for MCI and dementia, though the measure was too weak for prediction at the individual level.[20]

More work is needed to characterize the timeframe of changes in financial management, but detecting changes such as missed payments, bounced checks, or altered purchasing behavior (e.g., repeated purchases) presents another opportunity to identify individuals with preclinical AD. Banking and financial institutions already use algorithms, behavioral analytics, and artificial intelligence (AI)-powered technology to identify unusual transactions or spending behaviors that may be suggestive of fraud.[21] Similar techniques could be adapted to monitor older adults and notify them of behaviors indicative of dementia risk.

C *Smart Appliances*

Sensors can be deployed in the home to detect cognitive changes in older adults.[22] In a task-based study, individuals with MCI have been shown to spend more time in the kitchen when performing a set of home-based activities.[23] While in the kitchen, participants with MCI open cabinets and drawers, as well as the refrigerator, more often than cognitively unimpaired participants.[24] Researchers are exploring whether it is possible to use similar techniques to differentiate between healthy controls and individuals with preclinical AD.[25] A challenge for such monitoring studies (and, by extension, for real-life uptake) is the need to deploy multiple sensors in the home. One study attempted to circumvent this issue by focusing on passive in-home power usage for large appliances; the team found, on average, lower daily and seasonal usage of appliances among people with cognitive impairment.[26]

Smart appliances, like refrigerators and ovens, connect to the internet and can sync with smartphones or other devices. They are already in many homes and are another alternative to sensor-based systems for detecting early cognitive changes. Smart refrigerators could track the frequency with which they are opened and for

---

[20] Patricia A. Boyle et al., Scam Awareness Related to Incident Alzheimer Dementia and Mild Cognitive Impairment: A Prospective Cohort Study, 170 Annals Internal Med. 702 (2019).
[21] Benjamin Pimentel, Banks Watch Your Every Move Online. Here's How It Prevents Fraud, *Protocol* (June 1, 2021), www.protocol.com/fintech/behavioral-analytics-bank-fraud-detection.
[22] Yuriko Nakaoku et al., AI-Assisted In-House Power Monitoring for the Detection of Cognitive Impairment in Older Adults, 21 Sensors (Basel) 6249 (2021).
[23] Piau et al., supra note 11; Nakoku et al., supra note 22; Maxime Lussier et al., Smart Home Technology: A New Approach for Performance Measurements of Activities of Daily Living and Prediction of Mild Cognitive Impairment in Older Adults, 68 J. Alzheimers Dis. 85 (2019).
[24] Piau et al., supra note 11; Nakaoku et al., supra note 22; Lussier et al., supra note 23.
[25] The RADAR-AD Consortium et al., Remote Monitoring Technologies in Alzheimer's Disease: Design of the RADAR-AD Study, 13 Alzheimer's Rsch. & Therapy 89 (2021).
[26] Nakaoku et al., supra note 22.

how long. Similarly, smart ovens may track the time they are left on. Such usage information could then be shared with the consumer by the appliance itself, for example, via an app.

D *Speech*

Changes in speech have been used to characterize the progression of AD. Studies have often used active data collection in which individuals are recorded on a smartphone or similar device as they complete tasks associated with verbal fluency, picture description, and free speech. The voice recordings are then processed, sometimes using machine-learning techniques. Studies have found that short vocal tasks can be used to differentiate participants with MCI from those with dementia.[27] It remains an open question whether preclinical AD presents with detectable changes in speech. Yet, one study of speech changes found that cognitively unimpaired participants with AD biomarkers used fewer concrete nouns and content words during spontaneous speech.[28]

The interest in modalities for passive speech data collection – for example, conversations over the phone, communication with digital assistants, and texting related information – is mounting.[29] Improvements in machine-learning to reduce the burden of speech analysis, coupled with broad access to devices with microphones, are increasing the potential of passive speech data collection. Automatic speech recognition used for digital assistants like Amazon Alexa and Apple Siri has made strides in accuracy. As technological advancements further streamline transcription and analysis, speech data may be used to characterize changes related to preclinical AD. Simply put, Alexa may soon diagnose progression along the Alzheimer's continuum from preclinical AD to MCI to dementia.[30]

E *Device Use*

The ways people use their smartphones – including the amount of time spent on certain apps, login attempts, patterns of use, and disruptions in social interactions – may

---

[27] Alexandra König et al., Automatic Speech Analysis for the Assessment of Patients with Predementia and Alzheimer's Disease, 1 Alzheimer's & Dementia (Amst) 112 (2015); Alexandra Konig et al., Use of Speech Analyses within a Mobile Application for the Assessment of Cognitive Impairment in Elderly People, 15 Current Alzheimer Rsch. 120 (2018); Fredrik Öhman et al., Current Advances in Digital Cognitive Assessment for Preclinical Alzheimer's Disease, 13 Alzheimer's & Dementia (2021).
[28] Sander C.J. Verfaillie et al., High Amyloid Burden is Associated with Fewer Specific Words During Spontaneous Speech in Individuals with Subjective Cognitive Decline, 131 Neuropsychologia 184 (2019).
[29] Jessica Robin et al., Evaluation of Speech-Based Digital Biomarkers: Review and Recommendations, 4 Digit. Biomark 99 (2020); Lampros C. Kourtis et al., Digital Biomarkers for Alzheimer's Disease: The Mobile/Wearable Devices Opportunity, 2 npj Digit. Med. 9 (2019).
[30] David A. Simon et al., Should Alexa Diagnose Alzheimer's?: Legal and Ethical Issues with At-home Consumer Devices, Cell Reps. Med. 100692 (2022).

reveal signs of cognitive decline.[31] Studies examining patterns of smartphone use in older adults with and without cognitive impairment suggest that app usage is related to cognitive health.[32] There is much interest in leveraging device use as a potential marker of cognitive decline. The Intuition Study (NCT05058950), a collaboration between Biogen and Apple Inc., began in September 2021 with the aim of using multimodal passive sensor data from iPhone and Apple Watch usage to differentiate normal cognition from MCI; a secondary aim is to develop a function for predicting between individuals who will and will not develop MCI. With 23,000 participants, this observational longitudinal study will be the largest study to date collecting passive device use data.

Devices, like smartphones, could soon flag usage patterns that are suggestive of an increased risk of decline. Further, specific apps may be developed to detect concerning behavior changes by accessing meta-data from other apps and devices; this may streamline access to information and improve consumer friendliness.

IV CHALLENGES AHEAD

Here, we identify six ethical and legal challenges that will accompany the monitoring of digital biomarkers for AD. These are not exclusive, and many issues associated generally with measuring digital biomarkers will apply here as well. Moreover, the challenges outlined herein are not unique to digital biomarkers for AD. Rather, we would argue that they are heightened in this context because AD is a disease not just of the brain but the mind.

A Consent to Collect and Consent to Disclose

Although we hypothesize that preclinical AD will not be diagnosed clinically (i.e., using traditional biomarkers) until there is a disease-modifying therapy that renders the diagnosis medically actionable, in-home monitoring of digital biomarkers is not subject to this constraint. In fact, potential means of collecting and analyzing digital biomarkers for AD are already in our homes.

Yet, it is unlikely that individuals are aware that the GPS devices in their cars, the smart appliances in their kitchens, and the online banking apps on their phones can provide insights into their risk of cognitive and functional decline. Plugging in the GPS device, using the smart oven, or paying bills online, therefore, does not imply consent to having one's brain health measured. Nor can consent be presumed. Many individuals *do not* want to know about their risk of developing dementia

---

[31] Kourtis et al., supra note 29.
[32] Jonas Rauber, Emily B. Fox & Leon A. Gatys, Modeling Patterns of Smartphone Usage and Their Relationship to Cognitive Health (2019), https://arxiv.org/abs/1911.05683; Mitchell L. Gordon et al., App Usage Predicts Cognitive Ability in Older Adults, in *Proceedings of the 2019 CHI Conference on Human Factors in Computing Systems* 1 (2019), https://dl.acm.org/doi/10.1145/3290605.3300398.

caused by AD because there is little to be done about it.[33] Others eschew learning their dementia risk to avoid existential dread.[34] This all suggests that, if digital biomarkers for AD are to be collected, there must be explicit consent.

Even if individuals agree to having their digital biomarkers for AD monitored, they may ultimately choose against learning what is revealed therein. Some individuals who undergo testing to learn whether they are at risk for dementia caused by AD – whether due to genes or to biomarkers – subsequently decline to learn the results.[35]

This contrasts with – drawing an analogy to emergency medicine – our ability to presume consent for an Apple watch to monitor for and alert us to a possibly fatal arrythmia. But even there, where there is greater reason to presume consent, the evidence suggests we ought to eschew a "more is more" approach to disclosure. Apple watch monitoring for arrythmia can unduly worry people who receive a notification and subsequently follow-up with doctors, undergoing invasive and expensive tests only for the results to come back normal.[36] When the rate of false positives is unknown – or remains high – and when there are risks and burdens associated with disclosure, caution must accompany implementation.

B *Communicating Digital Biomarker Information*

To date, traditional AD biomarker information has been disclosed to cognitively unimpaired adults in highly controlled environments, mostly through research studies and with specialist clinical expertise.[37] Substantial work has gone into developing methods for disclosure, and the recommended steps include preparing people to learn about their biomarker information, maintaining sensitivity in returning the results, and following-up to ensure people feel supported after learning the results.[38] Digital biomarkers present an opportunity for individuals to learn that they are exhibiting subtle signs of cognitive decline or are at risk for dementia in the future from an app or from their banker or insurance agent – and without the option to speak directly and quickly about the results with a medical professional.

---

[33] Emily A. Largent et al., Disclosing Genetic Risk of Alzheimer's Disease to Cognitively Unimpaired Older Adults: Findings from the Study of Knowledge and Reactions to APOE Testing (SOKRATES II), 84 J. Alzheimer's Dis. 1015 (2021).

[34] Steven Pinker, My Genome, My Self, *The New York Times* (January 7, 2009), www.nytimes.com/2009/01/11/magazine/11Genome-t.html.

[35] Emily A Largent et al., "That Would be Dreadful": The Ethical, Legal, and Social Challenges of Sharing Your Alzheimer's Disease Biomarker and Genetic Testing Results with Others, J. Law & Biosciences lsab004 (2021).

[36] Larry Husten, Beware the Hype over the Apple Watch Heart App. The Device Could Do More Harm Than Good, *Stat* (March 15, 2019), www.statnews.com/2019/03/15/apple-watch-atrial-fibrillation/.

[37] Claire M. Erickson et al., Disclosure of Preclinical Alzheimer's Disease Biomarker Results in Research and Clinical Settings: Why, How, and What We Still Need to Know, 13 Alzheimer's; Dementia: Diagnosis, Assessment; Disease Monitoring (2021).

[38] Kristin Harkins et al., Development of a Process to Disclose Amyloid Imaging Results to Cognitively Normal Older Adult Research Participants, 7 Alzheimer's Rsch. & Therapy 26 (2015).

Although the disclosure of AD biomarkers has generally been found to be safe in pre-screened populations,[39] care should be taken when disclosing digital biomarker information more broadly. Here, the field may learn from discussions of direct-to-consumer genetic or biochemical testing.[40]

Another concern is that the monitoring of digital biomarker data could lead to the inadvertent disclosure of dementia risk. Imagine, for instance, that your changing device usage is flagged and then used to generate targeted advertisements for supplements to boost brain health or for memory games. You could learn you are at risk simply by scrolling through your social media feed. And, in that case, any pretense of thoughtful disclosure is dropped.

C Conflicting Desires for Monitoring

Studies suggest that some cognitively unimpaired older adults share their AD biomarker results with others because they would like to be monitored for – and alerted to – changes in cognition and function that might negatively affect their wellbeing.[41] Often, these individuals feel it is ethically important to share this information so as to prepare family members who might, in the future, need to provide dementia care or serve as a surrogate decision maker.[42] Other older adults, however, perceive monitoring as intrusive and unwelcomed.[43]

In an interview study of the family members of cognitively unimpaired older adults with AD biomarkers, some family members described watching the older adult more closely for symptoms of MCI or dementia after learning the biomarker results.[44] This may reflect family members' evolving understanding of themselves as pre-caregivers – individuals at increased risk for informal dementia caregiving.[45] Technology can allow family members to remotely monitor an older adult's location, movements, and activities, in order to detect functional decline and changes

---

[39] Erickson et al., supra note 37.
[40] Emily A. Largent, Anna Wexler & Jason Karlawish, The Future Is P-Tau – Anticipating Direct-to-Consumer Alzheimer Disease Blood Tests, 78 JAMA Neurol. 379 (2021).
[41] Sato Ashida et al., The Role of Disease Perceptions and Results Sharing in Psychological Adaptation after Genetic Susceptibility Testing: The REVEAL Study, 18 Eur. J. Hum. Genetics 1296 (2010); Largent et al., supra note 35.
[42] Largent et al., supra note 35.
[43] Clara Berridge & Terrie Fox Wetle, Why Older Adults and Their Children Disagree About In-Home Surveillance Technology, Sensors, and Tracking, Gerontologist (2020), https://academic.oup.com/gerontologist/advance-article/doi/10.1093/geront/gnz068/5491612; Marcello Ienca et al., Intelligent Assistive Technology for Alzheimer's Disease and Other Dementias: A Systematic Review, 56 J. Alzheimer's Disease 1301 (2017); Largent et al., supra note 35.
[44] Emily A Largent et al., Study Partner Perspectives on Disclosure of Amyloid PET Scan Results: Psychosocial Factors and Environmental Design/Living with Dementia and Quality of Life, 16 Alzheimer's & Dementia (2020).
[45] Emily A. Largent & Jason Karlawish, Preclinical Alzheimer Disease and the Dawn of the Pre-Caregiver, 76 JAMA Neurol. 631 (2019).

in cognition, as well as to intervene if needed. Despite these putative advantages, monitoring may be a source of friction if older adults and their families do not agree on its appropriateness or on who should have access to the resulting information.

V STIGMA AND DISCRIMINATION

Dementia caused by AD is highly stigmatized.[46] Research with cognitively unimpaired individuals who have the AD biomarker beta-amyloid suggests that many worry that this information would be stigmatizing if disclosed to others.[47] Unfortunately, this concern is likely justified; a survey experiment with a nationally representative sample of American adults found that, even in the absence of cognitive symptoms, a positive AD biomarker result evokes stronger stigmatizing reactions among members of the general public than a negative result.[48]

Discrimination occurs when stigmatization is enacted via concrete behaviors. Cognitively unimpaired individuals who have beta-amyloid anticipate discrimination across a variety of contexts – from everyday social interactions to employment, housing, and insurance.[49] It is not yet known whether – and if so to what extent – digital biomarkers will lead to stigma and discrimination. However, we must be aware of this possibility, as well as the scant legal protection against discrimination on the basis of biomarkers.[50]

VI INFORMATION PRIVACY

Digital biomarker information is health information. But it is health information in the hands of bankers and insurance agents or technology companies – individuals and entities that are not health care providers and are therefore not subject to the privacy laws that govern health care data. The Health Insurance Portability and Privacy Act (HIPAA) focuses on data from medical records; it does not, for instance, cover data generated by smartphone apps.[51] The need for privacy is intensified by the potential for stigma and discrimination, discussed above.

---

[46] Lynne Corner & John Bond, Being at Risk of Dementia: Fears and Anxieties of Older Adults, 18 J. of Aging Studs. 143 (2004); Perla Werner & Shmuel M. Giveon, Discriminatory Behavior of Family Physicians Toward a Person with Alzheimer's Disease, 20 Int. Psychogeriatr. 824 (2008); Alzheimer's Association, 2019 Alzheimer's Disease Facts and Figures, 15 Alzheimers Dementia 321 (2019).

[47] Largent et al., supra note 35.

[48] Shana D. Stites et al., The Relative Contributions of Biomarkers, Disease Modifying Treatment, and Dementia Severity to Alzheimer's Stigma: A Vignette-based Experiment, 292 Soc. Sci. & Med. 114620 (2022).

[49] Largent et al., supra note 35.

[50] Jalayne J. Arias et al., The Proactive Patient: Long-Term Care Insurance Discrimination Risks of Alzheimer's Disease Biomarkers, 46 J. Law. Med. Ethics 485 (2018).

[51] Nicole Martinez-Martin et al., Data Mining for Health: Staking Out the Ethical Territory of Digital Phenotyping, 1 npj Digit. Med. 68 (2018); Anna Wexler & Peter B. Reiner, Oversight of Direct-to-consumer Neurotechnologies, 363 Science 234 (2019).

Further, older adults with MCI and dementia are vulnerable – for example, to financial scammers. It is important to ensure that data generated by monitoring is not abused – by those who collect it or by those who subsequently access it – to identify potential targets for abuse and exploitation. Abuse and exploitation may occur at the hands of an unscrupulous app developer but also, or perhaps more likely, at the hands of an unscrupulous family member or friend.

VII DISPARITIES IN HEALTH AND TECHNOLOGY

The older population is becoming significantly more racially and ethnically diverse.[52] Black and Hispanic older adults are at higher risk than White older adults for developing AD, and they encounter disproportionate barriers to accessing health care generally, and dementia care specifically.[53] Health disparities are increasingly understood to reflect a broad, complex, and interrelated array of factors, including racism.[54] There are well-reported concerns about racism in AI.[55] Those are no less salient here and may be more salient, given disparities in care.

Further, monitoring may be cost prohibitive, impacted by the digital divide, or reliant on an individual's geographic location. For instance, older adults, especially adults from minoritized communities, may not have smart devices. According to a Pew report using data collected in 2021, only 61 percent of those aged 65 and older owned a smartphone and 44 percent owned a tablet.[56] As many of the digital biomarkers described in Section III require a smart device, uptake of monitoring methods may be unevenly distributed and exacerbate, rather than alleviate, disparities in AD care.

VIII CONCLUSION

The older adult we envisioned at the beginning of this chapter will not be the only face of AD much longer. We may soon come to think, too, of adults with preclinical AD. These individuals may learn about their heightened risk of cognitive and

---

[52] Sandra Colby & Jennifer Ortman, *Projections of the Size and Composition of the US Population: 2014 to 2060*, 13 (2015).
[53] María P. Aranda et al., Impact of Dementia: Health Disparities, Population Trends, Care Interventions, and Economic Costs, 69 J. Am. Geriatrics Soc'y 1774 (2021).
[54] Carl V. Hill et al., The National Institute on Aging Health Disparities Research Framework, 25 Ethn Dis 245 (2015); Camara P. Jones, Levels of Racism: A Theoretic Framework and a Gardener's tale, 90 Am. J. Pub. Health 1212 (2000).
[55] Effy Vayena, Alessandro Blasimme & I. Glenn Cohen, Machine Learning in Medicine: Addressing Ethical Challenges, 15 PLoS Med e1002689 (2018); Ravi B. Parikh, Stephanie Teeple & Amol S. Navathe, Addressing Bias in Artificial Intelligence in Health Care, 322 JAMA 2377 (2019).
[56] Michelle Faverio, Share of Those 65 and Older Who Are Tech Users Has Grown in the Past Decade, *Pew Rsch. Ctr.* (January 13, 2022), www.pewresearch.org/fact-tank/2022/01/13/share-of-those-65-and-older-who-are-tech-users-has-grown-in-the-past-decade/.

functional impairment from a clinician. Or they may learn about it because the GPS device plugged into their car has detected slight alterations in their driving patterns, because their smart refrigerator has alerted them to the fridge door staying open a bit longer, or because their phone has noted slight changes in speech.

AD is undergoing a biomarker transformation, of which digital biomarkers are a part. AD is a deeply feared condition, as it robs people of their ability to self-determine. Care must therefore be taken to address the multitude of challenges that arise when monitoring our minds.

PART III

The Shape of the Elephant for Digital Home Diagnostics

I. Glenn Cohen

INTRODUCTION

In the famous parable that originates in India of the blind men and the elephant, six blind men lived in a village and experienced the world by hearing stories about it. They learned about many things but become particularly fascinated by the elephant which (in stories they are told) tramples forests, carries huge burdens, and makes a loud trumpet call. But they also hear that the Rajah's daughter would ride the elephant when she travels around her father's kingdom. How could this thing be dangerous, if the Rajah lets his daughter ride it, and also be so loud? They would argue about what it was – a powerful giant, a large cow, a graceful ride for a princess, and so on. The villagers grew tired of the argument and arranged to have the blind men examine a real elephant. One touched its side and decided it was smooth and powerful like a wall, as he had believed. Another touched the tusk and announced it was like a sharp spear, as he had believed. Another touched the leg and decided it was nothing more than a large cow, as he had believed. Another touched its trunk and concluded it was a very large snake, as he had believed. And so on. They bickered until the Rajah overheard them. He chastised them for being so certain that they knew what an elephant was – they had each only felt a part of the elephant. Only by putting together all of the pieces could they understand what an elephant was.

The chapters in this part are far from the blind men; they are quite illuminating, indeed, and are very self-aware as to what each of their parts are doing and not doing. But if the elephant represents the legal issues with the way at-home diagnostic devices are actually put on the market, it remains true that each of the first three chapters in this part focus on one piece of the elephant, while the collective helps us better understand it.

David A. Simon and Aaron S. Kesselheim's "Physician and Device Manufacturer Tort Liability for Remote Patient Monitoring Devices" focuses on the ex post regulation of the US tort system. Focusing in particular on remote patient monitoring (RPM) devices, they examine how current US tort law applies to different players in the RPM device ecosystem: The manufacturers of the devices, physicians who prescribe them, patients who use them, and patients' caregivers. They also examine the way in which the various regulatory pathways to get an RPM Device to market – premarket notification approval (PMA), the 510(k) and the de novo pathway potentially – preempt certain kinds of tort claims in this space (manufacture, design, marketing) and more specific claim types, such as fraud on the FDA.

In their chapter, "Post-Market Surveillance of Software Medical Devices: Evidence from Regulatory Data," Alexander O. Everhart and Ariel D. Stern shift to a different ex post form of regulation – post-market surveillance of the subset of RPM and other software-driven products that meet the definition of a medical device in the United States and, therefore, are subject to regulation by the US Food and Drug Administration (FDA). While Simon and Kesselheim's primary way of touching the elephant is through case law analysis, Everhart and Stern offer an analysis of a large dataset they create. They identify all 510(k)-track and PMA-track medical devices – that is, moderate and high-risk devices – cleared or approved by the FDA from 2008–2018 in five common regulatory medical specialties that are most likely to include RPM devices. In that dataset they identify all the recalls and adverse events associated with these devices that occurred between 2008 and 2020. They find, among other things, that "software-driven medical devices" had higher adverse event and recall probabilities compared to devices without software components. They also argue that for us to truly understand this elephant better, we need a systematic collection of unbiased data describing the post-market performance of both medical devices and digital diagnostics.

Sara Gerke's chapter, "Labeling of Direct-to-Consumer Medical Artificial Intelligence Applications for 'Self-Diagnosis,'" shifts from ex post to ex ante regulatory mechanisms, with a focus on direct-to-consumer medical self-diagnosing artificial intelligence (AI) apps. She begins by showing that under the Federal Food, Drug, and Cosmetic Act (FDCA), Congress has given the FDA the power only to regulate software functions that are classified as medical devices under the FDCA. She then examines the guidance promulgated by the FDA for mobile medical apps and "software as a medical device" (SaMD), defined as "software intended to be used for one or more medical purposes that perform these purposes without being part of a hardware medical device." Apple's electrocardiogram (ECG) and irregular rhythms notification feature apps are good examples of SaMDs. Gerke then takes readers through the exceptions created by Congress through the 21st Century Cures Act to the medical device definition for certain software functions and explains the test the FDA has settled on for determining when it will apply regulatory oversight versus enforcement discretion. The chapter then shifts from the descriptive to the prescriptive in examining the labeling of direct-to-consumer medical self-diagnosing apps as information-only versus diagnostic, and the significant discrepancy between the user's perception of the intended use of the apps and the intended use put forward by the manufacturer. She argues for labeling standards for AI-based medical devices, including direct-to-consumer medical self-diagnosing AI apps that, among other things, would effectively inform consumers about the type of AI used (e.g., a black box, an adaptive algorithm, etc.), the various risks of bias, the risks of false positive and negative results, and when to seek medical help.

While these three chapters are up-close perspectives on pieces of the legal elephant described through various methods – doctrinal, empirical, regulatory – Zhang Yi and Wang Chenguang's chapter allows us to view the elephant from afar, by a comparison to how the same issues are handled in a very different legal system: China. In "'Internet Plus Health Care' as an Impetus for China's Health System Reform," the authors introduce non-Chinese readers to the regulatory category of "internet plus health care" (IPHC), the way that China regards "the use of digital technologies in support of the delivery of health care and health-related services, such as internet-based diagnosis, treatment, and medicine, and internet hospitals." While these technologies had some support in China even earlier, the 2009 round of health reform really brought them to the fore with increasing initiatives until 2019. The COVID-19 pandemic supercharged interests in these technologies in China, much as it did with telemedicine in the USA, leading the National Health Commission to publish its *Regulatory Rules on Internet-based Diagnosis and Treatment* in March 2022, among other forms of regulation. The authors then identify some of the remaining challenges – the way the regulations limit IPHC to "follow-up" diagnoses for "common diseases" and "chronic diseases," the affordability and insurance coverage of IPHC, and the difficulty of translating "physician multi-site practicing" to the online world in a way that is high-quality and accessible.

When read against the first three chapters in this part, the most striking takeaway from this fourth chapter is just how much China treats digital home diagnostics as the regulation of health care as opposed to the regulation of devices. The USA has centralized a lot of the ex ante and ex post regulation to the FDA and to the tort law around the products that is applicable to medical devices in general. In part because of the frequent shibboleth that the FDA does not regulate the practice of medicine, the agency does not directly regulate the integration of digital home diagnostics into health care let alone questions of affordability and insurance coverage. By contrast, it would seem that China views the devices as a means to health care delivery and, thus, leads with that. What would it mean if the US regulatory system started with health care system integration and incorporated that into its regulatory review?

8

Physician and Device Manufacturer Tort Liability for Remote Patient Monitoring Devices

David A. Simon[1] and Aaron S. Kesselheim[2]

I THE LANDSCAPE OF REMOTE AND DIAGNOSTIC DEVICES

New technologies allow patients to use, wear, or even have implanted remote patient monitoring (RPM) devices that collect data, which can be sent directly to physicians.[3] These data can be used to identify disease-related events that require medical intervention. RPM includes diagnostics performed by patients at home, without direct physician involvement, that had traditionally been performed in a clinical setting (such as a mobile sleep study), as well as services that combine routine monitoring and diagnosis (such as a heart rate monitor). For example, pacemakers that used to primarily support a patient's cardiac rhythm can now be used to transmit information to a cardiologist, potentially detecting arrhythmias that may lead to medical treatment at a presymptomatic stage.[4] Wearable glucose monitors, like Abbott's FreeStyle Libre 2, and seizure detection devices, like Empatica's Embrace2, can alert patients or caregivers to low glucose levels and seizure activity that require attention.[5]

With the increasing prevalence of RPM devices, questions remain about the liability protections for patients who use them. State laws, in particular tort law, provide some potential safeguards by enabling patients to sue device manufacturers and physicians for causing them harm. While a variety of state and federal laws impose

---

[1] Research Fellow, Petrie-Flom Center for Health Law Policy, Biotechnology, & Bioethics, Harvard Law School; Associate Professor of Law (July 2023), Northeastern University School of Law. This Author thanks the Gordon and Betty Moore Foundation for its support in writing this chapter (Grant #9977).
[2] Professor of Medicine at Harvard Medical School, Director, Program On Regulation, Therapeutics, and Law (PORTAL), Division of Pharmacoepidemiology and Pharmacoeconomics, Department of Medicine, Brigham and Women's Hospital. Dr. Kesselheim's research was supported by Arnold Ventures.
[3] For the purposes of this chapter, device means "intended for use in the diagnosis of disease or other conditions, or in the cure, mitigation, treatment, or prevention of disease, in man … or intended to affect the structure or any function of the body of man." 21 USC § 321(h)(1)(B).
[4] Stefan Simovic et al., The Use of Remote Monitoring of Cardiac Implantable Devices During the COVID-19 Pandemic: An EHRA Physician Survey, 24 EP Europace 473 (2022).
[5] *Freestyle Libre 2, Abbot*, www.freestyle.abbott/us-en/products/freestyle-libre-2; *Embrace2, Empatica*, www.empatica.com/embrace2/.

obligations on manufacturers,[6] tort law is a major tool to hold these actors accountable for injuries they cause to patients.[7]

The stakes are high. A cardiac monitor or a seizure detection device, like Embrace2, that malfunctions could result in brain damage or death, opening the manufacturer to large jury verdicts, particularly for widely used products. Physicians who improperly use or rely on RPM devices to notify them of such activity and fail to monitor patients could also face substantial damage claims.

Despite the significance of potential injury for patients and liability for manufacturers and physicians, it is not clear how these claims should be evaluated or resolved. To clarify when liability might arise, this chapter first explains how tort liability applies to manufacturers of RPM devices, physicians who prescribe them, and patients who use them (and their caregivers). It then proceeds to analyze how variation in device market entry, patient access, and use – through federal regulatory protections, physician prescriptions for devices, and patient and caregiver uses – can affect the viability of tort claims.

II LIABILITY FOR DEVICE MANUFACTURERS AND PHYSICIANS

Tort law contains two primary standards of liability typically applicable to devices like RPM devices (Table 8.1).[8] The first is negligence, which requires one to act with "reasonable care" when undertaking an activity. For a plaintiff to succeed in a lawsuit based on negligence, the plaintiff must prove that another failed to act with reasonable care, and that such failure caused harm to the plaintiff. The second is strict liability, which does not require such a showing; in theory, there is "no fault" because tort law imposes liability on the person who caused the injury regardless of whether that person acted with reasonable care. Both negligence and strict liability can apply to RPM manufacturers. Typically, only negligence applies to physicians.

A *Manufacturer Liability for Product Defects*

i Negligence

Manufacturers have a duty to use reasonable care in manufacturing, designing, and marketing a product.[9] They are, therefore, liable for injuries caused to users by

---

[6] For example, Iowa Code §155A.42 (2018).
[7] In the case of devices, contract law also plays a significant role in the liability analysis. Tort and contract law provide different legal tests, and some states allow contract but not tort claims. Nevertheless, the two are sufficiently similar that analyzing tort claims provides a reasonable overview of how courts are likely to respond to claims in contract, even if courts ultimately resolve claims differently. For this reason, and because of space limitations, we focus here only on tort claims. We also do not discuss various civil and criminal penalties for violations of federal and state statutes.
[8] Tort law also imposes liability on manufactures who make misrepresentations about their products, but we do not discuss such causes of action in this chapter.
[9] *Merrill v. Navegar, Inc.*, 28 P.3d 116, 124 (Cal. 2001).

TABLE 8.1 *Schematic of tort liability for manufacturers, physicians, and caregivers*

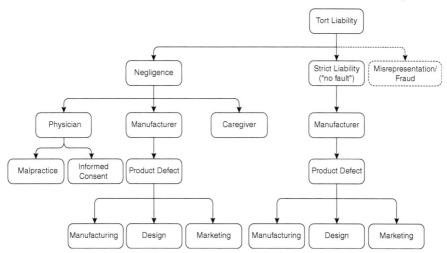

This table depicts the potential tort causes of actions against physicians, manufacturers, and caregivers arising from RPM devices. Misrepresentation/fraud claims are depicted in dotted lines to indicate potential causes of action that are not discussed in this chapter.

failing to reasonably warn of product risks or failing to use reasonable care in designing or manufacturing the product. The standard for negligence claims primarily focuses on the reasonableness of the manufacturer's behavior. Although evidence of industry custom is admissible in determining the relevant standard of care, industry custom does not determine the relevant standard of care.[10] That is a determination left to the fact-finder, and if it is a jury, with assistance from the judge.

ii Strict Liability

Manufacturers can also be liable under the theory of strict liability for the same three types of product defects (manufacturing, design, marketing) as they can be liable for in negligence. Unlike negligence, however, strict liability does not require the injured party to prove any negligent conduct by the manufacturer – only that the product defect existed when it left the manufacturer's hands.[11] Manufacturing defect claims allege that a defect arose in the production of the product that differed from the manufacturer's design, and that this defect caused harm to the plaintiff.[12] Design defect claims allege that, even if manufactured properly, the manufacturer's design was particularly unsafe and, therefore, defective, and that

[10] *Rossell v. Volkswagen of Am.*, 709 P.2d 517, 523 (Ariz. 1985).
[11] But see *Banks v. ICI Americas, Inc.*, 450 S.E.2d 671, 672 (Ga.1994) (applying reasonableness and negligence principles to evaluate design defect claims).
[12] *BIC Pen Corp. v. Carter*, 346 S.W.3d 533, 540 (Tex. 2011).

the defect caused injury to the plaintiff.[13] Finally, marketing defect claims – also called "failure to warn" or "inadequate warning" claims – allege that the manufacturer failed to provide to the patient with sufficient warnings about the risks of using the product.

iii Scope of Strict Liability Claims

Whether and how negligence or strict liability theories apply can depend on the type of defect alleged, the jurisdiction in which the lawsuit is filed, and the type of product at issue. The type of defect alleged can affect what the plaintiff must prove – with requirements occupying three places along a spectrum. At one end of the spectrum are manufacturing defect claims, for which the only questions are whether the product was manufactured according to the manufacturer's design and specifications and, if not, whether that defect caused the plaintiff's injury.[14] For example, liability under this theory would arise if a patient was injured by a pacemaker that malfunctioned because, during manufacturing, the manufacturer failed to install a computer chip required to process heart rhythms.

At the other end of the spectrum are failure to warn claims, for which the standards for strict liability and negligence are identical – the only question is whether the manufacturer reasonably warned the consumer of the product risks.[15] For example, a manufacturer of vaginal mesh may be liable on this theory for failing to warn that mesh removal may be required if the product fails.[16]

Somewhere in the middle are design defect claims. Here, the plaintiff must show either that "the product failed to perform as safely as an ordinary consumer would expect when used in an intended or reasonably foreseeable manner" or that "the product's design proximately caused his injury and the defendant fails to establish, in light of the relevant factors, that, on balance, the benefits of the challenged design outweigh the risk of danger inherent in such design."[17] In negligence, courts tend to ask how to balance the device's risk of harm against its utility, while in strict liability, they tend to emphasize the existence and monetary costs of using an alternative safer design.[18] For example, the manufacturer of an air conditioning compressor was found liable for injuries caused by an explosion it could have prevented by simply and costlessly relocating a safety groove from the inside to the outside of the

---

[13] In re Coordinated Latex Glove Litig., 121 Cal. Rptr. 2d 301 (Ct. App. 2002).
[14] Derienzo v. Trek Bicycle Corp., 376 F. Supp. 2d 537, 560 n. 28 (SDNY 2005).
[15] Nancy K. Plant, The Learned Intermediary Doctrine: Some New Medicine for an Old Ailment, 81 Iowa L. Rev 1007, 1012 (1995).
[16] Eghnayem v. Bos. Sci. Corp., 873 F.3d 1304, 1322 (11th Cir. 2017).
[17] Barker v. Lull Eng'g Co., 573 P.2d 443, 454–56 (Cal. 1978); Sparks v. Owens-Illinois, Inc., 38 Cal. Rptr. 2d 739 (Ct. App. 1995) (holding the tests were mutually exclusive); Dawson v. Chrysler Corp., 630 F.2d 950 (3d Cir. 1980) (outlining factors to consider).
[18] Toner v. Lederle Lab'ys, a Div. of Am. Cyanamid Co., 732 P.2d 297, 311 (Idaho 1987). But see Lance v. Wyeth, 85 A.3d 434, 459 (Pa. 2014) (refusing to apply this approach to prescription drugs).

compressor's insulating glass.[19] In some cases, medical devices like hip implants may be subject to a similar analysis when the device fails.[20]

Jurisdictions may differ, however, on whether strict liability applies. In some jurisdictions, a design defect claim for devices that are "incapable of being made safe for their intended and ordinary use"[21] will immunize a manufacturer from design defect claims if the manufacturer properly manufactures and warns consumers about the product's risks.[22] In such cases, adequate warnings immunize manufacturers from strict liability design defect claims.

All this suggests that the *type* of device – whether it is "incapable of being made safe" – can also influence whether strict liability applies. Some courts have found that prescription and implantable medical devices count.[23] Others disagree or think that the question must be resolved on a case-by-case basis by weighing the risk-utility tradeoff presented by the device,[24,25] sometimes casting the issue as one the defendant manufacturer must raise and prove as an affirmative defense.[26] Finally, there remains something of an open question about whether software itself can be a "product" subject to strict liability.[27]

Device type and jurisdictional issues can also interact to affect potential tort claims. So, even if immunity from strict liability applies, it may apply only to design defect claims (leaving strict liability claims for manufacturing and marketing defects),[28] or it may bar *all* strict liability claims.[29] In some jurisdictions, however, immunity from strict liability claims does not apply to negligence claims.[30]

---

[19] *Emerson Electric Co. v. Johnson*, 627 S.W.3d 197, 208 (Tex. 2021), reh'g denied (September 3, 2021); *Kaiser v. Johnson & Johnson*, 947 F.3d 996, 1002 (7th Cir. 2020).

[20] *Burningham v. Wright Med. Tech.*, Inc., 448 P.3d 1283, 1292 (Utah 2019).

[21] Restatement (Second) Torts § 402A cmt. k (Am. L. Inst. 1965). Most of the cases implicating comment k involve prescription drugs rather than devices.

[22] *Tansy v. Dacomed Corp.*, 890 P.2d 881, 885 (Okla. 1994); *Creazzo v. Medtronic, Inc.*, 903 A.2d 24, 31 (Pa. Super. Ct. 2006).

[23] Plant, supra note 13, at 1040; *Hufft v. Horowitz*, 5 Cal. Rptr. 2d 377 (Ct. App. 1992).

[24] *Burningham*, 448 P.3d at 1290 (holding that comment k does not apply to implantable devices cleared through the 510(k) process).

[25] *Johansen v. Makita USA, Inc.*, 128 N.J. 86, 96 (1992).

[26] For example, *Burningham*, 448 P.3d at 1290; *Tansy*, 890 P.2d at 886; *Mele v. Howmedica, Inc.*, 808 N.E.2d 1026, 1041 (Ill. 2004) (using risk-benefit analysis to determine if immunity applies).

[27] Bexis, New Decision Directly Addresses the "Is Software a Product" Question, *Drug & Device L. Blog* (May 2, 2022), www.druganddevicelawblog.com/2022/05/new-decision-directly-addresses-the-is-software-a-product-question.html. We assume, for the purposes of this chapter, that RPMs will include a physical device that incorporates software but not a standalone software that might fall outside the definition of "product" or "good" for the purposes of product liability law under either tort or contract.

[28] *Toner v. Lederle Lab'ys, a Div. of Am. Cyanamid Co.*, 732 P.2d 297, 308 (Idaho 1987); *Transue v. Aesthetech Corp.*, 341 F.3d 911, 917–19 (9th Cir. 2003); *Grundberg v. Upjohn Co.*, 813 P.2d 89, 92 (Utah 1991).

[29] *McPhee v. DePuy Orthopedics, Inc.*, 989 F. Supp. 2d 451, 461 (W.D. Pa. 2012).

[30] *Slisze v. Stanley-Bostitch*, 979 P.2d 317, 319 (Utah 1999) (product's liability statute did not preclude simultaneous strict liability and negligence claim); *Scott v. C.R. Bard, Inc.*, 180 Cal. Rptr. 3d 479, 489 (Ct. App. 2014); *Rogers v. Miles Lab'ys, Inc.*, 802 P.2d 1346, 1353 (Wash. 1991); *Toner v. Lederle Lab'ys, a Div. of Am. Cyanamid Co.*, 732 P.2d 297, 309–10 (Idaho 1987).

iv The Learned Intermediary Doctrine

Claim type and use, including the process by which a consumer use occurs, can also affect liability by shifting obligations from one party to another. Marketing defect claims, for instance, require the plaintiff to prove that a product was unreasonably dangerous because it lacked adequate warnings or instructions.[31] This duty ordinarily requires manufacturers to warn consumers directly. But when a physician prescribes the product, the "learned intermediary doctrine" requires a manufacturer to adequately warn only the prescribing physician subject to three limited exceptions.[32,33]

Because warning the physician may require different disclosures than warning a consumer, the learned intermediary doctrine can alter the manufacturer's explanation of device risks. This can also affect other claims. For example, a manufacturer that successfully defends a failure to warn claim may also be able to defeat liability for a design defect claim, since immunity from some design defect claims requires adequate warnings. At the same time, however, the learned intermediary doctrine will not affect manufacturing defect claims because they do not turn on whether the manufacturer gave proper warnings.

B Physician Liability for Lack of Informed Consent and Negligence

The learned intermediary doctrine is also related to the doctrine of "informed consent," which imposes on physicians a duty to obtain, prior to treatment, patient consent by informing them of the material risks associated with the treatment. In some jurisdictions, the sufficiency of informed consent is based on whether "the physician's failure to inform fell below the medical community's standard of care."[34] In others, the question of sufficiency is based on a record of the disclosure of facts that would influence the patient to consent to a particular procedure or treatment.[35]

Informed consent is often considered part of tort law's general requirement to act reasonably under the circumstances – a requirement that applies to physicians as

---

[31] *Lawson v. G. D. Searle & Co.*, 356 N.E.2d 779, 783 (Ill. 1976); *Ortho Pharm. Corp. v. Chapman*, 388 N.E.2d 541, 545 (Ind. Ct. App. 1979); *Hamilton v. Hardy*, 549 P.2d 1099, 1108 (Colo. App. 1976), overruled by *State Bd. of Med. Examiners v. McCroskey*, 880 P.2d 1188 (Colo. 1994).

[32] *O'Connell v. Biomet, Inc.*, 250 P.3d 1278, 1281–82 (Colo. App. 2010); *Ellis v. C.R. Bard, Inc.*, 311 F.3d 1272, 1280 (11th Cir. 2002) (applying Georgia law); *Beale v. Biomet, Inc.*, 492 F. Supp. 2d 1360, 1367–68 (S.D. Fla.2007) (collecting cases and applying Florida law); *Pumphrey v. C.R. Bard, Inc.*, 906 F. Supp. 334, 337 (NDW Va.1995) (applying West Virginia law).

[33] *Edwards v. Basel Pharms.*, 116 F.3d 1341 (10th Cir. 1997). New Jersey has created an exception for contraceptives marketed directly to consumers. *Perez v. Wyeth Lab'ys Inc.*, 734 A.2d 1245, 1259–60 (N.J. 1999).

[34] *Gorab v. Zook*, 943 P.2d 423, 427 (Colo. 1997).

[35] *Scott v. Bradford*, 606 P.2d 554 (Okla. 1979); *Hurley v. Kirk*, 398 P.3d 7, 9 (Okla. 2017).

well as manufacturers. Like the standard for manufacturers in negligence actions, the standard for physicians in negligence actions focuses on the reasonableness of the physician's behavior. Unlike the standard of negligence for manufacturers, however, the standard of negligence for physicians is often determined by custom. What is reasonable, in other words, is determined by the jury based on what an actual doctor in that field of expertise would actually have done in the situation, rather than on what a reasonable doctor under the circumstances would have done.[36] This standard of care, however it is determined, applies to physicians who prescribe and use RPM devices. Thus, tort law will hold physicians liable if their failure to warn of device risks (if the learned intermediary doctrine applies) or to take reasonable care in monitoring or treating a patient, which can include inadequate training on how to use a device, causes harm to the patient.[37]

C Defenses

Both physicians and manufacturers may have various defenses to claims involving defective products or negligent care. One is that the patient was negligent in using the device, and that negligence caused some or all of the harm suffered. In tort, a plaintiff's negligence can affect his or her claims by (1) barring recovery entirely (contributory negligence), (2) reducing recovery by the percentage the plaintiff is at fault (pure comparative negligence), or (3) reducing recovery if the plaintiff's fault is as great as or not greater than the defendant, otherwise barring recovery (modified comparative negligence). Most jurisdictions apply some version of modified comparative negligence when the plaintiff asserts a negligence claim. When the plaintiff asserts a claim in strict liability, contributory and comparative negligence defenses may still be available,[38] though they may be limited to certain evidentiary issues, such as risk-utility balancing or causation,[39] and circumscribed by statute.[40] Of course, even when comparative negligence applies, parceling liability may be challenging.

III FACTORS AFFECTING LIABILITY DETERMINATIONS

Building on the previous discussion, this part shows that how a device reaches the market and is used – through federal regulation, physician prescription, and patient and caregiver use – can also influence liability determinations.

---

[36] *Braswell v. Stinnett*, 99 So. 3d 175, 178 (Miss. 2012).
[37] *Manzi v Zuckerman*, 384 A.2d 541 (NJ Super. Ct. App. Div. 1978) (duty to monitor for conditions during pregnancy); *Marcano Rivera v. Turabo Med. Ctr. P'ship*, 415 F.3d 162 (1st Cir. 2005) (duty to monitor fetal heart signs using monitors, which includes proper training).
[38] *West v. Caterpillar Tractor Co.*, 336 So. 2d 80, 92 (Fla. 1976); *Gen. Motors Corp. v. Sanchez*, 997 S.W.2d 584, 587 (Tex. 1999); *Austin v. Raybestos-Manhattan, Inc.*, 471 A.2d 280, 288 (Me. 1984).
[39] *Johansen v. Makita USA, Inc.*, 607 A.2d 637, 645–46 (NJ 1992).
[40] *Emps. Mut. Ins. Co. v. Oakes Mfg. Co.*, 356 N.W.2d 719, 723 (Minn. Ct. App. 1984).

A Regulation

How a device reaches the market can influence manufacturer liability for injuries caused by the device. RPM devices reach the market in two principal ways. New, high-risk devices (class III) must file a premarket notification approval (PMA) application that requires the manufacturer to demonstrate "reasonable assurance of the safety and effectiveness" of the device.[41] By contrast, if a manufacturer can justify that its device is "substantially equivalent" to a device already legally on the market, the device qualifies for clearance under section 510(k) of the Food, Drug, and Cosmetic Act (FDCA), an exception to the PMA process (class II).[42] Almost all devices that require premarket review enter the market through the 510(k) pathway, though the FDA does have the power to reclassify devices based on data showing novel risks.[43]

Which of these two pathways applies to an RPM device can have important liability implications for the manufacturer and injured patient because the Supreme Court ruled that the Medical Device Amendments of 1976 (MDA) expressly or impliedly preempted state tort claims for high-risk devices that meet the "federal requirements" necessary for the approval of a PMA application.[44] Express preemption does not apply to devices cleared through the 510(k) pathway, which lacks the close regulatory review for safety and effectiveness present in a PMA review (Table 8.2).[45]

Implied preemption defeats only those parallel claims that would not exist but for the FDCA.[46] For 510(k)-devices, for example, implied preemption bars claims only when the manufacturer's fraudulent representations caused the FDA to allow the marketing of a device it otherwise would not have (so-called state-law "fraud-on-the-FDA claims") (Table 8.3).[47]

As a result, a manufacturer's liability exposure may turn on the type of product it manufactures and whether any similar product currently exists on the market. For example, if the heart rate monitoring feature of an implantable pacemaker is cleared through a 510(k) pathway, then the manufacturer would be liable for most harm that occurs as a result of a product defect.[48] If, by contrast, the feature required a PMA, then the manufacturer for which the PMA is granted would be immune from most lawsuits alleging injuries caused by the monitoring features of the device. Generally

---

[41] 21 USC § 351(f); 21 USC §§ 360e, (d)(1)(A)(ii), (d)(1)(B)(iii).
[42] 21 USC §§ 360c(a)(1)(B), (i), (f), 360(k), 360j.
[43] Inst. Med. Nat'l Acads., *Medical Devices and the Public's Health: The FDA 510(k) Clearance Process at 35 Years* (2011). Of all devices subject to FDA premarket review, 90 percent pass through the 510(k) pathway, but only about one-third of all devices entering the market pass through the 510(k) pathway. Id. at 4, 170. Most devices, however, require no review because they are low risk, class I devices.
[44] *Riegel v. Medtronic, Inc.*, 552 US 312 (2008); 21 USC § 360k(a).
[45] *Medtronic, Inc. v. Lohr*, 518 US 470, 471 (1996).
[46] For example, *Glover v. Bausch & Lomb, Inc.*, 275 A.3d 168, 175 (Conn. 2022).
[47] *Buckman Co. v. Plaintiffs' Legal Comm.*, 531 US 341, 352 (2001).
[48] We assume that preemption would not apply but recognize that this conclusion is complicated by devices with some components that are cleared and others that are approved. For example, *Shuker v. Smith & Nephew, PLC*, 885 F.3d 760, 773–76 n.14–15 (3d Cir. 2018).

TABLE 8.2 *Express preemptive effect of MDA on tort claims, by defect alleged*

	Type of claim expressly preempted		
FDA review	*Manufacture*	*Design*	*Marketing*
PMA	Yes*	Yes*	Yes*
510(k)	No	No	No
De Novo†	No (presumably)	No (presumably)	No (presumably)
None	No	No	No

"Yes" means the claim is expressly preempted; "No" means the claim is not expressly preempted.
* Preemption does not bar parallel state claims.
† The de novo process has not yet been the subject of a preemption analysis. Given that it is designed to provide a 510(k)-like process for new devices, however, it is reasonable to assume that preemption analysis for devices authorized under the de novo review would be the same (or substantially the same) as those cleared through the 510(k) process. Courts analyzing the issue, however, may disagree with this assumption and make a contrary holding.

TABLE 8.3 *Express and implied preemptive effect of MDA on tort claims, by claim type*

FDA review	Preemption type	Type of claim preempted		
Pathway	*Express or Implied*	*Fraud-on-FDA*	*Parallel*	*Other State Law*
PMA	Express and Implied	Yes	Some	Yes
510(k)	Implied	Yes	No	No
De Novo†	Implied	Yes (presumably)	No (presumably)	No (presumably)
None	Implied	Yes	No	No

"Yes" means the claim is expressly preempted; "No" means the claim is not expressly preempted. "(presumably)" means that courts would presumably find federal law impliedly preempted (or not) claims against manufacturers of devices authorized through the de novo pathway.
† The de novo process has not yet been the subject of a preemption analysis. Given that it is designed to provide a 510(k)-like process for new devices, however, it is reasonable to assume that preemption analysis for devices authorized under the de novo review would be the same (or substantially the same) as those cleared through the 510(k) process. Courts analyzing the issue, however, may disagree with this assumption and make a contrary holding.

speaking, then, devices that undergo a more complete FDA review before market entry are subject to less tort liability than devices that undergo a less complete or no FDA review before market entry.

Consider the Sunrise Sleep Disorder Diagnostic Aid, which uses jaw movements to detect sleep apnea.[49] The device had no analogue on the market, but Sunrise filed to

---

[49] FDA Device Classification Under Section 513(f)(2)(De Novo), Sunrise Sleep Disorder Diagnostic Aid, De Novo Number DEN210015 (January 7, 2022).

have its product cleared for the market without a PMA through an alternative mechanism, which may be treated similarly to the 510(k) process for preemption purposes.[50] While this choice likely saved Sunrise substantial capital, it could also increase its potential liability exposure. When deciding between a less stringent review and a PMA, Sunrise may have determined that the lower costs associated with less stringent review outweighed the benefits of liability protection afforded by a PMA.

Complicating things further, devices with a PMA are not immune from all lawsuits in all jurisdictions; such devices can be the subject of so-called "parallel claims" – state law causes of action that mirror FDA requirements but are not based solely upon them. For example, a state law manufacturing defect claim premised on, but not dependent on, a violation of federal manufacturing regulations could be a parallel claim provided that state law did not impose additional requirements on the manufacturer.[51] Here, jurisdictional issues can reappear because federal courts differ on what counts as a "parallel" claim that evades preemption.[52]

B *Path to Market and Patient*

How an RPM device reaches the consumer can also influence physician and manufacturer liability. For example, Phillips manufactures the BioSticker System, which is an RPM device that attaches to the skin and measures physiological data, such as heart rate, respiratory rate, skin temperature, and other symptomatic or biometric data. This information is displayed on a dashboard that physicians can access and monitor.

The device, which was cleared under the 510(k) process,[53] originally required a physician's prescription but, under a COVID-19 Emergency Use Authorization (EUA), is now available over the counter.[54] Before the EUA, this meant that the manufacturer could discharge its duty to warn by providing adequate instructions and warnings to the physician prescribing the device. The physician would then have an independent duty to obtain informed consent from the patient. After the EUA, however, consumers could access the device without a physician's prescription, requiring that the warnings be made to the patient directly.

Because the learned intermediary doctrine affects manufacturer liability only for failure-to-warn claims, Phillips could still be liable for harm caused by manufacturing defects in the BioSticker System even prior to the EUA. Consider a situation in

---

[50] 21 USC § 360c(f)(2); 21 CFR §§ 860.3, 860.200–860.260 (de novo classification request procedures).
[51] Some parallel claims may also be impliedly preempted. For example, Buckman, 531 US at 352.
[52] For example, Compare *Weber* v. *Allergan, Inc.*, 940 F.3d 1106, 1112 (9th Cir. 2019), cert. denied, 140 S. Ct. 2555 (2020) with *Bass* v. *Stryker Corp.*, 669 F.3d 501, 510 (5th Cir. 2012); compare *Mink* v. *Smith & Nephew, Inc.*, 860 F.3d 1319, 1330 (11th Cir. 2017) with *Bayer Corp.* v. *Leach*, 153 N.E.3d 1168, 1185 (Ind. Ct. App. 2020).
[53] FDA 10(k) Premarket Notification, BioSticker System, 510(K) Number K191614 (December 18, 2019).
[54] BioIntelliSense, *BioStickerTM Instructions for Use* (2022), https://biointellisense.com/assets/biosticker-supplemental-instructions-for-use.pdf?v=2.

which, because of a manufacturing defect, the Biosticker device failed to transmit information to a physician showing an irregular heart rate and respiratory function. If the patient died as a result of the physician's failure to intervene, and if the failure to intervene was caused by the device not having been manufactured according to specifications, then Phillips could be liable for the patient's death.

Manufacturers may also be liable for some design defect claims even when the learned intermediary doctrine applies. The scope of this liability may depend on whether the device is prescribed by a physician and the type of device at issue. Phillip's Biosticker was previously used by prescription, making it likely that Phillips could obtain immunity from strict liability design defect claims by adequately warning the physician of the risks posed by the device – for example, its inability to be used for more than a certain period of time or in water.[55]

Once the FDA issued the EUA authorizing the device to be sold directly to consumers without a prescription, no amount of warning to physicians would likely insulate Phillips from strict liability design defect claims; however, in some, but by no means all, jurisdictions, adequately warning consumers may immunize manufacturers from design defect claims. A company like Empatica, for example, may try to immunize itself by warning physicians and consumers about the Embrace2's ability to notify only emergency contacts, potentially foreclosing claims that Empatica defectively designed the Embrace2 since it lacked the capability to notify physicians or emergency responders. Regardless of whether strict liability immunity applies, a showing of adequate warning would not necessarily make Phillips immune from negligent design defect claims because of jurisdictional differences.

Besides the jurisdictional variations, it is unclear how courts would resolve such claims. While design defect claims often turn on the existence of available safer designs, along with the costs of developing and implementing them, some courts have been reluctant to apply this reasoning to prescription drugs.[56] Prescription RPM devices may be treated similarly. If they are not, however, such claims will turn on a fact-intensive analysis of the costs associated with changing the device to make it safer – rarely a question that can be resolved definitively and early in litigation.

In addition to its effect on manufacturer liability for information-based claims like failure to warn, the learned intermediary doctrine also opens physicians to more claims from patients injured by RPM devices. For example, suppose a physician prescribes to a patient, and the patient uses, a bracelet like the Embrace2 to detect seizure activity that automatically notifies designated caregivers.[57] If a seizure occurs and the device contacts a caregiver who cannot respond in time, the injured patient

---

[55] Id.
[56] Brown v. Super. Ct., 751 P.2d 470, 479 (Cal. 1988); Restatement (Third) of Torts: Prods. Liab. § 6(c) (Am. L. Inst. 1998). But see Freeman v. Hoffman-La Roche, Inc., 618 N.W.2d 827, 837 (Neb. 2000).
[57] See Embrace, supra note 388.

may attempt to sue the physician based on the theory that he or she would not have used the device if it was impossible for the device to alert someone who could more immediately help.[58]

To avoid liability, physicians will need to properly inform and educate patients and caregivers about the devices' risks and limitations. For devices like the Embrace2, part of this risk may be avoided by working with device manufacturers to notify parties who can respond in case of emergency and obtaining written and verbal consent, after explanation, for patient responsibilities in using the device and how the physicians can and will monitor the device data.

For example, physicians who recommend or prescribe a device like the Biosticker have a duty to understand how to use the product, including its limitations, as well as how and when they will be monitoring the data from the device. These physicians also have a duty to explain this clearly to the patient. If a physician will not be monitoring the device for real-time alerts, but instead using it as a data-gathering tool to obtain a more complete picture of the patient, they would do well to say so (and to document that conversation with the patient). The duty might include explaining to patients what to do if the device detects unusual behavior, including who they should contact and how they should interpret the data. Simply advising patients to "call 911" if there is an emergency may seem like a failsafe, but it also may create undue stress on the health care system if a device provides a variety of alerts. This may require new office procedures, points of contact, and protocols for reassessments of patients whose devices create particular kinds of alerts.

C Patient and Caregiver Use

Physicians are not the only individuals who can affect the liability of RPM device manufacturers. When patients use RPMs, they may be responsible for some or all of the harm the device causes, and their damages could be reduced or eliminated under the doctrine of comparative negligence. Similar to device manufacturers, how responsible patients are may turn on the type and nature of the device at issue.

Some RPM devices operate automatically and without any patient initiation, reducing the probability that a patient is responsible for harm suffered when using the device. RPM devices like the BioSticker or a pacemaker that monitors cardiovascular status, for example, collect information with minimal patient engagement. Without any patient action, it may be harder to show that the patient's negligence, rather than the device, is the cause of any harm that occurred while the patient used the device.

However, other devices may require the patient to initiate, operate, or respond to them, and to do so under particular conditions or in a particular manner. For example, Google announced that it was developing a dermatology app that deploys

---

[58] David A. Simon, et al., The Hospital-At-Home Presents Novel Liabilities for Physicians, Hospitals, Caregivers, and Patients, 28 Nat. Med. 438 (2022).

artificial intelligence and machine learning to analyze user-uploaded photographs to track skin lesions over time and provide diagnostic information.[59] Hyfe, a smartphone app that likely will apply for 510(k) clearance,[60] uses similar technology to monitor cough data that the patient captures by affirmatively initiating the application. Patients who fail to track skin lesions at certain intervals using Google's dermatology app or fail to initiate Hyfe may find that false negatives are their own fault, rather than the device's. Moreover, patients who do not reasonably act on alerts from devices like RPMs may reduce or eliminate their ability to recover if they are injured as a result.

Patients could also see damages reduced or claims eliminated entirely when they use and rely on these devices in environments where manufacturers specifically state that they will not operate accurately. Thus, a patient who does not operate Hyfe or Google's app in the recommended sound or lighting conditions, does not track coughs or skin lesions at the intervals required for the app to function optimally, or uses the device to predict asthma attacks or detect skin cancer (purposes for which they are not designed) may eliminate or reduce the probability of liability for manufacturers or physicians.

Similar issues apply to devices – like ResMed's AirSense Elite 10 continuous positive airway pressure (CPAP) machine with built-in RPM – which not only treats sleep apnea, but also collects information about the person wearing it, that could be used to detect important health events, including a lack of oxygen being delivered to the user.[61] Patients who improperly place the mask on their face or use the device only sporadically will encounter challenges when suing manufacturers because a device did not detect a respiratory event. This may be true even if the device itself did not function properly.

Additionally, RPM devices may require manual patient data input to function properly. Medtronic offers a patient management system that uses both sensor-based RPM and self-reporting by patients to monitor and evaluate respiratory health, in particular patients with COVID-19.[62] Patients who enter information incorrectly may cause the system to incorrectly not recommend further care or alert the appropriate parties. If that happens and the patient is injured or dies as a result of the delay or absence of care, the patient may bear some or all of the responsibility for the harm, reducing or eliminating their recovery under the doctrine of comparative negligence.

---

[59] Peggy Bui & Yuan Liu, Using AI to Help Find Answers to Common Skin Conditions, *Google, The Keyword* (2021), https://blog.google/technology/health/ai-dermatology-preview-io-2021/.
[60] Oral communication between David A. Simon and Peter Small (January 20, 2022).
[61] Resmed, *Devices* (May 19, 2022), www.resmed.com/en-us/healthcare-professional/products-and-support/devices/.
[62] Medtronic, *Virtual Care Solutions: Care Management Services* (May 10, 2022), www.medtronic.com/us-en/healthcare-professionals/services/medtronic-care-management-services/our-solutions/care-management-services.html.

Finally, third parties, like those who are "emergency contacts" alerted by a seizure detection device like the Embrace2, may have their phones turned off or may not respond to the patient in time to treat them. If their failure to respond causes harm to the patient, they could face liability, potentially reducing the liability of other actors. But if the third party's inaction is caused by the patient's failure to inform the third party that they would be notified, how they would be notified, or what they were expected to do when notified, then the patient may be responsible for the harm.

In short, the more patients can control what goes into the RPM, the more likely both the manufacturer and prescribing physician are to argue that any injury was caused not by them, but by the patient. To reduce the probability of patient-caused injury, manufacturers and physicians should carefully instruct patients on how, when, and for what purposes they should use RPM devices, and they should emphasize the limitations of the devices.

IV CONCLUSION

RPM devices may help patients self-manage conditions with fewer complications and at lower cost than traditional clinical care. But they also raise liability issues in tort law. While the doctrines used to assess these claims are quite old, their application to this new and changing area of medicine is unsettled. In this chapter, we have provided a framework for understanding these tort claims and how courts are likely to assess them based on a series of factors, including how the device reaches the market, the type of device, the type of claim, where it is brought, how it reaches the market and consumer, who uses it, and how they do so.

9

Post-Market Surveillance of Software Medical Devices

Evidence from Regulatory Data

Alexander O. Everhart and Ariel D. Stern[*]

I INTRODUCTION

Health care's digital transformation – accelerated, but by no means initiated, by the COVID-19 pandemic – has garnered attention as patients increasingly expect remote care options. A preponderance of digital health applications and connected sensors are poised to transform how health care is delivered in contexts outside of the hospital or clinic.[1]

The digitization of health care delivery and medical technology raises questions about the safety of digital medical devices and how regulators monitor and respond to safety questions. One concern is that introducing software components to previously analog medical devices may create unexpected complexity or harm. For example, patients have died due to drug overdoses caused by "key bounce" in infusion pump software, whereby software incorrectly interprets a single keystroke as multiple keystrokes, resulting in patients receiving far more medicine than intended.[2]

Even given the known safety concerns associated with digital products, the existing infrastructure for tracking medical device safety may not be well equipped to monitor the safety of products that are (increasingly) used outside of traditional health care facilities. Most post-market surveillance – that is, ongoing regulatory oversight beyond initial regulatory approval/clearance – in the United States takes the form of adverse event reporting by device manufacturers and (health care) user facilities or post-approval trials conducted by manufacturers.[3] Given that

---

[*] The authors are grateful to Melissa Ouellet for research assistance and to Jaye Glenn, Rebecca Kunau, and Olivia Staff for copyediting.
[1] Anna Essén et al., Health App Policy: International Comparison of Nine Countries' Approaches, 5 npj Digit. Med. 1 (2022); Jan Benedikt Brönneke et al., Regulatory, Legal, and Market Aspects of Smart Wearables for Cardiac Monitoring, 21 Sensors 4937 (2021).
[2] Institute of Medicine, *Public Health Effectiveness of the FDA 510(k) Clearance Process: Measuring Postmarket Performance and Other Select Topics* (2011), https://nap.nationalacademies.org/catalog/13020/public-health-effectiveness-of-the-fda-510k-clearance-process-measuring.
[3] Noam Tau & Daniel Shepshelovich, Assessment of Data Sources that Support US Food and Drug Administration Medical Devices Safety Communications, 180 JAMA Internal Med. 1420 (2020).

post-market surveillance primarily relies on the vigilance of manufacturers and health care providers, regulators may miss important safety signals as medical technologies are moved from health care facilities to patients' homes.

These safety challenges have important implications for remote patient monitoring (RPM) tools. RPM is the collection of physiological measures that can be shared with health care providers – both actively by patients (e.g., by taking measurements and entering data at home) or passively with connected devices (which may automatically enter such data into a relevant database).[4] RPM encompasses the use of both combined hardware–software products, such as connected sensors, as well as standalone software tools.

Here, we focus specifically on the subset of RPM and other software-driven products that meet the definition of a medical device in the United States and, therefore, are subject to regulation by the US Food and Drug Administration (FDA). By focusing on regulated diagnostic and therapeutic devices, we specifically focus on products used in patients' formal health care delivery instead of more consumer-health/wellness-oriented digital products. In other words, this chapter does not consider the overwhelmingly large set of consumer health apps that may or may not be verified or validated.[5] Importantly, we consider *all* medical devices containing software – both standalone software tools (often called "software as medical devices," or SaMDs) as well as combination hardware–software products ("software in medical devices," or SiMDs). In doing so, we follow the definition of "software-driven medical devices" (SdMDs) introduced by Gordon and Stern (2019) (which includes both SaMDs and SiMDs) and consider all SdMDs subject to FDA oversight.[6] Relative to digital diagnostics and therapeutics used outside of traditional clinical settings, our sample represents a highly relevant set of products, but is almost certainly a "super-set" of those regulated devices used in remote diagnosis and care.

The chapter proceeds as follows. First, we provide a brief overview of post-market surveillance of regulated medical devices in the United States and present data on post-market outcomes from recent years. Next, in detailed regulatory data, we identify SdMDs among regulated devices and document trends in their approvals, as well as the associated post-market safety issues. Finally, we conclude with a discussion of the implications of our findings for regulatory policy and the future of post-market surveillance for SdMDs.

---

[4] Mitchell Tang et al., Trends in Remote Patient Monitoring Use in Traditional, 182 JAMA Internal Med. 1005 (2022).
[5] Jennifer C. Goldsack et al., Verification, Analytical Validation, and Clinical Validation (V3): The Foundation of Determining Fit-for-Purpose for Biometric Monitoring Technologies (BioMeTs), 3 npj Digit. Med. 1 (2020).
[6] William J. Gordon & Ariel D. Stern, Challenges and Opportunities in Software-driven Medical Devices, 3 Nature Biomedical Eng'g 493 (2019).

II POST-MARKET SURVEILLANCE ACTIVITIES AND REGULATORY DATA

For regulated medical technologies, post-market surveillance plays an important role in ensuring that products continue to be safe and effective. The FDA's Center for Devices and Radiological Health (CDRH) notes that post-market surveillance activities may include "tracking systems, reporting of device malfunctions, serious injuries or deaths, and registering the establishments where devices are produced or distributed." Further, post-market requirements may also include surveillance studies and additional post-approval studies that were deemed to be required at the time of device approval.[7] We briefly summarize these activities and the types of publicly available data that they generate before turning to an empirical analysis.

Under 21 USC § 360I, the FDA has the authority to require manufacturers to engage in various post-market activities. These may be required at either the time of approval/clearance of a new device or sometime thereafter. An FDA Guidance Document further outlines best practices for the medical device industry with respect to several aspects of post-market surveillance,[8] including surveillance planning, interim reporting, and the implications of failing to comply with post-market reporting requirements. The following sections provide an overview of the various post-market activities that the FDA may require.

A Post-Market Trials and Registries

Two common ways in which manufacturers and regulators continue to monitor the ongoing safety and effectiveness of medical devices are via post-market clinical trials and patient registries.

One or more post-approval studies may be required by regulators at the time of a Pre-Market Approval (PMA), Humanitarian Device Exemption (HDE), or Product Development Protocol (PDP) application. The FDA may require that manufacturers commit to conducting such studies before it grants regulatory approval, and failure to complete studies may be grounds for the FDA to withdraw a device's approval.[9] For example, the *Post-Approval Study on Patients Who Received a HeartWare HVAD® During IDE Trials (HW-PAS-03)*, a multi-center study sponsored by the device's manufacturer, provided continued evaluation and follow-up

---

[7] US Food and Drug Admin., *Postmarket Requirements (Devices)* (updated September 27, 2018), www.fda.gov/medical-devices/device-advice-comprehensive-regulatory-assistance/postmarket-requirements-devices.

[8] US Food and Drug Admin., *Postmarket Surveillance Under Section 522 of the Federal Food, Drug, and Cosmetic Act: Guidance for Industry and Food and Drug Administration Staff* (October 7, 2022), www.fda.gov/media/81015/download.

[9] US Food and Drug Admin., *Post-Approval Studies Program* (updated October 6, 2022), www.fda.gov/medical-devices/postmarket-requirements-devices/post-approval-studies-program.

on patients who had received the HeartWare® Ventricular Assist System during earlier clinical trials.[10] The FDA may request that post-approval studies be conducted for both moderate- and high-risk devices. In practice, post-market studies are often delayed or terminated after the manufacturer changes the indication for use of the studied medical device.[11]

Patient registries may be device-specific or embedded in larger surveillance initiatives. For example, as a condition for the approval of transcatheter heart valves, the FDA required all manufacturers to "continue to follow patients enrolled in their randomized studies for 10 years to further monitor transcatheter aortic valve safety and effectiveness...." As part of this initiative, the manufacturers agreed to participate in the Society of Thoracic Surgeons/American College of Cardiology Transcatheter Valve Therapy (TVT) Registry.[12]

B Plant Inspections

Another important component of post-market medical device regulation includes the inspection of plants where devices with hardware components are manufactured. Ball et al. (2017) summarized the rationale for manufacturing plant inspections by noting that "governments cannot feasibly sample every manufactured product before its release to customers; therefore, they frequently depend on plant inspections to appraise a plant's quality systems."[13]

Generally speaking, device-manufacturing plant inspections are conducted according to the process described in the *Quality System Inspection Technique Guide*, which, in turn, follows the requirements contained within 21 CFR § 820.[14] Such plant inspections involve the detailed documentation of various processes – including those associated with quality system requirements, various forms of controls (e.g., design, production, and process), corrective and preventative actions, and so on. Notably, investigators do not inspect actual products, but, instead, examine the systems that guide the device manufacturing process.

---

[10] US National Library of Medicine, *Post- Approval Study on Patients Who Received a HeartWare HVAD® During IDE Trials (HW-PAS-03)* (updated July 11, 2019), www.clinicaltrials.gov/ct2/show/NCT01832610.

[11] Vinay K. Rathi et al., Postmarket Clinical Evidence for High-Risk Therapeutic Medical Devices Receiving Food and Drug Administration Premarket Approval in 2010 and 2011, 3 JAMA Network Open e2014496 (2020); US Government Accountability Office, *FDA Ordered Postmarket Studies to Better Understand Safety Issues, and Many Studies Are Ongoing* (October 29, 2015), www.gao.gov/assets/gao-15-815.pdf.

[12] US Food and Drug Admin., *FDA Expands Indication for Several Transcatheter Heart Valves to Patients at Low Risk for Death or Major Complications Associated with Open-heart Surgery* (August 16, 2019), www.fda.gov/news-events/press-announcements/fda-expands-indication-several-transcatheter-heart-valves-patients-low-risk-death-or-major.

[13] George Ball et al., Do Plant Inspections Predict Future Quality? The Role of Investigator Experience, 19 Mfg. & Serv. Operations Mgmt. 534 (2017).

[14] US Food and Drug Admin., *Guide to Inspections of Quality Systems* (1999).

Inspectors typically arrive at a plant unannounced, tour the facility, interview managers, and perform a process documentation review. There are three different types of such inspections: (1) Surveillance inspections – those that occur regularly and routinely to assess plant quality; (2) compliance inspections – those that are part of the establishment of new or modified manufacturing processes or new product launches; and (3) complaint inspections – those that occur in response to serious complaints by customers/device users.[15] In response to inspections, remedial actions may or may not be indicated; remedial actions may be "voluntary" or "official," depending on the severity of issues identified.[16]

C Medical Device Reporting

Once devices are legally marketed, a system of voluntary and mandatory medical device reporting serves to track adverse events and identify emergent safety issues. The FDA receives several hundred thousand medical device reports (MDRs) related to suspected device-associated malfunctions, injuries, and deaths annually.[17] These reports are collected in the Manufacturer and User Facility Device Experience (MAUDE) database, which is maintained by the FDA. Reports are mandatory for certain users – namely device manufacturers, importers, and health care facilities – and voluntary for others, including patients, consumers, and clinicians.

MDRs are input into the MAUDE database along with detailed product information, which includes a device's manufacturer, product code, and FDA clearance/approval identifiers. This information allows individual MDRs to be linked to specific products. Although MDRs and the accompanying MAUDE database represent rich and well-organized sources of information, the FDA warns that the surveillance system may be incomplete, unverified, or inaccurate because of biased reporting, reporting lags, and other factors, and therefore cautions against using MAUDE data to understand the frequency or causality of adverse events. Nevertheless, MAUDE remains an important source of information about product quality issues, and its open-source format lends itself to empirical research in medicine and health policy.[18]

---

[15] Ball et al., supra note 15.
[16] Id.
[17] US Food and Drug Admin., *MAUDE – Manufacturer and User Facility Device Experience* (updated September 30, 2023), www.accessdata.fda.gov/scripts/cdrh/cfdocs/cfmaude/search.cfm.
[18] Jessica M. Andreoli et al., Comparison of Complication Rates Associated with Permanent and Retrievable Inferior Vena Cava Filters: A Review of the MAUDE Database, 25 J. of Vascular and Interventional Radiology 1181 (2014); Shawn E. Gurtcheff & Howard T. Sharp, Complications Associated with Global Endometrial Ablation: The Utility of the MAUDE Database, 102 Obstetrics & Gynecology 1278 (2003); Ariel D. Stern et al., Review Times and Adverse Events for Cardiovascular Devices, 1 Nature Biomedical Eng'g 1 (2017).

D Recalls

Finally, post-market regulation includes the oversight of formal medical device recalls. Although recalls are typically manufacturer-initiated, they are overseen by the FDA, which classifies recalls according to risk/severity:

- Class I recalls (most severe) occur where "there is a reasonable chance that a product will cause serious health problems or death" – for example, a faulty pacemaker lead that would prevent proper functioning.
- Class II recalls (moderate severity) occur where "a product may cause a temporary or reversible health problem or where there is a slight chance that it will cause serious health problems or death" – for example, an insufficiently tight surgical clamp.
- Class III recalls (low severity) occur where "a product is not likely to cause any health problem or injury" but where an issue nevertheless should be corrected – for example, a labeling issue.[19]

The FDA's medical device recall database publishes data on all classes of product recalls. The database links recall information to specific clearance/approval decision identifiers, enabling researchers to link a recall to at least one specific previously regulated product.

III METHODS FOR DATA COLLECTION AND ANALYSIS

In this section we describe the datasets we used to quantify the likelihood of post-market safety events associated with SdMDs and other devices over recent years.

A Data Sources and Sample Construction

We identified all 510(k)-track and PMA-track medical devices (i.e., moderate and high-risk devices) cleared or approved by the FDA from 2008–2018 in the five common regulatory medical specialties (associated with CDRH Advisory Committees of the same name) most likely to include RPM devices: Cardiology, clinical chemistry, gastroenterology, general hospital, and general and plastic surgery. We then identified all recalls and adverse events associated with these devices that occurred between 2008 and 2020 using the FDA's MAUDE and recall databases, respectively. We limited data from MAUDE to only include adverse events from mandatory reporters to reduce non-random differences in reporting across device types.

---

[19] US Food and Drug Admin., *What is a Medical Device Recall?* (updated September 26, 2018), www.fda.gov/medical-devices/medical-device-recalls/what-medical-device-recall.

B Identifying Software-Driven Medical Devices

We employed a supervised document classification algorithm to identify SdMDs. For each medical device in our sample, we downloaded its associated public statement or summary document from the FDA's website. These documents are required for all submissions and each "includes a description of the device such as might be found in the labeling or promotional material for the device."[20] We then used optical character recognition software to search each document for the word "software" to identify devices with a software component.

This text search technique was demonstrated to work well in manual review: In comparison to a manually coded random sample of summary documents, the document classification had a 0 percent false negative rate, meaning devices flagged as including a software component via supervised document classification always included a software component. Accordingly, we identified a medical device as including a software component if "software" appeared at least once in its public summary of evidence. Additional details on the supervised document classification are provided elsewhere.[21]

C Outcomes of Interest

We focused on two primary outcomes of interest: (1) Class I/II recalls (i.e., those of moderate or greater severity) and (2) mandatorily reported adverse events. For recalls, we identified all class I/II recalls that occurred within two years of regulatory approval/clearance for each device. We chose to use two years of follow-up, as most medical device recalls occur shortly after a medical device comes to market.[22] For adverse events, we similarly created a count of all adverse events from mandatory reporters in the two years following a device's clearance/approval.

D Statistical Analysis

We compared differences in adverse events and recalls by software status by performing two-sided, two-sample t-tests comparing the outcomes between SdMDs vs. non-SdMDs. To understand the changes over time, we plotted the number of recalls or adverse events in a given calendar year divided by the number of approvals/clearances in the two preceding years, such that the frequency of outcomes was

---

[20] US Food and Drug Admin., *Content of a 510(k)* (updated April 26, 2019), www.fda.gov/medical-devices/premarket-notification-510k/content-510k.

[21] Cirrus Foroughi & Ariel D. Stern, Who Drives Digital Innovation? Evidence from the US Medical Device Industry, 19–120 *Harvard Business School Working Paper* 15 (2019).

[22] William Maisel, *510(k) Premarket Notification Analysis of FDA Recall Data* (2011), www.ncbi.nlm.nih.gov/books/NBK209655.

scaled by the number of devices recently placed on the market in each year. All statistical analyses were performed using data from the entire sample, as well as within individual medical specialties.

IV RESULTS

Our sample included 13,186 medical devices, or 39.46 percent of all medical devices approved or cleared by the FDA during the sample period. During this time, software became increasingly prevalent in medical devices: While we observed variation over time in the total number and share of new SdMDs cleared/approved, all five medical specialties had a greater number and proportion of cleared/approved devices that included a software component in 2020 vs. 2010 (Figure 9.1). For example, 25.7 percent of the cardiovascular devices cleared or approved in 2010 included a software component, vs. 27.8 percent in 2020.

SdMDs in our sample experienced more adverse events (Figure 9.2) and class I/II recalls (Figure 9.3) than devices without software. The average SdMD had 14.516 associated adverse events from mandatory reporters in the MAUDE database (in

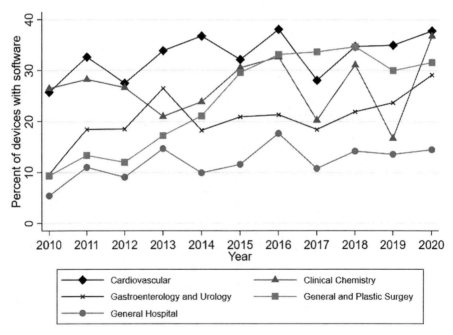

FIGURE 9.1 Proportion of devices with software by specialty over time
Note: Authors' analysis of FDA approval and clearance data from 2010–2020. Software identified based on keyword searches of FDA documents. Analysis restricted to medical specialties likely to include remote patient monitoring devices (39.46 percent of devices approved/cleared).

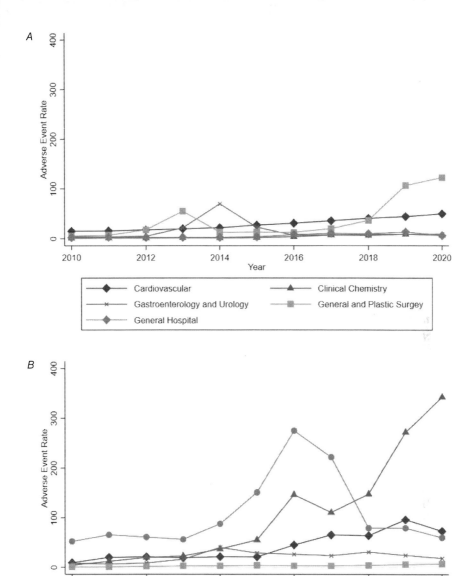

FIGURE 9.2 Two-year adverse event rates by specialty over time. A: *No software*; B: *Software*

Note: Authors' analysis of FDA approval and clearance data and the FDA's MAUDE database from 2010–2020. Software identified based on keyword searches of FDA documents. Analysis restricted to medical specialties likely to include remote patient monitoring devices (39.46 percent of all devices approved/cleared). For each year–specialty observation, the total adverse events from mandatory reporters were calculated and then divided by the number of approvals and clearances within that specialty in the preceding two years.

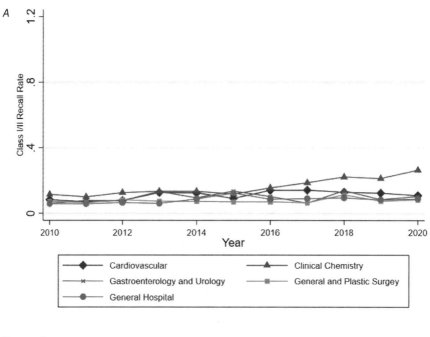
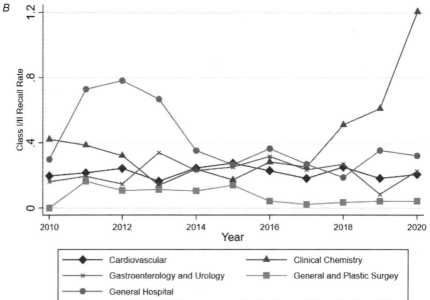

FIGURE 9.3 Two-year class I and class II recall rates by specialty over time.
A: *No software*; B: *Software*
Note: Authors' analysis of FDA approval and clearance data and the FDA's MAUDE database from 2010 to 2020. Software identified based on keyword searches of FDA documents. Analysis restricted to medical specialties likely to include remote patient monitoring devices (39.46 percent of all devices approved/cleared). For each year–specialty observation, total class I/II recalls were calculated and then divided by the number of approvals and clearances within that specialty in the preceding two years.

TABLE 9.1 *Two-year adverse event rates by specialty*

Specialty	Statistic	No software	Software	p
Cardiovascular	N	3,055	1,341	
	Mean	8.998	10.247	0.723
	(SD)	(97.243)	(111.656)	
Clinical chemistry	N	1,067	332	
	Mean	0.384	67.744	0.050
	(SD)	(3.786)	(622.820)	
Gastroenterology and urology	N	1,530	329	
	Mean	1.548	5.991	0.108
	(SD)	(13.286)	(49.618)	
General hospital	N	2,214	263	
	Mean	0.745	10.989	0.047
	(SD)	(8.197)	(83.094)	
General and plastic surgery	N	2,424	631	
	Mean	1.791	1.498	0.486
	(SD)	(16.036)	(6.694)	
Total	N	10,290	2,896	
	Mean	3.524	14.516	0.010
	(SD)	(54.059)	(226.749)	

Note: Authors' analysis of the FDA's MAUDE and recall databases for devices approved/cleared from 2008 to 2018. Software identified based on keyword searches of FDA approval/clearance documents. Analysis restricted to medical specialties likely to include remote patient monitoring devices (39.46 percent of all devices approved/cleared). Adverse events limited to mandatory reports. For each device, the total number of adverse events in two years following regulatory approval or clearance was calculated. Differences in means within specialties by software presence were assessed using two-sided t-tests under the assumption of unequal variance.

its first two years on the market), while the average device without software had 3.524 associated adverse events reported (p = 0.010) (Table 9.1). Similarly, 8.1 percent of SdMDs experienced at least one class I/II recall in the two years following regulatory approval/clearance, vs. 3.6 percent of devices without software (p < 0.001) (Table 9.1).

While devices with software generally experienced more adverse events and recalls, we observed significant heterogeneity in these differences by medical specialty area. When examining adverse events within individual medical specialties, only clinical chemistry and general hospital devices had statistically significant differences in adverse event rates in SdMDs vs. other devices. Among clinical chemistry devices, SdMDs had a mean 67.744 associated adverse events reported in the two years following regulatory approval or clearance, while non-SdMDs had a mean of just 0.384 adverse events reported in the two years following regulatory approval or clearance (p = 0.050) (Table 9.1). The difference between SdMDs and non-SdMDs, while statistically significant, was smaller

TABLE 9.2 *Two-year class I and class II recall rates by specialty*

Specialty	Statistic	No software	Software	p
Cardiovascular	N	3,055	1,341	
	Mean	0.050	0.080	<0.001
	(SD)	(0.219)	(0.271)	
Clinical chemistry	N	1,067	332	
	Mean	0.028	0.093	<0.001
	(SD)	(0.165)	(0.291)	
Gastroenterology and urology	N	1,530	329	
	Mean	0.041	0.097	0.001
	(SD)	(0.199)	(0.297)	
General hospital	N	2,214	263	
	Mean	0.024	0.118	<0.001
	(SD)	(0.153)	(0.323)	
General and plastic surgery	N	2,424	631	
	Mean	0.031	0.052	0.025
	(SD)	(0.173)	(0.223)	
Total	N	10,290	2,896	
	Mean	0.036	0.081	<0.001
	(SD)	(0.187)	(0.273)	

Note: Authors' analysis of the FDA's MAUDE and recall databases for devices approved/cleared from 2008 to 2018. Software identified based on keyword searches of FDA approval/clearance documents. Analysis restricted to medical specialties likely to include remote patient monitoring devices (39.46 percent of all devices approved/cleared). For each device, a binary indicator for a class I or class II recall was calculated. Differences in means within specialties by software presence were assessed using two-sided t-tests under the assumption of unequal variance.

among general hospital devices, where SdMDs had a mean of 10.989 associated adverse events in the two years following regulatory approval/clearance, while non-SdMDs had a mean of 0.745 adverse events reported over the same window of time ($p = 0.047$) (Table 9.1).

In contrast to adverse events, we observed significant differences in the number of recalls per approved device between SdMDs and non-SdMDs in each medical specialty studied. However, here too, the magnitude of the difference in recall rates varied meaningfully by specialty. General and plastic surgery devices had the smallest differences in recall rates (5.2 percent for SdMDs vs. 3.1 percent for non-SdMDs) ($p = 0.025$) (Table 9.2). General hospital devices had the largest difference in recall rates (11.8 percent of SdMDs vs. just 2.4 percent of non-SdMDs) ($p < 0.001$) (Table 9.2).

We also observed that the differences in outcomes between SdMDs and non-SdMDs were driven in part by large increases in recalls and adverse events for specific types of devices over relatively short periods of time. For example, a large increase in recalls of general hospital devices between 2011 and 2013 was

TABLE 9.3 *Example recalls*

Infusion pump recall description:	Glucose monitor recall description:
"Moog Inc. ... announced today that the [FDA] has classified the voluntary correction of the Curlin 6000 CMS, Curlin 6000 CMS IOD, PainSmart, and PainSmart IOD as a Class I recall... The decision to conduct the device recall is due to a software anomaly which leads to software Error Code 45 (EC45), resulting in a shutdown of the pump. This failure may result in a delay or interruption of therapy, which could result in serious injury and/or death."	"... Dexcom... issued a voluntary recall on the G6 CGM App due to the alarm feature on the iOS application failing to properly alert users. In particular, alarms were not detecting severe hypoglycemic (low glucose) or hyperglycemic (high glucose) events and therefore consumers were not being notified of fluctuations to blood glucose levels."

primarily driven by recalls of infusion pumps and sterilizers. A large increase in recalls of clinical chemistry devices in 2018 through 2020 was primarily driven by recalls of blood glucose monitors. Table 9.3 presents illustrative examples of such recalls.[23]

V DISCUSSION

Overall, we observed that SdMDs had higher adverse event and recall probabilities compared to devices without software components. Further, we documented heterogeneity in the difference between SdMDs and non-SdMDs, both over time and across medical specialties.

It should be noted that there are several limitations on the current post-market surveillance system in the United States that prevent us from concluding that SdMDs are less safe than non-SdMDs. For example, even if SdMDs experience more recalls and adverse events, software-based recalls may have a smaller impact on patient wellbeing vs. other types of recalls. For example, manufacturers may be able to address (some) software recalls more quickly by issuing software patches, rather than physically removing defective products from the market. However, in supplemental analyses (not reported here), we found no evidence that recalls of SdMDs were terminated more quickly (on average) than those of non-SdMDs.

In addition to limitations in our ability to extrapolate patient impact from adverse event and recall-based measures, there is almost certainly imprecision

---

[23] *Moog Recalls Curlin Ambulatory Infusion Pump Models 6000 CMS, 6000 CMS IOD, PainSmart, and PainSmart IOD* (Apr. 8, 2011), www.moog.com/news/corporate-press-releases/2011/moog-recalls-curlin-ambulatory-infusion-pump-models-6000-cms-6000-cms-iod-painsmart-painsmart-iod.html; *Lawyers Investigate Potential Device Defects after Recall of Dexcom Glucose Monitoring Systems* (June 19, 2020), www.leighday.co.uk/latest-updates/news/2020-news/lawyers-investigate-potential-device-defects-after-recall-of-dexcom-glucose-monitoring-systems/.

in how we estimated the rates of these outcomes. The FDA's MAUDE database for reporting adverse events does not include the number of devices in use at any given time – that is to say, there is no "denominator" to calculate the frequency of adverse events and/or recalls per device in circulation. As such, it is impossible to calculate a true adverse event rate, defined as adverse events per medical device in use. Rather, we calculate the rates of adverse events and recalls per device approved, but this is an imperfect measure. Devices with more units in circulation may have had more adverse events simply because they were used in more patients, which in turn, could impact the interpretation of our findings. Specifically, if SdMDs were used more (or less) frequently than non-SdMDs, the true per device used probability of such events could be substantially lower (or higher, respectively).

Further, both adverse event reporting and recalls rely on users and manufacturers identifying product problems. The salience of product issues is therefore likely to influence the probability with which true product failures are reported as adverse events and result in product recalls. One could imagine that certain types of product issues may be more noticeable in SdMDs – for example, issues with a digital display or internet connectivity. To the extent that this is true, it could also influence the results reported here and would drive up the likelihood that adverse events associated with SdMDs are reported and, as a corollary, the likelihood that a manufacturer recall is issued.

Our findings, therefore, also speak to the limitations of the current post-market surveillance and adverse event reporting infrastructure in the United States. While we found that on a per-new-device basis, SdMDs were more likely to experience recalls compared to non-SdMDs, we did not always detect differences in adverse events between SdMDs and non-SdMDs. Adverse events are a noisy signal of post-market safety and are not necessarily a reliable predictor of subsequent medical device recalls. The user-reported nature of the information collected in MAUDE may limit its ability to detect unsafe products, as regulators have already acknowledged.

Precisely because of these limitations, we believe that a key policy recommendation from our findings is the need for the systematic collection of unbiased data describing the post-market performance of both medical devices and digital diagnostics specifically. The FDA, the Centers for Medicare and Medicaid Services, and other bodies should work to include standardized medical device identifiers in administrative claims data (i.e., records of provider services reimbursed by health insurers).[24] Doing so would allow researchers and regulators to reliably track the use of SdMDs and their subsequent outcomes, thus differentiating safety issues from data artifacts caused by differences in device circulation.

---

[24] Kadakia et al., For Safety's Sake, It's Time to Get Medical Device Identifiers Over the Finish Line, STAT (July 18, 2022), www.statnews.com/2022/07/18/medica-device-identifiers-claims-forms-safety/.

It may also be beneficial for the FDA to consider implementing a broader and more robust set of post-market surveillance activities as software becomes increasingly integrated into medical devices and diagnostic technologies. Such activities could involve more direct evaluations of safety. For example, the FDA could potentially initiate periodic audits of randomly selected SdMDs to ensure that devices are performing as intended.

However, future post-market surveillance initiatives need not necessarily involve data collection by the FDA. The digitization of medical devices may raise safety issues, but it also presents new opportunities to collect data on device use and safety. SdMDs intrinsically generate "digital exhaust," or metadata through their use. Regulators should consider how they might encourage manufacturers to leverage such data (including data on frequency and duration of device use) as part of post-market surveillance strategies, potentially by tying pre-market approval to a clear post-market data monitoring plan when appropriate.

The FDA alone will not be able to execute some of these changes. As the FDA acknowledged in a recent report, the "faster cycles of innovation and the speed of change for medical device software would benefit from a new regulatory approach,"[25] but the FDA is constrained in the actions it can currently take. The scope of the FDA's regulatory activities is largely determined by the original 1976 legislation that gave the agency the authority to regulate devices. New legislative authority is needed for the FDA to design regulatory approaches that best address the unique nature of medical device software.[26]

As the FDA considers new regulatory approaches to SdMDs, patients and providers should be aware that the introduction of software into previously analog devices may present new safety concerns. These concerns will not always be readily identifiable through existing post-market surveillance mechanisms. Accordingly, health care providers should consider how they might "monitor the monitors" and ensure that newly adopted remote patient monitoring technologies work as intended.

VI CONCLUSION

In an analysis focusing on five key medical specialties and using over a decade of data, we found that medical devices with software components had more adverse events and recalls (per new device) as compared to devices without software. While these findings hint at potential safety challenges associated with SdMDs, the data available do not allow us to extrapolate further and calculate safety issues per device in circulation, a measure that would be more appropriate for informing

---

[25] US Food and Drug Admin., *The Software Precertification (Pre-Cert) Pilot Program: Tailored Total Product Lifecycle Approaches and Key Findings* (September 26, 2022), www.fda.gov/media/161815/download.
[26] Id.

individual patient/provider safety concerns. That said, the data analyzed here demonstrate that it is vital to continue to monitor the safety and effectiveness of SdMDs going forward. Further, patients and providers should not assume that existing post-market surveillance mechanisms are sufficient for detecting safety concerns in the early years following market entry for new products with software components.

10

Labeling of Direct-to-Consumer Medical Artificial Intelligence Applications for "Self-Diagnosis"

Sara Gerke

I INTRODUCTION

Artificial intelligence (AI), particularly its subcategory, machine learning, is changing our daily lives and the way we receive health care. The digital health apps market is booming, with over 350,000 health apps available to patients and consumers, ranging from wellness and fitness apps to disease management apps.[1] In particular, many direct-to-consumer medical AI apps for "self-diagnosis" (DTC medical self-diagnosing AI apps) are emerging that help individuals to identify a disease or other condition based on entering, for example, symptoms.[2] DTC medical self-diagnosing AI apps offer new opportunities, but they also raise issues. While the current legal debate has mainly focused on the poor accuracy of DTC medical self-diagnosing apps,[3] this chapter will discuss the labeling challenges associated with these apps that have received little attention in the literature.

This chapter will first explore the current and future landscape of DTC medical self-diagnosing AI apps. It will then focus on their regulation and discuss whether DTC medical self-diagnosing AI apps are medical devices under section 201(h)(1) of the Federal Food, Drug, and Cosmetic Act (FDCA). This will be followed by a discussion of two labeling challenges raised by DTC medical self-diagnosing AI apps:

---

[1] Emily Olsen, Digital Health Apps Balloon to More Than 350,000 Available on the Market, According to IQVIA Report, *Mobi Health News* (August 4, 2021), www.mobihealthnews.com/news/digital-health-apps-balloon-more-350000-available-market-according-iqvia-report.

[2] The term "consumer" is here understood broadly and includes healthy individuals and patients. Aleksandar Ćirković et al., Evaluation of Four Artificial Intelligence–Assisted Self-Diagnosis Apps on Three Diagnoses: Two-Year Follow-Up Study, 22 J. Med. Internet Res. e18097 (2020).

[3] See, for example, Boris Babic et al., Direct-to-Consumer Medical Machine Learning and Artificial Intelligence Applications, 366 Nature Mach. Intel. 283 (2021); Sara Gerke et al., Germany's Digital Health Reforms in the COVID-19 Era: Lessons and Opportunities for Other Countries, 3 npj Digit. Med., 94 (2020); Stephanie Aboueid et al., The Use of Artificially Intelligent Self-Diagnosing Digital Platforms by the General Public: Scoping Review, 7 JMIR Med. Info. e13445 (2019). For privacy aspects of DTC AI/machine learning health apps, see Sara Gerke & Delaram Rezaeikhonakdar, Privacy Aspects of Direct-to-Consumer Artificial Intelligence/Machine Learning Health Apps, 6 Intelligence-Based Med. 100061 (2022).

First, the concern of labeling DTC medical self-diagnosing AI apps as what I call "information-only" tools, and second, particular issues associated with the use of AI, ranging from bias to adaptive algorithms.

This chapter concludes that the labeling of DTC medical self-diagnosing AI apps as "information-only" rather than "diagnostic" tools is unknown to most consumers. The Food and Drug Administration (FDA) should create user-friendly labeling standards for AI-based medical devices, including those that are DTC. For example, these standards should ensure that consumers are adequately informed about the indications for use, model characteristics, and the risks and limitations of the respective DTC medical self-diagnosing AI apps. Based on a risk-based approach, some of these apps should also be prescribed by physicians rather than being offered directly to consumers over the counter. Physicians can help direct the use of the app in question and point out material facts, such as the risk of false positives and negatives, in the patient–physician conversation. In the long run, it may also be helpful to set up a new federal entity responsible for (at least for the coordination of) all issues raised by mobile health apps, from regulation to privacy to reimbursement. While this chapter focuses on FDA regulation for DTC medical self-diagnosing AI apps, some of the suggested solutions here may also have implications for other DTC apps.

II THE CURRENT AND FUTURE LANDSCAPE OF DTC MEDICAL SELF-DIAGNOSING AI APPS

The US mobile health market is expected to grow continuously over the next decade, with medical apps (compared to fitness apps) representing the bulk of the market.[4] Before, or instead of, visiting a doctor's office, consumers are trying more than ever before to self-diagnose their conditions by putting keywords of their symptoms into search engines like Google or using DTC medical self-diagnosing AI apps.[5] Approximately 80 percent of patients use the Internet for health-related searches.[6] According to a 2017 US survey, only 4 percent (ages 61 and older) to 10 percent (ages 18 to 29) of adults used apps for self-diagnosis, but 32 percent (ages 18 to 29) to 62 percent (ages 61 and older) of adults said that they could imagine using them.[7] Since the COVID-19 pandemic, digital health technologies have gained

---

[4] Grand Review Research, *mHealth Apps Market Size, Share & Trends Analysis Report By Type (Fitness, Medical), By Region (North America, Europe, Asia Pacific, Latin America, Middle East & Africa), and Segment Forecasts, 2022–2030*, www.grandviewresearch.com/industry-analysis/mhealth-app-market.

[5] The Smart Clinics, *Rise in Internet Self-Diagnosis*, www.thesmartclinics.co.uk/rise-in-internet-self-diagnosis.

[6] Maria Clark, 37 Self Diagnosis Statistics: Don't Do It Yourself, *Etactics* (December 10, 2020), https://etactics.com/blog/self-diagnosis-statistics.

[7] Statista, *Percentage of US Adults That Use Apps for Self-Diagnosis as of 2017, by Age*, www.statista.com/statistics/699505/us-adults-that-use-apps-to-self-diagnose-by-age.

popularity to mitigate the spread of the virus,[8] and the use of medical self-diagnosing apps, including those based on AI, has become a reality for more adults in the USA.[9]

In 2021, Google announced the planned launch of a pilot study of its "AI-powered dermatology tool" to help consumers find answers to their skin, nail, and hair condition questions.[10] With their phone's camera, consumers simply need to take three photos of their skin, nail, or hair concerns from different perspectives and answer a few questions, such as their skin type and other symptoms.[11] The app will then offer a list of possible conditions.[12] Google's app, dubbed DermAssist, is currently CE-marked as a low-risk (so-called class I) medical device in the European Union (EU) but is being further tested via a limited market release.[13] The CE marking indicates that the device conforms with the applicable legal requirements.[14] DermAssist is not yet available in the USA and has not undergone an FDA review for safety and effectiveness.[15]

But Google is not the only company that is investing in dermatology apps. Indeed, a quick search in mobile app stores like Apple and Google Play reveals that there are already similar apps available to download for US consumers, such as AI Dermatologist: Skin Scanner by the developer Acina. Once consumers download this AI app, they can check their skin by taking a photo of, for example, their mole with their phone's camera.[16] Within one minute, consumers will receive a risk assessment from AI Dermatologist, including some advice concerning the next steps.[17] It appears that AI Dermatologist is CE-marked as a medical device in the EU but has not undergone premarket review by the FDA.[18]

---

[8] See, for example, Sara Gerke et al., Regulatory, Safety, and Privacy Concerns of Home Monitoring Technologies During COVID-19, 26 Nature Med. 1176 (2020).

[9] See, for example, Raquel Correia, How Doctors Can Benefit from Symptom Checkers, Infermedica (March 2, 2021) https://blog.infermedica.com/how-doctors-can-benefit-from-symptom-checkers.

[10] Peggy Bui & Yuan Liu, Using AI to Help Find Answers to Common Skin Conditions, Google, The Keyword (May 18, 2021), https://blog.google/technology/health/ai-dermatology-preview-io-2021.

[11] Id.

[12] Id.

[13] Google Health, DermAssist, https://health.google/consumers/dermassist.

[14] For more information on CE marking, see the new EU Medical Device Regulation (2017/745 – MDR), Art. 2(43) and, for example, Sara Gerke et al., Ethical and Legal Challenges of Artificial Intelligence-Driven Healthcare, in Artificial Intelligence in Healthcare (1st edn.) 295, 312 (Adam Bohr & Kaveh Memarzadeh eds., 2020).

[15] Google Health, supra note 13.

[16] AI Dermatologist, Say No To Skin Diseases!, https://ai-derm.com.

[17] Id.

[18] Id. AI Dermatologist is not listed on the FDA's website for AI/machine learning (ML)-enabled medical devices marketed in the USA. See US Food and Drug Admin., Artificial Intelligence and Machine Learning (AI/ML)-Enabled Medical Devices, www.fda.gov/medical-devices/software-medical-device-samd/artificial-intelligence-and-machine-learning-aiml-enabled-medical-devices (last updated October 5, 2022). This app can also not be found in the FDA's databases Devices@FDA, see US Food and Drug Admin., www.accessdata.fda.gov/scripts/cdrh/devicesatfda/index.cfm (last updated October 9, 2023), and DeNovo, see US Food and Drug Admin., www.accessdata.fda.gov/scripts/cdrh/cfdocs/cfPMN/denovo.cfm (last updated October 9, 2023).

There are also other DTC medical self-diagnosing AI apps already available on the US market. A classic example is Apple's electrocardiogram (ECG) and irregular rhythms notification feature apps.[19] Both apps are moderate-risk (so-called class II) medical devices that received marketing authorization from the FDA in September 2018.[20] They are used with the Apple Watch and are addressed directly to consumers. While Apple's ECG app is intended to store, create, transfer, record, and display a single channel ECG,[21] Apple's irregular rhythms notification feature app detects irregular heart rhythm episodes suggestive of atrial fibrillation.[22] Another example is the AI symptom checker Ada. Consumers can manage their health by answering Ada's health questions about their symptoms, such as headaches and stomach problems.[23] Ada's AI will then use its medical dictionary of medical conditions and disorders to deliver possible causes for the symptoms and offer advice.[24] Ada's consumer app is currently CE-marked as a class I medical device in the European Economic Area,[25] but, similar to AI Dermatologist, it does not appear that the app has undergone a premarket review by the FDA.[26]

III DTC MEDICAL SELF-DIAGNOSING AI APPS AS MEDICAL DEVICES

Can the FDA regulate DTC medical self-diagnosing AI apps? The answer is yes, if they are classified as medical devices under FDCA section 201(h)(1). This section will discuss the definition of a medical device, the FDA's enforcement discretion, and a relevant exception to the medical device definition.

A *The Medical Device Definition and the FDA's Enforcement Discretion*

Under FDCA section 201(h)(1), a "device" is

> an instrument, apparatus, implement, machine, contrivance, implant, in vitro reagent, or other similar or related article, including any component, part, or

---

[19] Letter from the FDA to Apple Inc., *ECG App* (September 11, 2018), www.accessdata.fda.gov/cdrh_docs/pdf18/DEN180044.pdf; Letter from the FDA to Apple Inc., *Irregular Rhythm Notification Feature* (September 11, 2018), www.accessdata.fda.gov/cdrh_docs/pdf18/DEN180042.pdf.
[20] Letters from the FDA to Apple Inc. (September 11, 2018), supra note 19.
[21] Letter from the FDA to Apple Inc., *ECG App* (September 11, 2018), supra note 19, at 1.
[22] Letter from the FDA to Apple Inc., *Irregular Rhythm Notification Feature* (September 11, 2018), supra note 19, at 1.
[23] Ada, *Take Care of Yourself With ADA*, https://ada.com/app. For further examples of DTC medical self-diagnosing AI apps, see Ćirković et al., supra note 2; Aboueid et al., supra note 3.
[24] Ada, supra note 23.
[25] Class IIa under the EU MDR is currently pending; see Ada, *5.1 Is Ada a Medical Device?*, https://ada.com/help/is-ada-a-medical-device. The European Economic Area consists of all 27 EU member states, Liechtenstein, Norway, and Iceland.
[26] Ada is not listed on the FDA's website for AI/ML-enabled medical devices marketed in the USA, see FDA, supra note 18. This app can also not be found in the FDA's databases Devices@FDA and DeNovo, supra note 18. For more information, see also infra Section III.A.

accessory, which is ... *intended for use in the diagnosis of disease or other conditions, or in the cure, mitigation, treatment, or prevention of disease*, in man ..., and which does not achieve its primary intended purposes through chemical action within or on the body of man ... and which is not dependent upon being metabolized for the achievement of its primary intended purposes....[27]

From the outset, the FDA can only regulate software functions that are classified as medical devices under FDCA section 201(h)(1) (so-called "device software functions").[28] In other words, the FDA has no statutory authority to regulate software functions that are *not* considered medical devices under FDCA section 201(h)(1).[29] There are different types of software classifications. A relevant one is "Software as a Medical Device" (SaMD), which is standalone software and, as such, counts as a medical device.[30] The International Medical Device Regulators Forum defines SaMD as "software intended to be used for one or more medical purposes that perform these purposes without being part of a hardware medical device."[31] For example, Apple's ECG and irregular rhythms notification feature apps are both SaMD because they are software-only apps intended for a medical purpose.[32]

Only recently, in September 2022, the FDA updated its *Guidance for Device Software Functions and Mobile Medical Applications* (*Mobile Medical App Guidance*) to reflect recent changes, such as the issuance of the FDA's final *Guidance on Clinical Decision Support Software*.[33] Although the *Mobile Medical App Guidance* contains nonbinding recommendations, it represents the FDA's current thinking on its regulatory approach to device software functions, including mobile medical apps.[34] The FDA defines "mobile medical apps," as mobile apps

---

[27] 21 USC § 321(h)(1) (emphasis added).
[28] Sara Gerke, Health AI For Good Rather Than Evil? The Need For a New Regulatory Framework For AI-Based Medical Devices, 20 Yale J. Health Pol'y L. & Ethics 433, 446 (2021).
[29] See US Food and Drug Admin., *FDA's Legal Authority* (April 24, 2019), www.fda.gov/about-fda/changes-science-law-and-regulatory-authorities/fdas-legal-authority.
[30] Gerke, supra note 28, at 446. For more information on the different types of software, see, for example, US Food and Drug Admin., *Software as a Medical Device (SaMD)* (December 4, 2018), www.fda.gov/medical-devices/digital-health-center-excellence/software-medical-device-samd.
[31] International Medical Device Regulators Forum, *Software as a Medical Device (SaMD): Key Definitions* 6 (2013), www.imdrf.org/sites/default/files/docs/imdrf/final/technical/imdrf-tech-131209-samd-key-definitions-140901.pdf.
[32] Letters from the FDA to Apple Inc., supra note 19; Gerke, supra note 28, at 447.
[33] US Food and Drug Admin., *Policy for Device Software Functions and Mobile Medical Applications: Guidance for Industry and Food and Drug Administration Staff* (2022), www.fda.gov/media/80958/download; US Food and Drug Admin., *Device Software Functions Including Mobile Medical Applications* (September 29, 2022), www.fda.gov/medical-devices/digital-health-center-excellence/device-software-functions-including-mobile-medical-applications. For the new Clinical Decision Support Software Guidance, see US Food and Drug Admin., *Clinical Decision Support Software: Guidance for Industry and Food and Drug Administration Staff* (2022), www.fda.gov/media/109618/download.
[34] US Food and Drug Admin., *Mobile Medical App Guidance*, supra note 33, at 1, 3.

that incorporate device software functionalities that meet the medical device definition in the FDCA, and either are "intended ... to be used as an accessory to a regulated medical device; or ... to transform a mobile platform into a regulated medical device."[35]

The "intended use" is relevant for determining whether a mobile app is considered a medical device.[36] The term means "the objective intent of the persons legally responsible for the labeling of devices."[37] Such persons are usually the manufacturers whose expressions determine the intent.[38] The intent can also be shown by the circumstances surrounding the product's distribution.[39] For instance, the objective intent can be derived from advertising materials, labeling claims, and written or oral statements by the product's manufacturer or its representatives.[40]

In its *Mobile Medical App Guidance*, the FDA clarifies that it intends to focus its regulatory oversight on only those device software functions whose functionality could present a risk to the safety of patients if they were not to function as intended.[41] This means that the FDA intends to exercise enforcement discretion over those software functions that are or may be medical devices under FDCA section 201(h)(1) but present a lower risk to the public.[42] Enforcement discretion means that the agency does not aim to enforce requirements under the FDCA.[43]

For example, the FDA intends to apply its regulatory oversight to device software functions that analyze images of skin lesions using mathematical algorithms and provide users with risk assessments of the lesions.[44] In contrast, for instance, the FDA considers apps exclusively intended for patient education, such as an app that helps guide patients to ask the right questions to their physician concerning their disease, as *not* being medical devices, and, thus, those apps fall outside of the FDA's statutory authority.[45] An example of a mobile app that may meet the medical device definition, but for which the FDA intends to exercise enforcement discretion because it poses a lower risk to the public, is an app that provides a "Skill of the Day" behavioral technique that patients with diagnosed psychiatric conditions can access when experiencing increased anxiety.[46]

---

[35] US Food and Drug Admin., *Mobile Medical App Guidance*, supra note 33, at 5. A mobile app is "a software application that can be executed (run) on a mobile platform (i.e., a handheld commercial off-the-shelf computing platform, with or without wireless connectivity), or a web-based software application that is tailored to a mobile platform but is executed on a server." Id. at 5.
[36] Id. at 6.
[37] Id. at 6 and n.20. See also 21 CFR § 801.4 (defining the words "intended uses").
[38] US Food and Drug Admin., *Mobile Medical App Guidance*, supra note 33, at 6 and n.20.
[39] Id.
[40] Id.; 21 CFR § 801.4.
[41] US Food and Drug Admin., *Mobile Medical App Guidance*, supra note 33, at 2, 11.
[42] Id. at 2, 14, 24.
[43] Id. at 2, 13.
[44] Id. at 27.
[45] Id. at 18.
[46] Id. at 24.

When applying the FDA's current thinking in the *Mobile Medical App Guidance* to DTC medical self-diagnosing AI apps, some of these apps are considered device software functions that are the focus of the agency's regulatory oversight. Take as an example Apple's ECG and irregular rhythms notification feature apps. Both apps are considered class II (moderate-risk) medical devices and had to undergo a premarket review by the FDA via the so-called De Novo process before being placed on the US market.[47]

However, even if DTC medical self-diagnosing AI apps are considered medical devices because they help individuals identify a disease or other condition and are considered to be "intended for use in the diagnosis of disease or other conditions, or in the cure, mitigation, treatment, or prevention of disease,"[48] the FDA may exercise enforcement discretion over some of them if they are considered to pose a low risk to the public. For example, as mentioned previously, the consumer app Ada is currently CE-marked as a class I (low-risk) medical device in the European Economic Area.[49] However, it seems that Ada has not undergone a premarket review by the FDA.[50] One option why this is likely the case is that Ada (may) meet(s) the medical device definition in FDCA section 201(h)(1),[51] but falls within the FDA's enforcement discretion because it is considered to pose a lower risk to the public. This analysis also seems to be consistent with the *Mobile Medical App Guidance*. In Appendix B of its *Guidance*, the FDA lists examples of software functions that may meet the medical device definition but for which the agency exercises enforcement discretion, including:

- "Software functions that use a checklist of common signs and symptoms to provide a list of possible medical conditions and advice on when to consult a health care provider" and
- "Software functions that guide a user through a questionnaire of signs and symptoms to provide a recommendation for the type of health care facility most appropriate to their needs."[52]

In addition, most class I medical devices under the FDCA are also a priori exempt from premarket notification (510(k)) requirements.[53]

---

[47] See supra Section II and Letters from the FDA to Apple Inc., supra notes 19.
[48] FDCA section 201(h)(1). See also infra Section III.B. (discussing whether DTC medical self-diagnosing AI apps fall under the medical device exception in FDCA section 520(o)(1)(B)).
[49] See supra Section II; Ada, supra note 25.
[50] See supra Section II.
[51] See infra Section III.B. (discussing whether DTC medical self-diagnosing AI apps fall under the medical device exception in FDCA section 520(o)(1)(B)).
[52] US Food and Drug Admin., *Mobile Medical App Guidance*, supra note 33, at 24–25.
[53] US Food and Drug Admin., *Class I and Class II Device Exemptions* (February 23, 2022), www.fda.gov/medical-devices/classify-your-medical-device/class-i-and-class-ii-device-exemptions. For more information on health-related products that straddle the line between devices and general wellness products, see also David Simon et al., At-Home Diagnostics and Diagnostic Excellence, 327 JAMA 523 (2022).

B The Medical Device Exception, FDCA Section 520(o)(1)(B)

Section 3060(a) of the 21st Century Cures Act introduced five exceptions to the medical device definition for certain software functions. One of these exceptions is particularly relevant for DTC AI apps – namely FDCA section 520(o)(1)(B), which states that "the term device, as defined in section 201(h), shall not include a software function that is intended … for maintaining or encouraging a healthy lifestyle and is unrelated to the diagnosis, cure, mitigation, prevention, or treatment of a disease or condition; … ."

In 2019, the FDA issued nonbinding *Guidance on Changes to Existing Medical Software Policies Resulting from Section 3060 of the 21st Century Cures Act* (*Cures Act Guidance*), in which the agency, among other things, expresses its current interpretation of FDCA section 520(o)(1)(B).[54] In particular, the FDA clarifies that FDCA section 520(o)(1)(B) means software functions that belong to the first category of general wellness intended uses, as defined in the FDA's nonbinding *Guidance on General Wellness: Policy for Low Risk Devices* (*General Wellness Guidance*),[55] and that are "unrelated to the diagnosis, cure, mitigation, prevention, or treatment of a disease or condition."[56] Software functions that fall within the first category of general wellness intended uses are intended for "maintaining or encouraging a general state of health or a healthy activity."[57] For example, an app that assists users with weight loss goals and does not make any reference to diseases or conditions falls under FDCA section 520(o)(1)(B), and, thus, is *not* considered a medical device under FDCA section 201(h)(1).[58]

In its *Cures Act Guidance*, the FDA also clarifies that software functions that fall within the second category of general wellness intended uses, as defined in the *General Wellness Guidance*, are not covered by FDCA section 520(o)(1)(B).[59] Software functions that fall within the second category of general wellness intended uses have "an intended use that relates the role of healthy lifestyle with helping to reduce the risk or impact of certain chronic diseases or conditions and where it is well understood and accepted that healthy lifestyle choices may play an important role in health outcomes for the disease or condition."[60]

In contrast to the first category of general wellness intended uses, this second category relates to the prevention or mitigation of a disease or condition, and, thus, software functions that fall within this second category are *not* excluded from the

---

[54] US Food and Drug Admin., *Changes to Existing Medical Software Policies Resulting from Section 3060 of the 21st Century Cures Act: Guidance for Industry and Food and Drug Administration Staff* 4–7 (2019), www.fda.gov/media/109622/download.
[55] US Food and Drug Admin., *General Wellness: Policy for Low Risk Devices: Guidance for Industry and Food and Drug Administration Staff* (2019), www.fda.gov/media/90652/download.
[56] US Food and Drug Admin., supra note 54, at 5.
[57] US Food and Drug Admin., supra note 55, at 3.
[58] See id.; US Food and Drug Admin., supra note 54, at 5–6.
[59] US Food and Drug Admin., supra note 54, at 5–6.
[60] US Food and Drug Admin., supra note 55, at 3.

medical device definition.[61] For example, if the app in the previous example makes reference to diseases or conditions – for instance, if it claims that maintaining a healthy weight will aid living well with type 2 diabetes – this app falls outside of the scope of FDCA section 520(o)(1)(B).[62]

As understood here, DTC medical self-diagnosing AI apps help users to identify a disease or other condition based on entering, for example, symptoms. They are related "to the diagnosis, cure, mitigation, prevention, or treatment of a disease or condition" and, thus, do *not* fall under the medical device exception in FDCA section 520(o)(1)(B).[63] To sum up, DTC medical self-diagnosing AI apps are medical devices under FDCA Section 201(h)(1) that are either the focus of the FDA's regulatory oversight or for which the agency exercises its enforcement discretion. Figure 10.1 summarizes the regulation of mobile health apps, including DTC medical self-diagnosing AI apps.

IV LABELING CHALLENGES FOR DTC MEDICAL SELF-DIAGNOSING AI APPS

As established above, DTC medical self-diagnosing AI apps, as understood here, are medical devices that are either the focus of the FDA's regulatory oversight or for which the agency exercises its enforcement discretion. This section will focus on the labeling challenges for DTC medical self-diagnosing AI apps. It will first give an overview of medical device labeling and the relevant terminology. It will then focus on labeling challenges for DTC medical self-diagnosing AI apps and make suggestions on how to overcome them.

A Labeling

Device software functions are organized into one of three classes based on their risk level, ranging from class I (lowest risk) to class III (highest risk).[64] Depending on the device classification, manufacturers must follow the associated controls – that is, General Controls, Special Controls, and/or Premarket Approval.[65] In principle, General Controls apply to all device software functions.[66] For instance, the General Device Labeling Requirements in Part 801 of Title 21 of the Code of Federal Regulations (CFR) are General Controls.[67] 21 CFR Part 801 includes, among other

---

[61] US Food and Drug Admin., supra note 54, at 6.
[62] See id.; US Food and Drug Admin., supra note 55, at 4–5.
[63] See US Food and Drug Admin., supra note 54, at 5–6; US Food and Drug Admin., supra note 55, at 4–5.
[64] US Food and Drug Admin., *Mobile Medical App Guidance*, supra note 33, at 11.
[65] Id. For more information on the regulatory controls, see also US Food and Drug Admin., *Regulatory Controls* (March 27, 2018), www.fda.gov/medical-devices/overview-device-regulation/regulatory-controls.
[66] For exemptions by regulations, see US Food and Drug Admin., supra note 65.
[67] For more information on device labeling, see, for example, US Food and Drug Admin., *Device Labeling* (October 23, 2020), www.fda.gov/medical-devices/overview-device-regulation/device-labeling.

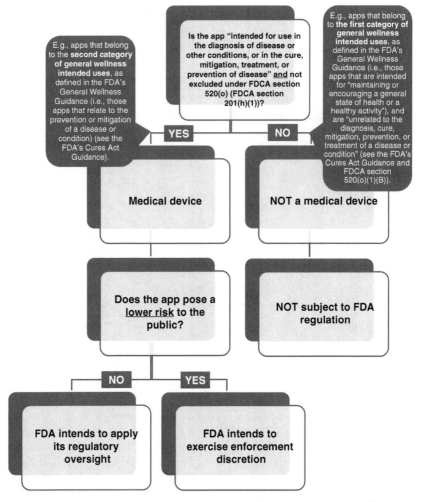

FIGURE 10.1 Regulation of mobile health apps, including DTC medical self-diagnosing AI apps[a]

[a] Figure inspired by the FDA's *Mobile Medical App Guidance*, supra note 33; the FDA's *Cures Act Guidance*, supra note 54; the FDA's *General Wellness Guidance*, supra note 55.

things, general labeling provisions, such as the name and place of business, adequate directions for use, and the use of symbols, as well as special requirements for specific devices, such as hearing aids, and labeling requirements for unique device identification and over-the-counter devices.[68]

[68] For more information, see Sara Gerke, "Nutrition Facts Labels" for Artificial Intelligence/Machine Learning-Based Medical Devices – The Urgent Need for Labeling Standards, 91 Geo. Wash. L. Rev 79, Section III.A.3 and Box 1.

Labeling is defined in FDCA section 201(m) as "all labels and other written, printed, or graphic matter (1) upon any article or any of its containers or wrappers, or (2) accompanying such article." It is a generic term that also includes all labels.[69] Under FDCA section 201(k), the term "label" means

> a display of written, printed, or graphic matter upon the immediate container of any article; and a requirement made by or under authority of this Act that any word, statement, or other information appear on the label shall not be considered to be complied with unless such word, statement, or other information also appears on the outside container or wrapper, if any there be, of the retail package of such article, or is easily legible through the outside container or wrapper.

In the context of DTC medical self-diagnosing AI apps, the label will usually be available in non-physical form through the app itself.

It is also worth noting that if the "labeling is false or misleading in any particular," the device is considered misbranded under FDCA section 502(a)(1). The term "misleading" means that the labeling proves deceptive to device users and creates or leads to a false impression in their minds.[70] For example, this can be the case if the label contains exaggerated claims or if it fails to inform users about relevant facts.[71]

B Challenges

DTC medical self-diagnosing AI apps raise labeling challenges. This section will discuss two: First, the concern of labeling DTC medical self-diagnosing AI apps as what I call "information-only" tools, and second, particular issues associated with the use of AI, ranging from bias to adaptive algorithms. It will also make suggestions on how to address these challenges. While the following remarks focus on medical devices, they may also have implications for those DTC apps that fall outside the FDA's statutory authority.

i Labeling as "Information-Only" Tools

Apple's ECG and irregular rhythms notification feature apps used with the Apple Watch are both over-the-counter class II medical devices that received marketing authorization from the FDA in September 2018.[72] As previously mentioned, Apple's ECG app is intended to store, create, transfer, record, and display a single channel ECG.[73] The indications for use, however, also include, among other things, the following sentences:

---

[69] Id. at 123.
[70] US Food and Drug Admin., *Labeling: Regulatory Requirements for Medical Devices* (1989) 4, www.fda.gov/media/74034/download.
[71] Id. For more information on misbranding, see also Gerke, supra note 68, at Section III.A.2.
[72] See supra Section II and letters from the FDA to Apple Inc., supra notes 19.
[73] See supra Section II and the letter from the FDA to Apple Inc., *ECG App*, supra note 19, at 1.

The user is *not intended to interpret or take clinical action based on the device output without consultation of a qualified healthcare professional.* The ECG waveform is meant to supplement rhythm classification for the purposes of discriminating AFib [atrial fibrillation] from normal sinus rhythm and *not intended to replace traditional methods of diagnosis or treatment.*[74]

The FDA created a new device type, namely "electrocardiograph software for over-the-counter use," regulated in 21 CFR 870.2345, for Apple's ECG app and substantially equivalent devices.[75] Interestingly, 21 CFR 870.2345(a) also states that "this device is not intended to provide a diagnosis."

Moreover, as mentioned, Apple's irregular rhythms notification feature app detects irregular heart rhythm episodes suggestive of atrial fibrillation.[76] But, much like Apple's ECG app, this app's indications for use include, inter alia, the following phrases:

> It is *not intended to provide a notification on every episode of irregular rhythm suggestive of AFib and the absence of a notification is not intended to indicate no disease process is present*; rather the feature is intended to opportunistically surface a notification of *possible AFib* when sufficient data are available for analysis. These data are only captured when the user is still. Along with the user's risk factors, the feature can be used to supplement the decision for AFib screening. The feature is *not intended to replace traditional methods of diagnosis or treatment.*[77]

The FDA also created a new device type, namely "photoplethysmograph analysis software for over-the-counter use," laid down in 21 CFR 870.2790, for Apple's irregular rhythms notification feature app and substantially equivalent devices.[78] Similar to 21 CFR 870.2345, this regulation also clarifies that "this device is not intended to provide a diagnosis."[79]

But Apple's apps are not the only DTC medical self-diagnosing AI apps that articulate that their device "is not intended to provide a diagnosis." For example, Google's 2021 announcement of its AI-powered dermatology tool says:[80] "The tool is *not intended to provide a diagnosis* nor be a substitute for medical advice as many conditions require clinician review, in-person examination, or additional testing like a biopsy. Rather we hope *it gives you access to authoritative information so you can make a more informed decision* about your next step."[81]

---

[74] Letter from the FDA to Apple Inc., *ECG App*, supra note 19, at 1 (emphasis added).
[75] Id. at 1–2.
[76] See supra Section II and the letter from the FDA to Apple Inc., *Irregular Rhythm Notification Feature*, supra note 19, at 1.
[77] Letter from the FDA to Apple Inc., *Irregular Rhythm Notification Feature*, supra note 19, at 1 (emphasis added).
[78] Id. at 1–2.
[79] 21 CFR § 870.2790(a).
[80] For more information on this tool, see supra Section II.
[81] Bui & Liu, supra note 10 (emphasis added).

In addition, Google's website states: "DermAssist is intended for informational purposes only and does not provide a medical diagnosis."[82] The same is also true for the AI Dermatologist: Skin Scanner app.[83] When looking up information about the app in an app store, the preview states: "It is essential to understand that an AI-Dermatologist is not a diagnostic tool and cannot replace or substitute a visit to your doctor."[84] App store previews of Ada say something similar: "CAUTION: The Ada app cannot give you a medical diagnosis.... The Ada app does not replace your healthcare professional's advice or an appointment with your doctor."[85]

Consequently, DTC medical self-diagnosing AI apps are labeled as "information-only" rather than "diagnostic" tools.[86] Irrespective of whether DTC medical self-diagnosing AI apps are medical devices that are the focus of the FDA's regulatory oversight or for which the agency exercises its enforcement discretion, these apps seem to have in common that their manufacturers claim they are "not intended to provide a diagnosis." This is likely due to their over-the-counter nature, although Apple's clinical study of the ECG app, for example, showed that the app correctly diagnosed atrial fibrillation with 98.3 percent sensitivity and 99.6 percent specificity.[87] As a comparison, a prescription device is a "device which, because of any potentiality for harmful effect, or the method of its use, or the collateral measures necessary to its use is not safe except under the supervision of a practitioner licensed by law to direct the use of such device."[88] But do patients and consumers really understand that Apple's ECG app and similar apps are not intended to replace traditional diagnosis and treatment methods, let alone that some have been FDA reviewed and others have not?

There appears to be a significant discrepancy between the user's perception of the intended use of DTC medical self-diagnosing AI apps and their actual intended use (i.e., not to diagnose). Indeed, a recent study on AI-assisted symptom checkers revealed that 84.1 percent of respondents perceive them as diagnostic tools.[89] In addition, 33.2 percent of respondents use symptom checkers for deciding whether to seek care, and 15.8 percent of respondents said they use them to receive medical advice without seeing a doctor.[90] However, as seen above, apps like the ones from Apple

---

[82] Google Health, supra note 13.
[83] For more information on this app, see supra Section II.
[84] AI Dermatologist, *App Store Preview*, https://apps.apple.com/mt/app/ai-dermatologist-skin-scanner/id1511472597.
[85] Ada, *App Store Preview*, https://apps.apple.com/app/id1099986434?mt=8. For more information on Ada, see also supra Section II.
[86] The indications for use are usually included in the directions for use and part of the labeling requirements of over-the-counter devices; see 21 CFR § 801.61(b).
[87] US Food and Drug Admin., *De Novo Classification Request for ECG App*, 11, www.accessdata.fda.gov/cdrh_docs/reviews/DEN180044.pdf.
[88] 21 CFR § 801.109.
[89] Ashley ND Meyer et al., Patient Perspectives on the Usefulness of an Artificial Intelligence–Assisted Symptom Checker: Cross-Sectional Survey Study, 22 J. Med. Internet Res. e14679 (2020).
[90] Id.

and other companies have clear indications for use, and, thus, are likely *not* considered deceptive to device users and, thus, not "misleading" under FDCA section 502(a)(1).[91] Nevertheless, even if one cannot establish misleading labeling under the FDCA, there is this misperception among users that these apps are diagnostic tools.

This misperception can also be due, among other things, to the fact that many users may not read the labels. Labeling has many benefits, including helping patients and consumers to make more informed decisions, such as by informing them about the potential limitations of an app. But if users do not read the labels and accompanying statements and language like "this device is not intended to provide a diagnosis" is buried somewhere within them, using DTC medical self-diagnosing AI apps can become risky and jeopardize patient health. For example, imagine a patient uses an app like AI Dermatologist and screens herself for skin cancer. What if the AI misses a melanoma, and the patient does not see a doctor because she perceives the app as a diagnostic tool and believes everything is alright?

Regulators and stakeholders, such as app developers, need to better educate users of DTC medical self-diagnosing AI apps, for example, about the indications for use, whether the app has undergone FDA review, and its risks. With the right design, labels could help to achieve these goals. Several groups have already shown the benefits of "eye-popping" label designs, such as with the help of "nutrition" or "model facts" labels.[92] In particular for apps, there is a multitude of possible design options (e.g., pop-up notifications in plain language) to make users more effectively aware of important information.[93] Thus, regulators like the FDA could – with the help of stakeholders and label designers – develop user-friendly label design options for DTC medical self-diagnosing AI apps.[94] Once created, additional educational campaigns could be used to promote the proper reading of the label.[95] Human factors testing would also be helpful, particularly to see whether users understand when to seek medical help.[96]

In addition, as part of its regulatory review, the FDA should consider whether some of these apps should be prescribed by doctors rather than being offered directly to consumers over the counter.[97] The advantage could be that physicians could

---

[91] For more information on misleading labeling, see supra Section IV.A.
[92] See, for example, Mark P. Sendak et al., Presenting Machine Learning Model Information to Clinical End Users With Model Facts Labels, 3 npj Digit. Med., 41, 3 (2020); Andrea Coravos et al., Modernizing and Designing Evaluation Frameworks for Connected Sensor Technologies in Medicine, 3 npj Digit. Med., 37, 8 (2020). For more information, see Sara Gerke, supra note 68, at Section IV.B.
[93] See Sara Gerke, *Digital Home Health During the COVID-19 Pandemic* (1st edn.) 141, 160 (I. Glenn Cohen et al. eds., 2022).
[94] See also Gerke, supra note 68, at Section IV.B (suggesting "nutrition facts labels" as a promising label design for AI/ML-based medical devices).
[95] See id.
[96] See id.; Gerke et al., supra note 8, at 1178.
[97] See Babic et al., supra note 3, at 286; Gerke et al., supra note 3, at 1–2.

assist patients with the use of the app in question and point out material facts in the patient–physician conversation. A risk-based approach may likely be useful here to determine such "prescription apps."

Moreover, there is a general question of whether the FDA's current approach to practice enforcement discretion over many DTC medical self-diagnosing AI apps is convincing. Other countries have come up with different regulatory designs to better protect consumers. For example, Germany incentivizes manufacturers of even low-risk apps (i.e., class I devices) to produce high-quality apps that comply with specific standards (e.g., safety, privacy, etc.) by offering insurance coverage for their apps in return.[98] While the FDA does not currently seem to have the resources to execute a similar approach and review all DTC medical self-diagnosing AI apps, the flood of mobile health apps and all the associated issues,[99] ranging from poorly designed products to inadequate data protection, to labeling issues and misperceptions concerning their use, requires a new regulatory approach in the long run. A better option might be to create a new federal entity in the future that would be responsible for (at least the coordination of) all issues raised by mobile health apps, including DTC medical self-diagnosing AI apps, from regulation over privacy to enforcement actions and reimbursement.

ii Particular Issues of AI: From Bias to Adaptive Algorithms

Another labeling challenge that DTC medical self-diagnosing AI apps raise is that they are not only directly addressed to consumers without a licensed practitioner's supervision, but that they also operate using AI. Indeed, AI-based medical devices, including DTC medical self-diagnosing AI apps, are very different from traditional medical devices, such as simple tongue depressors.[100]

First, DTC medical self-diagnosing AI apps may use methods like deep learning that make them opaque (often dubbed "black boxes").[101] This means that the end users of the DTC medical self-diagnosing AI app (and likely even the app developers) cannot understand how the AI reached its recommendations and/or decisions. Second, DTC medical self-diagnosing AI apps may be biased. AI tools are prone to different types of bias, ranging from biased data fed to them (e.g., a skin cancer screening app that is largely trained on white skin images) to label choice biases (e.g., the algorithm uses an ineffective proxy for ground truth).[102] Third, DTC

---

[98] Gerke et al., supra note 3, at 1–2.
[99] See, for example, Babic et al., supra note 3; Gerke, supra note 68; Gerke & Rezaeikhonakdar, supra note 3; Simon et al., supra note 53.
[100] See Gerke, supra note 68, at Section III.B.
[101] See id. at Sections I.A.2 and III.B.2. For more information on deep learning, see, for example, Kun-Hsing Yu et al., Artificial Intelligence in Healthcare, 2 Nature Biomed. Eng'g 719, 720 (2018).
[102] See Gerke, supra note 68, at Section III.B.1; Ziad Obermeyer et al., Dissecting Racial Bias in an Algorithm Used to Manage the Health of Populations, 366 Science 447 (2019).

medical self-diagnosing AI apps may continuously learn from new data (e.g., health information, images, etc.) supplied by consumers using such apps (so-called "adaptive algorithms").[103] These apps are, thus, much more unpredictable in terms of their reliability and would preferably need constant monitoring to avoid introducing new biases, for example.[104] Lastly, the human–AI interaction is complex. In particular, DTC medical self-diagnosing AI apps that have unique characteristics as their outputs are often probabilistic and, thus, require consumers to incorporate the information received into their own beliefs.[105] In addition, DTC medical self-diagnosing AI apps are usually available for little money or even for free.[106] They can easily be used as often as consumers wish.[107] For example, consumers of a skin scanner app may decide to scan their moles many times (rather than just once), which increases the chance of false-positive results – that is, the app detects a potential disease that is not actually present.[108] Because consumers are typically risk-averse about their health outcomes, they may seek medical help when it is not needed, further overburdening the health care system and taking away limited resources from patients who are more likely to need them.[109]

Despite the differences between AI-based medical devices, such as DTC medical self-diagnosing AI apps, and traditional medical devices, such as simple tongue depressors, there are currently no labeling requirements for medical devices specifically aimed at AI (see Title 21 of the CFR).[110] The FDA has not yet developed any labeling standards for AI-based medical devices, let alone those directly addressed to consumers.[111] Thus, when creating the optimal design labels for DTC medical self-diagnosing AI apps,[112] the FDA should also focus on the content and use this opportunity to develop labeling standards for AI-based medical devices, including those that are DTC.[113]

It is crucial that consumers know and understand, among other things, the indications for use, model characteristics, and the risks and limitations of AI-based medical devices.[114] For example, users of DTC medical self-diagnosing AI apps should be made aware of the type of AI used (e.g., a black box, an adaptive algorithm, etc.) and the risks associated with using the app in question. They should also be informed about the various risks of bias and warned against blindly relying on the app's

---

[103] See Gerke, supra note 68, at Sections III.B.3.
[104] See Boris Babic et al., Algorithms on Regulatory Lockdown in Medicine, 366 Science 1202, 1204 (2019).
[105] Babic et al., supra note 3, at 284.
[106] Id. at 283.
[107] Id.
[108] Id. at 284–85.
[109] Id. at 283.
[110] See Gerke, supra note 68, at Section III.A.3.
[111] Id.
[112] See supra Section IV.B.i.
[113] See Gerke, supra note 68, at Section IV.A.
[114] Id.

outputs. Moreover, consumers should be alerted to the fact that increased testing can lead to an increased chance of false positives and generally be educated about the risks of false-positive and false-negative results, including when to see a doctor. A discussion with stakeholders needs to occur as soon as possible on the content of the labels of AI-based medical devices, including DTC medical self-diagnosing AI apps.[115] In particular, the language used for the labeling of these devices will need to be plain when they are DTC.[116]

V CONCLUSION

The digital health apps market is booming, and DTC medical self-diagnosing AI apps are emerging that help users to identify a disease or other condition based on entering, for instance, symptoms. Examples of such apps include Apple's ECG and irregular rhythm notification feature apps, Google's AI-powered dermatology tool, the AI Dermatologist: Skin Scanner app, and the symptom checker Ada. DTC medical self-diagnosing AI apps raise a multitude of challenges, including questions of labeling. What should labels directly addressed to consumers look like? What information should be included in such a label?

This chapter has argued that the FDA should develop user-friendly labeling standards for AI-based medical devices, including DTC medical self-diagnosing AI apps. For example, consumers need to be effectively informed about the type of AI used (e.g., a black box, an adaptive algorithm, etc.), the various risks of bias, the risks of false-positive and negative results, and when to seek medical help. In particular, the design of such labels needs to promote their reading so that users are made aware that the DTC medical self-diagnosing AI app in question is an "information-only" tool and is "not intended to provide a diagnosis." Additionally, some of these apps should be prescribed by a doctor, not offered over the counter, based on a risk-based approach so that the doctor can point out key facts. In the long run, it may also be helpful to create a new federal entity responsible for (at least the coordination of) all issues raised by mobile health apps, ranging from regulation to privacy to reimbursement.

---

[115] Id.
[116] Id. at 145, 160.

11

"Internet Plus Health Care" as an Impetus for China's Health System Reform[*]

Zhang Yi and Wang Chenguang

I INTRODUCTION

Digital technologies are integrated into all areas of life. The field of health is no exception. Some of the earliest uses of digital technology for health can be dated back to the 1960s.[1] In its 2005 resolution, the World Health Assembly (WHA) acknowledged the value of digital health and encouraged its member states to incorporate digital technologies into their health systems.[2] The important role of digital health was reiterated in the 2018 resolution, in which the WHA urged member states to prioritize the development and greater use of digital technologies for promoting equitable, affordable, and universal access to health for all.[3] During the COVID-19 pandemic, many countries have accelerated the utilization and development of digital health so as to guarantee the continued provision of health services with minimum in-person contact. As a result, there is now a growing consensus among countries that digital health has the potential to strengthen health systems and improve access to health.[4]

China embraced the new digital technology and attempted to use it for health as early as the 1990s.[5] As will be discussed in the following sections, the government, encouraged by the rapid development of internet technology in China, has made great efforts to support digital health in the past three decades for solving the problem of uneven geographic and health resources distribution. In 2018, the General Office of the State Council released an overarching document, entitled *Opinions on Promoting the Development of "Internet Plus Health Care,"* with an aim to promote

---

[*] Acknowledgement: This study is funded by the National Social Science Fund of China (no. 20CFX018).
[1] Maryam A. Hyder & Junaid Razzak, Telemedicine in the United States: An Introduction for Students and Residents, 11 J Med Internet Res. e20839 (2020).
[2] World Health Assembly Resolution 58.28 (May 25, 2005).
[3] World Health Assembly Resolution 71.7 (May 26, 2018).
[4] Ilona Kickbusch et al., The Lancet and Financial Times Commission on Governing Health Futures 2030: Growing up in a Digital World, 398 The Lancet 1727, 1727–76 (2021).
[5] Hui Cai et al., Application of Telemedicine in Gansu Province of China, 11 PLoS ONE e0158026 (2016).

the innovative integration of digital technologies into the health system as a means of improving equitable, affordable, and universal access to health.[6] The term "internet plus health care" (IPHC) was introduced as a blanket term to mean the use of digital technologies in support of the delivery of health care and health-related services, such as internet-based diagnosis, treatment, and medicine, and internet hospitals. In this article, we use IPHC as an umbrella term for general discussion and refer to specific terms such as internet-based diagnosis where necessary.

This article intends to provide an overview of the development of IPHC in China, from its origins to its widespread use during the COVID-19 pandemic, with focuses on its regulatory landscape and, particularly, on digital diagnosis. In Section III, we identify three major regulatory challenges to IPHC. We conclude with a few recommendations for furthering the development and implementation of IPHC in the post-COVID-19 era.

II LANDSCAPE ANALYSIS OF "INTERNET PLUS HEALTH CARE"

A *The Development of "Internet Plus Health Care" in China*

China's health system has long been criticized for its inequitable distribution of health resources and unequal access to health care. To address these deeply rooted problems, particularly the weak provision of primary health care at grassroots level, the Chinese central government initiated a new round of health reform in 2009. Digital technologies, across a range of measures, have been employed as a feasible modern channel for promoting equitable, affordable, and universal access to health for all.[7]

As far back as the 1990s, some of the first attempts at using digital technologies to improve access to quality health services were initiated. In 1988, the first remote consultation center was founded, which enabled the discussion of neurosurgery cases between Chinese and German hospitals via satellite.[8] With the development of information technology (IT), many medical institutions in urban areas started to establish remote consultation centers for exchanging knowledge and sharing experience with lower-level medical institutions. More importantly, the government made special efforts to support remote diagnosis in rural and mountainous regions as a means of addressing geographic barriers to access health care services. For example, many village clinics were equipped with computer terminals, despite the then poor IT infrastructure in these regions. As a result, a relatively robust physical and IT infrastructure was deployed for IPHC.

---

[6] General Office of the St. Council, 关于促进"互联网+医疗健康"发展的意见 [*Opinions on Promoting the Development of "Internet Plus Health Care"*] (April 28, 2018) www.gov.cn/zhengce/content/2018-04/28/content_5286645.htm.

[7] Yi Zhang, *Advancing the Right to Health Care in China: Towards Accountability* 162–66 (Intersentia 2019).

[8] Cai, supra note 5, at e0158026.

Since the beginning of the twenty-first century, a variety of regulatory and policy instruments have been adopted to facilitate the development of IPHC. With supportive policies, giant IT companies such as Alibaba and Tencent began to leverage their advances in digital technologies to establish online platforms and mobile applications to provide health-related services. In the meantime, public medical institutions also started to establish their own internet platforms. In 2012, the first public online hospital platform was founded in Guangdong Province.[9] Provinces with scarce health resources took the initiative to issue favorable policies to attract medical companies to set up internet hospitals as a means of improving access to health for their residents. The favorable policies and innovative technologies have stimulated the rapid development of IPHC during this period. In 2018, the aforementioned *Opinions on Promoting the Development of "Internet Plus Health Care"* (*Opinions*) document was released, with an overall aim to promote IPHC and guarantee equitable, affordable, and universal access to health for all. For quality assurance purposes, platform-based internet hospitals with no offline facilities were no longer allowed. In particular, this document required authorities to develop implementation rules and action plans for governing IPHC. A preliminary regulatory framework was thus established (see details in Section II.B). In September 2018, the National Health Commission (NHC) and the Government of Ningxia Hui Autonomous Region signed a strategic agreement to establish the first national IPHC pilot demonstration area, and in May 2019, the NHC signed similar agreements with another ten provinces and municipalities. In short, tremendous efforts had been made to promote the development and use of IPHC before the COVID-19 pandemic. However, the use of IPHC remained limited in practice due to regulatory restrictions and poor technical maintenance.

The COVID-19 outbreak has become a turning point in this area. The Chinese government has made several regulatory changes to make IPHC more widely used and to ensure the continued provision of health care when in-person services were not available during the health emergency. These changes include the relaxation of limitations on the scope of IPHC services and the expansion of health insurance coverage. The NHC also issued guidelines urging public hospitals to introduce or further develop IPHC as a means of relieving pressure on overloaded offline facilities. As a result, IPHC has obtained greater acceptance and its use surged during the pandemic. Statistical reports show that, by 2021, the number of licensed internet hospitals in China exceeded 1,600, while the user size of IPHC amounted to 298 million, accounting for 28.9 percent of all Internet users.[10]

---

[9] Dan Wu et al., Description of an Online Hospital Platform, China, 97 Bull World Health Org. 578, 578–79 (2019).

[10] China Internet Network Information Center, *The 49th Statistical Report on China's Internet Development* 57 (2022).

B Current Regulatory Framework of "Internet Plus Health Care"

In 2018, the NHC and National Administration of Traditional Chinese Medicine (NATCM) issued three consecutive normative documents for trial implementation as a response to the requirements of the *Opinions* mentioned above: The *Administrative Measures for Internet-based Diagnosis and Treatment* (AMIDT), *Administrative Measures for Internet Hospital* (AMIH), and *Administrative Regulations on Remote Medical Service* (ARRMS).[11] The AMIDT and ARRMS provide norms and guidelines for the provision of "internet-based diagnosis and treatment" and "remote diagnosis and treatment."[12] These two documents also make it clear that medical institutions and qualified health personnel are eligible to provide such services. According to the AMIH, there are two different operating models of internet hospitals. The AMIH stipulates stringent licensing and operation requirements for each type of internet hospital. It also sets out registration and practicing requirements for physicians who practice at internet hospitals.

In addition, as will be discussed further in Section III.C, the National Health Security Administration (NHSA) issued a series of guidance documents regarding the reimbursement and coverage of internet-based medical services during the pandemic, so as to make IPHC more widely affordable to patients.

Safety is at the heart of health care services, and internet-based diagnoses are no exception. After three years of trial implementation, the NHC published its *Regulatory Rules on Internet-based Diagnosis and Treatment* in March 2022, with an aim to reinforce governance structures and oversight mechanisms for internet-based diagnosis as well as the related medical institutions and health personnel.[13] The new *Regulatory Rules* set out guiding principles for the supervision of internet-based diagnosis and outlined explicit regulatory requirements for medical institutions providing such services. This regulatory document requires provincial health administrations to establish their own regulatory platforms and implement real-time supervision of medical institutions that provide internet-based diagnosis within their jurisdiction, to ensure that internet-based diagnoses meet the same quality as

---

[11] National Health Commission and National Administration of Traditional Chinese Medicine, 互联网诊疗管理办法（试行）[*Administrative Measures for Internet-based Diagnosis and Treatment (for Trial Implementation)*]; 互联网医院管理办法（试行）[*Administrative Measures for Internet Hospital (for Trial Implementation)*]; 远程医疗服务管理规范（试行）[*Administrative Regulations on Remote Medical Services (for Trial Implementation)*] (July 17, 2018) www.gov.cn/gongbao/content/2019/content_5358684.htm. Normative documents (i.e., "*guifanxing wenjian*") are promulgated by competent national authorities with general legal effects which are generally at the lower end of the hierarchy of Chinese laws. Many Chinese legal scholars regard normative documents as *soft law*.

[12] Given the theme of this book, internet-based treatment will not be further elaborated in this chapter.

[13] National Health Commission and National Administration of Traditional Chinese Medicine, 互联网诊疗监管细则（试行）[*Regulatory Rules on Internet-based Diagnosis and Treatment (for Trial Implementation)*] (February 8, 2022), www.nhc.gov.cn/yzygj/s3594q/202203/fa87807fa6e1411e9afeb82a4211f287.shtml.

TABLE 11.1 *A selection of legal and policy documents that impact IPHC*

2012	Administrative Measures for Remote Medical Care (for Trial Implementation)
2014	Opinions on Promoting Medical Institutes' Delivery of Remote Medical Services
2015	Guiding Opinions of the State Council on Actively Advancing the "Internet Plus Action"
2016	"Healthy China 2030" Plan
2017	Administrative Regulations on the Application of Electronic Medical Records (for Trial Implementation)
2018	Administrative Measures for Internet-based Diagnosis and Treatment (for Trial Implementation)
	Administrative Measures for Internet Hospital (for Trial Implementation)
	Administrative Measures on the Standards, Security and Services of National Healthcare Big Data (for Trial Implementation)
	Administrative Regulations on Remote Medical Service (for Trial Implementation)
	Opinions on Promoting the Development of "Internet Plus Health Care"
2019	Basic Medical and Health Care and Health Promotion Law
	Guiding Opinions on Improving the "Internet Plus" Medical Service Price and Medical Insurance Coverage Policy
2020	Guiding Opinions on Actively Promoting Medical Insurance Coverage of "Internet Plus" Medical Service
	Guiding Opinions on Promoting "Internet Plus" Medical Insurance Service during the Prevention and Control of COVID-19
	Information Security Technology-Guide for Health Data Security (GB/T 39725-2020)
2022	Law on Physicians
	Regulatory Rules on Internet-based Diagnosis and Treatment (for Trial Implementation)

in-person services. Built on these documents, a preliminary regulatory framework for IPHC has been created. Table 11.1 summarizes the legal and policy documents that have an impact on IPHC.

C Types of "Internet Plus Health Care" Services

i Internet-Based Diagnosis

Internet-based diagnosis, or online diagnosis, is a particular type of medical service precisely defined by the AMIDT as "a follow-up diagnosis for some common and chronic diseases delivered by a medical institution's own registered physicians via internet or other digital technologies."

Several restrictions in the AMIDT have been imposed on internet-based diagnosis for quality assurance purposes. First, only medical institutions with valid licenses and registered physicians with more than three years of independent clinical practice are qualified to provide internet-based diagnoses. Second, the scope of diseases is limited to certain common and chronic diseases. The types of chronic disease are determined by provincial health commissions and health security administrations, and generally include hypertension, coronary heart disease, diabetes, epilepsy, and so on. Third, a first diagnosis or diagnoses of sophisticated diseases are not permitted. This means that if a person becomes ill and in need of medical services, the person has to have a face-to-face diagnosis first. A physician in an offline hospital should diagnose that the patient has a common or chronic disease, then follow-up diagnoses and treatment can be given online. First diagnoses or patients with no medical records are not eligible for an internet-based diagnosis. Requiring an in-person diagnosis for a first diagnosis is a particular procedural and institutional requirement for safety assurance in the field of digital health.

ii Remote Diagnosis

In the Chinese context, remote diagnosis is a type of medical service provided by two or more medical institutions that are generally in the same medical consortium. According to the ARRMS, one medical institution can invite another to provide technical support for the diagnosis of its patients by means of digital technologies. In practice, normally the inviter is a community-level medical institution that has a close partnership (e.g., medical consortium) with the invitee, which, in most cases, is a top-tier medical institution. The invited medical institution will provide remote diagnosis on the basis of physical examinations and diagnostic tests, such as X-ray, ultrasound, and electrocardiogram, conducted by the inviting institution. For example, a township-level medical center may be equipped with an X-ray unit but lack the expertise to diagnose on the basis of an X-ray film. If a person living in this kind of rural area breaks a leg, they can still visit the center, the physician there will upload the X-ray film to the invited medical institution, and the diagnosis will be conducted remotely. If the center is equipped with a portable X-ray unit, then the patient can be diagnosed at home. Remote medical services promote the intra-group sharing of expertise and ensure that patients living in rural and remote areas have access to the same standards of medical care as those living in urban areas.

iii Online Consultation

Online consultation is the most common type of IPHC provided for first-visit patients with common conditions. Patients can consult physicians or other health professionals at any location about personal medical or psychiatric conditions, or simply seek advice on routine health management, healthy lifestyle, and so on through digital technologies. Online consultation enables patients to receive ongoing care where face-to-face or internet-based diagnoses are not necessary or easily accessible. It is worth pointing out that, while online consultation has much in common with online diagnosis, it lies outside the scope of internet-based diagnosis in the Chinese context. If an online consultation involves diagnosis-making or drug prescriptions, it is indeed classed as an internet-based diagnosis.

Due to space constraints, other IPHC services, such as online health management, electronic medical records management, appointment scheduling, and online payment are not elaborated here.

III REMAINING CHALLENGES

Despite considerable progress, the widespread implementation of IPHC remains difficult in practice. Regulatory challenges include restrictions on internet-based diagnosis, physicians practicing at multiple medical institutions, and medical insurance coverage and reimbursement. Technology-related barriers include digital literacy and internet infrastructure, among others. Due to space constraints, the following sections focus on the regulatory challenges.

A *Restrictions on Internet-Based Diagnosis*

As internet-based diagnosis is a brand-new model of medical service delivery, the NHC has taken a deliberate approach and limited it to "follow-up" diagnoses for "common diseases" and "chronic diseases" in the interests of patient safety and quality of care. Yet, after years of trial implementation, this restriction has raised considerable controversy.

First, the definition and scope of common and chronic diseases is not clear. The AMIDT stipulates that internet-based diagnosis is restricted to "certain" common and chronic diseases, without specifying which diseases fall within that scope. Even though detailed implementation plans of the AMIDT were formulated by provincial health administrations, the wording remained the same. In real practice, the interpretation of this guidance depends largely on the discretion of physicians due to the lack of legal clarity.

Second, it is difficult to verify whether a common or chronic disease was first diagnosed in an offline hospital. According to the AMIDT and other provincial implementation plans, internet hospitals should request to see medical records directly from patients or from other medical institutions with patients' authorization before diagnosis. Yet, for information security, internet hospitals are less likely to access other institutions' EMR databases, unless there is a preexisting partnership (e.g., a medical consortium). Patients, in particular the elderly, may neither reserve paper medical records nor understand how to upload their records onto the Internet. In practice, physicians collect patient medical records simply to fulfil regulatory requirements. It is not feasible for them to authenticate patients' first in-person diagnoses. During the COVID-19 emergency, the NHC lifted the requirement for first in-person diagnoses. Patients with suspected coronavirus symptoms would have an internet-based diagnosis before going to the hospital. This gives rise to the question: Is it still necessary to prohibit internet hospitals from providing a first diagnosis, even just for common or chronic diseases?

After many years of IPHC development, there are plenty of discussions in academia and industry about relaxing the restrictions on the scope of internet-based diagnosis. Arguably, internet hospitals have an obvious limitation: Medical services, such as physical examinations and diagnostic tests, must be conducted in-person in offline hospitals. Therefore, because of quality and safety concerns, strict measures have been taken to regulate the operation of internet hospitals. Prior to the COVID-19 pandemic, internet hospitals just served as a supplement to offline hospitals. Yet the demand for IPHC significantly increased during the health emergency. As such, national and provincial health administrations have issued a number of guidance documents to provide temporary regulatory flexibility, so as to make internet hospitals more widely accessible. Internet hospitals have now become a part of mainstream medical service delivery, and the NHC, in its newly released *National Health Informatization Program in the Fourteenth Five-year Plan*, intends to set up electronic health files and electronic medical records for every citizen. These provide a good opportunity to conduct further research on the potential and proper trades-offs between convenience of access to health care and safety of service and privacy, while loosening the regulations on internet-based diagnosis.

B *Physician Multi-site Practicing*

Physician multi-site practicing (PMP) is expected to advance the implementation of IPHC.[14] PMP is designed as a mechanism to address health professional shortages and improve efficient and equitable allocation of medical resources.[15] For example, as Haodaifu ("good doctor" in Mandarin) Online (one of the biggest platform-based internet hospitals in China) claims, there are more than 240,000 physicians registered on its platform, more than 70 percent of whom are from tertiary hospitals across the country.[16] PMP makes it possible for patients living in remote rural areas to receive internet-based diagnoses provided by physicians in big cities, such as Beijing and Shanghai, at home.

---

[14] Physician multi-site practicing refers to physicians practicing at various medical institutions. Before China's new round of health system reforms in 2009, a physician could only register and practice at one medical institution, which in most cases would be a public medical institution. To this extent, physicians are often regarded as quasi-civil servants. After the reforms, physicians were encouraged to register at one primary medical institution and practice at different institutions as a means to address the shortage of human resources in health care.

[15] Imam M. Xierali, Physician Multisite Practicing: Impact on Access to Care, 31 J. of Am. Bd. of Fam. Med. 260, 260–69 (2018).

[16] China has a three-tiered medical service delivery system with primary health centers providing primary health care, secondary hospitals providing general outpatient and inpatient services, and tertiary comprehensive hospitals providing high-level specialized outpatient and inpatient services. See Zhang, supra note 7, at 80.

PMP needs regulatory clarification. Since the new round of health system reforms in 2009, the Chinese government has issued various guidance documents to encourage physicians to practice at multiple sites. In 2017, the *Administrative Measures for the Registration of Practicing Medical Doctors* took effect and released limitations on the number and geographic location of medical institutions at which a physician is permitted to practice.[17] More importantly, the measures simplified the registration procedures for PMP. Approval from the primary practice institution is no longer necessary. Nevertheless, this requirement was once again included in the 2018 *Administrative Measures for Internet-based Diagnosis and Treatment*. As a result, physicians have to obtain the approval from their primary practice institution before practicing at any internet hospital. Therefore, further clarification is needed regarding the regulation of PMP.

To a lesser extent, even though prior approval would not be necessary for multi-practicing online, it does not mean that the primary practice institution has no de facto discretion when it comes to PMP. In China, most physicians are hired by medical institutions (in most instances their primary practice institution) and are, thus, subject to the personnel management of the institution. Physicians are the most valuable medical resources and the core competence of any medical institution. Arguably, PMP would have a considerable impact on the operation of the primary practice institution. Also, given the high workload in public medical institutions and especially tertiary hospitals, some institutions may take administrative measures to restrict de facto PMP, except for in their affiliated online or offline institutions.

There are also concerns over the affordability and quality of care regarding PMP. On the one hand, prices for medical services provided by public medical institutions, whether online or offline, are capped by governments, while those provided by non-public medical institutions (e.g., platform-based internet hospitals) are self-determined. In addition, as will be discussed further in the next section, medical services provided by non-public medical institutions are generally not covered by the country's mandatory basic medical insurance (BMI) schemes, unless these institutions choose to negotiate prices and sign contracts with local health insurance bureaus (i.e., insurers).[18] Consequently, the service fees charged by non-public medical institutions are higher than public ones and patients have to pay all the service fees out-of-pocket, unless the patient has extra commercial insurance to cover all or parts of the expenses. For instance, for the same specialist, the outpatient service fee charged by the aforementioned Haodaifu Online could be ten times higher than that of the tertiary hospital. On the other hand, physicians are better

---

[17] National Health and Family Planning Commission, 医师执业注册管理办法 [*Administrative Measures for the Registration of Practicing Medical Doctors*] (February 28, 2017, effective April 1, 2017) www.nhc.gov.cn/cms-search/xxgk/getManuscriptXxgk.htm?id=ad4008212c48418199d2d613087d7977.

[18] "Basic medical insurance" is the mandatory insurance scheme in China which covers over 95 percent of the entire population. See Zhang, supra note 7, at 166.

paid under this circumstance. Financial incentives could motivate them to allocate more (free) time to platform-based internet hospitals, and waiting times for hospital admission would, thus, be significantly reduced. However, there is a dilemma for patients: PMP at platform-based internet hospitals makes medical services provided by specialists more accessible, yet less affordable. In other words, patients need to pay more money in exchange for a shorter waiting time for specialist medical services. PMP may also have a negative impact on the quality of care provided by the specialist's primary practice institution. Therefore, national and provincial health administrations have made some principal guidelines on PMP, requiring physicians to give priority to the work at their primary practice institution. It would thus be important for policy makers to consider complementary measures to encourage as well as to regulate PMP, so as to further improve the accessibility, affordability and quality of health care.

C Affordability of IPHC

Affordability is one of the key determinants of IPHC. The NHSA has, therefore, issued a series of policies to make IPHC more affordable to patients. In 2019, the NHSA announced for the first time that all eligible "internet plus" medical services would gradually be covered by medical insurance in the *Guiding Opinions on Improving the "Internet Plus" Medical Service Price and Medical Insurance Coverage Policy*.[19] This document authorizes provincial health insurance bureaus to set prices for internet-based diagnoses and other medical services provided by public medical institutions, while non-public medical institutions are allowed to set their own service prices. Nevertheless, prior to the COVID-19 pandemic, internet-based medical services had not started to be covered by BMI schemes.

In response to the COVID-19 outbreak, the NHSA and NHC issued their *Guiding Opinions on Promoting "Internet Plus" Medical Insurance Service during the Prevention and Control of COVID-19*, expanding the BMI coverage to make internet-based diagnosis and other medical services more affordable.[20] The pricing policy remains unchanged in this guidance document. BMI programs would cover and reimburse internet-based diagnoses for common and chronic diseases provided by designated public medical institutions that voluntarily signed a supplementary contract with local health insurance bureaus. Internet-based diagnoses provided by designated non-public medical institutions would also be reimbursed, but at the

---

[19] National Health Security Administration, 关于完善"互联网＋"医疗服务价格和医保支付政策的指导意 [*Guiding Opinions on Improving the "Internet Plus" Medical Service Price and Medical Insurance Coverage Policy*] (August 30, 2019), www.nhsa.gov.cn/art/2019/8/30/art_14_1705.html.

[20] National Health Security Administration and National Health Commission, 关于推进新冠肺炎疫情防控期间开展"互联网＋"医保服务的指导意见 [*Guiding Opinions on Promoting "Internet Plus" Medical Insurance Services during the Prevention and Control of COVID-19*] (March 2, 2020), www.nhsa.gov.cn/art/2020/3/2/art_71_2753.html.

same rate as public medical institutions if non-public institutions choose to provide such services. Multiple provinces and municipalities have also taken actions to temporarily broaden provincial BMI schemes to cover internet-based diagnoses, as well as expand the types of internet hospitals which may provide such services.

Several months later, the NHSA issued another document, *Guiding Opinions on Actively Promoting Medical Insurance Coverage of "Internet Plus" Medical Service*, establishing concrete measures to promote the reimbursement and coverage of internet-based medical services.[21] The new *Guiding Opinions* make clear that a voluntary supplementary contract between designated medical institutions and local health insurance bureaus is a prerequisite for BMI coverage. Payment parity is granted, which means that internet-based diagnoses will be reimbursed at the same rate as the equivalent in-person services provided by public medical institutions offline. However, this document does not require service parity. Provincial health insurance bureaus are authorized to determine the coverage of services in their own insurance plans. Research suggests that twenty-one Chinese provinces have so far expanded their provincial BMI coverage of internet-based diagnoses, while the scope of coverage varies from province to province.[22] In addition, as just explained, non-public medical institutions could set their own pricing for medical services, no matter whether they are provided online or offline. Such services will not be covered nor reimbursed by BMI schemes, unless these institutions choose to negotiate prices and sign contracts with local health insurance bureaus.[23]

To sum up, affordability was, is, and may still be a major barrier for the utilization of IPHC. Although the NHSA has issued a number of polices to expand coverage, most of them only provide principal guidelines, without an integrated regulatory framework for "internet plus" health insurance coverage and reimbursement.

IV CONCLUSION: THE WAY FORWARD

IPHC has proven to be critical and full of potential for strengthening the Chinese health system, transforming health care services, and improving equitable, affordable, and universal access to health. The Chinese government has taken a variety of measures to accelerate the utilization of IPHC before, during, and after COVID-19, such as the establishment and revision of regulations, the removal of restrictions, and adjustments to reimbursement mechanisms. However, gaps remain in the legal and regulatory framework for governing the use of IPHC. Many of the reimbursement

---

[21] National Health Security Administration, 关于积极推进"互联网+"医疗服务医保支付工作的指导意见 [*Guiding Opinions on Actively Promoting Medical Insurance Coverage of "Internet Plus" Medical Services*] (November 2, 2020), www.nhsa.gov.cn/art/2020/11/2/art_37_3801.html.
[22] Cui Wenbin et al.,"互联网+"医疗服务纳入医保支付范围研究 [*Research on "Internet +" Medical Service Included in Medical Insurance Reimbursement*], 3 中国医院 4–6 (2020).
[23] Xinfa Zhou & Lu Chen, Digital Health Care in China and Access for Older People, 12 Lancet Public Health e873, e873–74 (2021).

mechanisms have been established as exceptions rather than permanent changes. Also, most IPHC-related regulations are still in trial the phases of implementation. Therefore, it is necessary to develop a clear legal and regulatory framework for supporting the development and sustained use of IPHC, and for eventually developing an "internet plus" health ecosystem in the post-COVID-19 era. Additional research on the potential trades-offs in loosening the regulations on internet-based diagnoses, as well as PMP, is needed. In addition, the use of digital technologies for health helps to improve geographic access to health, yet it may exacerbate other inequalities due to digital literacy. For example, the elderly living alone face greater challenges when it comes to using digital technologies to access internet hospitals. Further research should pay particular attention to the special needs of vulnerable groups and focus on how to improve their digital literacy and access to the Internet. Also, additional studies on how to strike the balance between data sharing and privacy protection are much needed.

PART IV

Reimbursement Considerations for Digital Home Health

Julia Adler-Milstein

INTRODUCTION

Health care reimbursement is complex. At its core, reimbursement requires defining both the unit that is the basis of payment and the amount. However, health care reimbursement layers on top of this adjustments for varied factors, such as the setting of care, differences in local labor costs, severity of the patient population, the degree of technology involved, and myriad others. Further, in the USA, payers are fragmented, with each defining their own approach to these decisions. The COVID-19 pandemic ushered in a new era in which digitally enabled home-based care is a mainstream modality. However, the approach to reimbursement for this care remains a work-in-progress, with significant unanswered questions that will determine whether this modality expands or disappears if it is determined to be financially unsustainable.

It is important to acknowledge that reimbursement is only a challenge because of the continued reliance on a fee-for-service approach. Under a fully capitated approach, the risk-bearing entity would deploy the mix of care modalities most optimally suited to care for their population within the per member per year fee they receive. Indeed, a key opportunity for ongoing work is to understand the relationships between the payment model and level of use of digitally enabled home-based care. However, under today's system that uses a mix of payment models, whether and how digitally enabled home-based care is reimbursed is an open question and one that will shape future offerings.

Zawada and colleagues describe their efforts at Mayo Clinic to build (and then expand under pandemic-relaxed regulations) a home hospital program that allows patients to shift to home-based care for lower-acuity conditions. Beyond the value from understanding in detail how the model works, and which specific regulatory relaxations allowed its expansion, the authors emphasize the critical need to maintain current levels of payment parity – in other words, patients in the hospital at home are reimbursed at the same level as if they were in the inpatient setting. While this makes sense at a high level (i.e., lower reimbursement would naturally create incentives to decrease use in favor of keeping people in the hospital), more deeply it raises the question of whether the cost structure of the hospital at home is fundamentally different from the inpatient cost structure. While hospital at home does not need to maintain the same level of physical infrastructure, the technology and staffing needs are arguably greater (e.g., home health visits by nurses, telemedicine consultations by physicians, remote monitoring technologies). Ultimately, given the many benefits of the hospital-at-home model described by Zawada and colleagues (including increased access, lower utilization, better understanding of the home environment and social determinants of health, and smoother transitions to post-acute care), they make a strong case for maintaining payment parity (as well as continuing to waive regulatory barriers) – at least until it becomes clear whether there are major differences in terms of cost structure.

Huber and Sklar's chapter offers a similar assessment but in the broader context of home and community-based services (HCBS) that allow older adults to reside at home as opposed to in an institutional setting, such as a skilled nursing facility. It has long been known that the demand for HCBS far outpaces supply. Huber and Sklar make the argument that digitally enabled HCBS could alleviate this imbalance by allowing models of HCBS that more readily scale. Unlike the hospital-at-home model that is in current use, digitally enabled HCBSs are still largely conceptual. The technologies exist but the organizations delivering HCBS – many of which focus on custodial care – have not yet widely embraced them. Therefore, in their chapter, Huber and Sklar suggest the need to use reimbursement as a motivator, coupled with regulatory accommodations, better evidence on benefits, and an approach to ensure consent and the security of the data that would be shared under digital approaches. Ultimately, it seems unclear whether reimbursement is the key lever, as the technologies (with their associated costs) are highly varied. If digitally enabled HCBS could be delivered to more individuals at a lower cost, then today's reimbursement environment should accommodate this. Given that this is not happening, it suggests instead that the costs are too high and/or that the benefits are too uncertain. Nonetheless, with such an urgent need to expand HCBS capacity, there is an argument for experimentation with payment models that would specifically incentivize digitally enabled HCBS alongside an assessment of the costs and benefits to inform future reimbursement policy.

Van Delm's chapter takes the topic of reimbursement for digitally enabled care – specifically telemedicine – to the European Union (EU) context. With frequent instances of individuals living in (or traveling to) an EU country that is not their home and, vice versa, the opportunity for telemedicine to be delivered by a person or entity based outside the home country, there are myriad situations in which payment parity must be considered. As stated by Van Delm, "To safeguard the national social security systems, the EU legal framework strictly coordinates the reimbursement options for cross-border care, without touching upon the question of which type of health care falls within patients' basket of health care. It clarifies which member state bears the financial burden for the cross-border care, and when the patient must request prior authorisation to qualify for reimbursement." Unfortunately, two different legal bases for claiming reimbursement for cross-border care have emerged within the EU and they are not in sync. Van Delm explains these differences, including the many conditions under which cross-border care may be delivered. For some dimensions one is more favorable and for other dimensions, it is flipped. Most concerning is her argument that these differences create disincentives for the development and use of telemedicine across EU borders, despite it being a lower-cost option. Taken together, her chapter makes a strong case for a single, harmonized EU policy to secure the ongoing use of cross-border telemedicine in the EU.

12

A Pathway for High-Value Home Hospital Care in the United States

Statutory, Reimbursement, and Cybersecurity Strategies in the Age of Hybrid Care

Stephanie Zawada, Nels Paulson, Margaret Paulson, Michael Maniaci, and Bart Demaerschalk

I INTRODUCTION

Prior to the emergence of modern health insurance programs after World War I, house calls were standard practice for physicians in the United States.[1] The end of the twentieth century saw a resurgence of interest in health care at home, partly fueled by the expansion of home health services by Medicare.[2] By the 1990s, pilot hospital-at-home (H@H) programs demonstrated the potential to provide similar levels of inpatient care at home while decreasing costs.[3]

Although before 2020 most payers offered plans covering home health services for older adults, a population that experiences a disproportionate share of hospitalizations, only a handful of hospitals around the country offered H@H programs.[4] Among those were world-renowned health systems, like Brigham and Women's Hospital and the Johns Hopkins Hospital, capable of securing pilot study funding to demonstrate the safety and effectiveness of their individual H@H models. In turn, these studies allowed the programs to receive reimbursement for H@H services from the Centers for Medicare & Medicaid Services (CMS), the federal entity responsible for setting health care service costs and coverage under the nation's

---

[1] Bruce Leff & John R. Burton, The Future History of Home Care and Physician House Calls in the United States, 56 J. Gerontology: Series A M603–08 (2001).
[2] Nelda McCall et al., Utilization of Home Health Services Before and After the Balanced Budget Act of 1997: What Were the Initial Effects?, 38 Health Serv. Rsch. 85–106 (2003).
[3] Sasha Shepperd et al., Avoiding Hospital Admission Through Provision of Hospital Care at Home: A Systematic Review and Meta-analysis of Individual Patient Data, 180 Can. Med. Ass'n J. 175–82 (2009).
[4] Alexander L. Janus & John Ermisch, Who Pays for Home Care? A Study of Nationally Representative Data on Disabled Older Americans, 15 BMC Health Servs. Rsch. (2015); Maureen Anthony, Hospital-at-Home, 39 Home Healthcare Now 127 (2021).

insurance program for adults ages 65 and older.[5] Since 2005, the majority of H@H programs have demonstrated noninferior or superior outcomes to in-hospital care;[6] however, the widescale implementation of H@H by community and regional hospitals remained elusive, chiefly due to a lack of coverage and guaranteed reimbursement under the Medicare fee-for-service (FFS) program.[7] It is estimated that only a few thousand patients had received care through the limited number of H@H programs in the USA before 2020.[8]

According to the CMS's Conditions of Participation, Medicare-certified hospitals must staff nurses 24/7 and on-site to be eligible for the reimbursement of services provided to hospitalized patients. During the COVID-19 Public Health Emergency (PHE), the CMS solicited applications from hospitals to deliver inpatient-level care at home under its temporary Acute Hospital Care at Home (AHCaH) waiver, which lifts the on-premises requirement for nurses providing acute care.[9] From its launch in November 2020 through October 2021, the waiver enabled H@H programs to care for 1,878 patients in thirty-three states.[10] As of March 2023, the program has expanded to thirty-seven states at 123 health systems and 277 hospitals.[11] This waiver allowed hospitals to partner with software platforms and vendors to develop care pathways that blended in-person, telehealth, and remote patient monitoring (RPM) services and were adjusted to reflect the local and geographic constraints associated with a hospital's location.

Today, hospitals are negotiating with private payers to develop H@H models beyond the scope of the CMS's H@H definition, which exclusively focuses on acute care.[12] However, there are many concerns about the future viability of H@H

---

[5] Alisa L. Niksch, Hospital at Home: Transformation of an Old Model with Digital Technology, in Leveraging Technology as a Response to the COVID-19 Pandemic, 1, 18 (Harry Pappasv and Paul Frisch eds., 2022).

[6] Man Qing Leong et al., Comparison of Hospital-at-Home Models: A Systematic Review of Reviews, 11 *BMJ Open* (2021).

[7] Linda V. DeCherrie et al., Hospital at Home services: An Inventory of Fee-for-service Payments to Inform Medicare Reimbursement, 69 J. Am. Geriatrics Soc'y 1982–92 (2021); Shikha Garg et al., Hospitalization Rates and Characteristics of Patients Hospitalized with Laboratory-Confirmed Coronavirus Disease 2019 – COVID-NET, 14 States, March 1–30, 2020, 69 MMWR Morbidity and Mortality Weekly Report, 458–64 (2020); Marilyn Moon, What Medicare Has Meant to Older Americans, 18 Health Care Financing Rev. 49–59 (1996); Sarah Klein et al., The Hospital at Home Model: Bringing Hospital-Level Care to the Patient, *Commonwealth Fund* (August 22, 2016), www.commonwealthfund.org/publications/case-study/2016/aug/hospital-home-model-bringing-hospital-level-care-patient.

[8] Am. Hosp. Ass'n, *Hospital at Home* (2023), www.aha.org/hospitalathome.

[9] Ctr. to Advance Palliative Care, *Acute Hospital Care at Home Frequently Asked Questions*, www.capc.org/documents/download/882/.

[10] Douglas V. Clarke et al., Acute Hospital Care at Home: The CMS Waiver Experience, *NEJM Catalyst Innovations in Care Delivery* (December 7, 2021), https://catalyst.nejm.org/doi/full/10.1056/CAT.21.0338.

[11] Eli Adashi et al., Hospital at Home Receives a New Lease on Life: A Promising if Uncertain Future, 136 Am. J. Med. 958–59 (2023).

[12] Pamela Pelizzari et al., Hospital At Home Is Not Just For Hospitals, *Health Affs. Forefront* (May 24, 2022), doi:10.1377/forefront.20220520.712735.

programs. Notably, the effectiveness of these models and their patient eligibility criteria are tied to the technology-enabled services they deliver, including telehealth and RPM.[13] While numerous federal flexibilities for telehealth remain temporarily waived and all fifty states have expanded access to telehealth services, it is unclear which services will secure permanent reimbursement in the future. Though patient satisfaction with H@H and telehealth services remains uniquely high, questions about the long-term effectiveness of these pandemic-era initiatives in the context of value-based care, defined as care that improves patient health outcomes, remain.[14]

Based on our experiences at Mayo Clinic, we recommend that H@H care be integrated into the continuum of care, rather than delivered as a separate instance of care, after which patients are traditionally discharged to primary care. Beyond the AHCaH waiver, a flexible telehealth policy framework that allows providers to tailor care plans balancing patient need and convenience is vital to ensuring H@H programs yield high-value outcomes. This approach allows at-home patients recovering from an acute episode to receive post-acute care linked to improved patient outcomes, including rehabilitation, medication management, and patient education, via telehealth. Facilitating a gradual transition to primary care, the H@H model with subsequent hybrid services allows clinicians to monitor and intervene with timelier services during the post-acute period, thereby preventing adverse events and avoidable readmissions.

II HOW THE AHCAH WAIVER AND RELATED FLEXIBILITIES FACILITATED THE CONTINUUM OF CARE

Although the delivery of care at home had grown increasingly popular in the years before the pandemic, reimbursement uncertainty and low patient and provider willingness to use such services limited their adoption.[15] Restrictive regulations, such as the CMS's explicit categorization of telephones as a non-eligible tool for telehealth, also limited patient options.[16] Furthermore, while numerous studies found that RPM of real-time vital signs and symptoms could reduce costs and improve outcomes, its implementation was limited and complicated by the need to integrate device data with electronic health records.[17] Recognizing the technical difficulties associated

---

[13] Bruce Leff et al., A Research Agenda for Hospital at Home, 70 J. Am. Geriatric Soc'y 1060–69 (2022).
[14] NEJM Catalyst, What Is Value-based Healthcare?, NEJM Catalyst: Innovations in Care Delivery (January 1, 2017), https://catalyst.nejm.org/doi/full/10.1056/CAT.17.0558.
[15] Asim Kichloo et al., Telemedicine, the Current COVID-19 Pandemic and the Future: A Narrative Review and Perspectives Moving Forward in the USA, 8 Fam. Med. & Cmty. Health, 3 (2020).
[16] Ross D'Emanuele, Medicare Payment Rules Changed to Allow Broad Use of Remote Communications Technology, JDSupra (April 8, 2020), www.jdsupra.com/legalnews/medicare-payment-rules-changed-to-allow-93032/.
[17] Catherine Dinh-Le et al., Wearable Health Technology and Electronic Health Record Integration: Scoping Review and Future Directions, 7 JMIR Mhealth Uhealth 9 (2019), https://mhealth.jmir.org/2019/9/e12861.

TABLE 12.1 *Frequent H@H program condition inclusion criteria*

Common acute phase conditions treated in H@H programs (Levine et al., 2020)	
Chronic kidney disease with volume overflow	Atrial fibrillation with rapid ventricular response
Urinary tract infection	Hypertension urgency
Pneumonia	Anticoagulation needs
Heart failure	Diabetes complications
Asthma	Gout flare
COPD	Cellulitis

with delivering care remotely, the Secretary of Health and Human Services (HHS) temporarily waived Health Insurance Portability and Accountability Act (HIPAA) sanctions and penalties for the PHE, allowing providers to use any software available to offer telehealth services, including those delivered in H@H.[18]

With the 2020 establishment of the AHCaH waiver, a hospital could launch an H@H program with guaranteed reimbursement equal to traditional in-hospital payment for acute care services delivered at a patient's home, provided that 24/7 monitoring by nurses was completed using telehealth and RPM.[19] To be eligible for enrolment in a hospital's H@H program under this waiver, patients first need to be admitted to a hospital and assessed by an on-site physician. The inclusion criteria for admission consider a range of chronic conditions presenting in an acute episode, that is, one that qualifies for inpatient-level care, to ensure a patient's status is sufficiently stable for at-home care (Table 12.1).[20]

Additional personal mobility, environmental, and social screening measures are implemented on a site-by-site basis. After a carefully evaluated patient enrols in H@H, hospitals must provide twice daily in-person visits from a registered nurse or paramedic at the patient's home and deliver daily telehealth evaluations by a clinician.[21] With the AHCaH waiver, all Medicaid and Medicare patients, as well as dually eligible beneficiaries, qualified for consideration of H@H care during the PHE.[22]

---

[18] HHS Office for Civil Rights (OCR), *Notification of Enforcement Discretion for Telehealth Remote Communications During the COVID-19 Nationwide Public Health Emergency*, US Dep't of Health and Hum. Servs. (2021), www.hhs.gov/hipaa/for-professionals/special-topics/emergency-preparedness/notification-enforcement-discretion-telehealth/index.html.

[19] Andis Robeznieks, Tech that Provides High-acuity Home Care Gets High-profile Boost, *Am. Med. Ass'n* (June 23, 2021), www.ama-assn.org/practice-management/digital/tech-provides-high-acuity-home-care-gets-high-profile-boost.

[20] David M. Levine et al., Hospital-Level Care at Home for Acutely Ill Adults: A Randomized Controlled Trial, 172 Annals Internal Med. 77–85 (2018).

[21] Press Release, CMS, *CMS Announces Comprehensive Strategy to Enhance Hospital Capacity Amid COVID-19 Surge* (November 25, 2020), www.cms.gov/newsroom/press-releases/cms-announces-comprehensive-strategy-enhance-hospital-capacity-amid-covid-19-surge.

[22] Clarke et al., supra note 10.

Patients in the prehospitalized, restorative (postacute) or ambulatory phases of care are not eligible for H@H care reimbursed under the AHCaH waiver; however, H@H models negotiated for reimbursement with private payers, like Presbyterian Health's program under Medicare Advantage, are not restricted to acute care.[23] Likewise, some individual hospitals using the AHCaH waiver to cover H@H acute services have designed postacute models of care that combine hybrid services, like at-home rehabilitation therapy and telehealth medication management visits, for different insurance populations, subject to state regulations governing home health and telehealth services.[24]

Before the pandemic, multiple regulatory barriers restricted access to telehealth services for Medicare beneficiaries at home. Among these were CMS requirements that patients reside in rural areas and be physically present at a designated site to receive telehealth services eligible for reimbursement. For the PHE, the CMS waived these requirements, allowed payment parity for telehealth, and expanded its list of services eligible for telehealth.[25] Policies regulating telehealth and H@H programs also vary by state, insurance coverage, and program. In some states, policies apply to both public and private payers delivering care to patients in-state, while in other states there are separate regulatory frameworks for telehealth delivered to public versus private beneficiaries.[26] During the pandemic, all fifty states and the District of Columbia introduced reforms to expand access to telehealth at home.[27] For instance, states introduced statutory flexibilities to incorporate a broader range of devices eligible for telehealth (Table 12.2). The nation's leading private payer plans also expanded telehealth access by offering payment parity or cost-sharing waivers.[28]

Combined with the AHCaH waiver, these telehealth flexibilities freed clinical care teams to identify optimal software and monitoring devices to integrate into care pathways for H@H patients in the acute as well as postacute phases. The design of hybrid care models that deliver H@H as a part of the continuum of care, providing services beyond the scope of acute care, was guided by relevant state and federal telehealth and RPM flexibilities (Table 12.3).

---

[23] Klein et al., supra note 7.
[24] Nels Paulson et al., *Why US Patients Declined Hospital-at-Home during the COVID-19 Public Health Emergency: An Exploratory Mixed Methods Study*, 10 J. Patient Exp. 23743735231189354 (2023).
[25] Press Release, CMS, *Trump Administration Makes Sweeping Regulatory Changes to Help US Healthcare System Address COVID-19 Patient Surge* (March 30, 2020), www.cms.gov/newsroom/press-releases/trump-administration-makes-sweeping-regulatory-changes-help-us-healthcare-system-address-covid-19.
[26] Ctr. for Connected Health Pol'y, *An Analysis of Private Payer Telehealth Coverage During the COVID-19 Pandemic* (2021), www.cchpca.org/2021/04/Private-Payer-Telehealth-Coverage-Reportfinal.pdf.
[27] *US States and Territories Modifying Requirements for Telehealth in Response to COVID-19*, Fed'n of State Med. Bds. (2022), www.fsmb.org/siteassets/advocacy/pdf/states-waiving-licensure-requirements-for-telehealth-in-response-to-covid-19.pdf.
[28] Ctr. for Connected Health Pol'y, supra note 26.

TABLE 12.2 *Example telehealth use cases*

Telehealth modality	Technology example
Asynchronous/Store-and-forward	Sharing patient images via a HIPAA-secure patient portal
Synchronous	Videoconference with provider and patient
Remote patient monitoring (RPM)	Wireless ECG streams patient data to provider
Autonomous	Smartphone app AI chatbot classifies patient symptoms for triage

AI, artificial intelligence; ECG, electrocardiogram.

TABLE 12.3 *Scope of current H@H models*

AHCaH waiver only (no state or federal telehealth flexibilities)	AHCaH waiver paired with state and federal telehealth flexibilities
Covers acute phase care	*Covers acute phase care and can include pre-hospital, post-acute, and ambulatory care*
Allows for the use of telehealth and remote monitoring services as necessary for acute phase management only	Allows for the use of telehealth and remote monitoring services before or after an acute episode of care
Daily in-person visits by nurses	Daily in-person visits by nurses
Daily physician evaluation by telehealth	Daily physician evaluation by telehealth
Daily vitals monitoring at multiple timepoints	Daily vitals monitoring at multiple timepoints
Delivery of point-of-care testing, mobile imaging, and IV therapies, as needed	Delivery of point-of-care testing, mobile imaging, and IV therapies, as needed
Skilled nursing services, as needed	Skilled nursing services, as needed

III CHARACTERISTICS OF HIGH-VALUE H@H PROGRAMS THAT SPAN THE CARE CONTINUUM

The characteristics listed below emerged from evidence generated before and during the pandemic, corroborating our experiences at Mayo Clinic, and can be used to evaluate the design of value-based H@H and other hybrid care models as regulatory and reimbursement frameworks evolve.

A Increased Access to Care

H@H programs allow providers to scale hospital capacity beyond the facility walls and reserve inpatient beds for the most critical patients.[29] In areas with inpatient

---

[29] Shereef Elnahal et al., How US Health Systems Can Build Capacity to Handle Demand Surges, *Harvard Bus. Rev.* (October 4, 2021), https://hbr.org/2021/10/how-u-s-health-systems-can-build-capacity-to-handle-demand-surges.

capacity shortages, driven particularly by patients waiting to be discharged to restorative care, H@H programs with hybrid postacute services can more efficiently transition patients to postacute services at home, ensuring that they receive timelier rehabilitative care.[30] These postacute hybrid services also can expand access to patients residing in rural locations by substituting in-person visits with telehealth and, thereby, reducing travel requirements for follow-up services.[31] Integrating telehealth into H@H and postacute services also connects patients to specialists they might otherwise be unable to access in their local community hospital.[32]

B *Enhanced Quality of Care*

Patient and family member satisfaction rates are often higher with H@H programs.[33] Moreover, patients in H@H are less sedentary compared to those treated in brick-and-mortar hospitals, a finding associated with faster recovery times, and multiple H@H programs have demonstrated lower mortality rates compared to in-hospital care, partially attributed to the increased physical activity that naturally occurs at home.[34] Timelier and preventative care is also a potential benefit for H@H, as RPM technology evolves and can alert providers to early signs of patient health deterioration.[35]

Notably, when H@H programs are offered with hybrid models of postacute or other transitional care, reduced readmission rates and improved patient outcomes are possible.[36] While limited data about H@H patient outcomes during the pandemic has been published, a single-site analysis found no difference in readmission rates for H@H or in-hospital patients. Although H@H patients experienced

---

[30] Emily Hanson, Why Many Hospitals Are Over Capacity Two Years into the Pandemic, KING5 (July 29, 2022), www.king5.com/article/sponsor-story/hospitals-over-capacity-pandemic-evergreen-health/281-ad20857e-2017-4cee-b647-a351fd41fdb6; CMS, *Medicare Telemedicine Health Care Provider Fact Sheet*,(2020), www.cms.gov/newsroom/fact-sheets/medicare-telemedicine-health-care-provider-fact-sheet.
[31] Bart M. Demaerschalk et al., Quality Frameworks for Virtual Care: Expert Panel Recommendations, 7 Mayo Clin. Proc. Innov. Qual. Outcomes. 31–44 (2022).
[32] Nat'l Advisory Comm. on Rural Health & Hum. Servs., *Telehealth in Rural America* (2015), www.hrsa.gov/sites/default/files/hrsa/advisory-committees/rural/publications/2015-telehealth.pdf.
[33] Sarah Klein, "Hospital at Home" Programs Improve Outcomes, Lower Costs but Face Resistance from Providers and Payers, *Commonwealth Fund* (2019), www.commonwealthfund.org/publications/newsletter-article/hospital-home-programs-improve-outcomes-lower-costs-face-resistance; Lesley Cryer et al., Costs for "Hospital at Home" Patients Were 19 Percent Lower, With Equal or Better Outcomes Compared to Similar Inpatients, 31 Health Affs. 1237–43 (2012); Klein et al., supra note 7.
[34] Klein et al., supra note 7; Levine et al., supra note 20.
[35] Jared Conley et al., Technology-enabled Hospital at Home: Innovation for Acute Care at Home, 3 NEJM Catalyst Innovations in Care Delivery, 3, 2022.
[36] Cecile Davis et al., Feasibility and Acute Care Utilization Outcomes of a Post-Acute Transitional Telemonitoring Program for Underserved Chronic Disease Patients, 21 Telemedicine and e-Health 705–13 (2015); Stephanie A Hicks & Verena R Cimarolli, The Effects of Telehealth Use for Post-acute Rehabilitation Patient Outcomes, 24 J. Telemedicine & Telecare 179–84 (2018).

shorter inpatient lengths of stay (LOS), they also experienced longer total LOS, suggesting that H@H care may reduce inpatient-level care costs but require longer recovery times, a percentage of which might be appropriately delivered by post-acute hybrid models focusing on telehealth and monitoring, a strategy employed by Mayo Clinic H@H.

C Reduced Costs

Reducing costs remains of interest as payers and health systems continue to shift from fee-for-service (FFS) to value-based care.[37] Evidence supporting H@H's potential to decrease costs without compromising care quality includes a randomized clinical trial that showed H@H patients required fewer laboratory orders and imaging studies.[38] Compared to traditional acute care, multiple H@H programs have shown the potential to decrease costs per patient by nineteen or more percent.[39] Reduced hospital lengths of stay, fewer readmissions, and decreased skilled nursing facility utilization are also associated with H@H programs.[40] The chief method of cost containment proffered by H@H with hybrid postacute services is the more comprehensive management of chronic diseases during the transition period from hospital to primary care.[41]

D Robust Understanding of Social Determinants of Health (SDoH)

H@H programs afford providers the chance to observe patients in their homes. Although a telehealth visit is limited by the lack of a hands-on physical examination, video telehealth is valuable in assisting with physical exams, especially when augmented by connected devices, such as a stethoscope to assess lung and heart sounds. Pairing in-home and virtual clinicians can help providers gain new insights into a patient's daily life, observing family interactions, domestic environments, and information about food and medication availability.[42] Such information can help providers design more effective treatment plans tailored to a patient's unique circumstances, such as balancing patient need with convenience by substituting routine follow-up visits with telehealth and RPM for patients who cannot take time off work.[43]

---

[37] Allison H. Oakes & Thomas R. Radomski, Reducing Low-Value Care and Improving Health Care Value, 325 JAMA 1715–16 (2021).
[38] Levine et al., supra note 20.
[39] Klein, supra note 33; Cryer et al., supra note 33.
[40] Alex D. Federman et al., Association of a Bundled Hospital-at-Home and 30-Day Postacute Transitional Care Program With Clinical Outcomes and Patient Experiences, 178 JAMA Internal Med., 1033–40 (2018).
[41] Demaerschalk et al., supra note 31.
[42] Nicole Warda & Shannon M. Rotolo, Virtual Medication Tours with a Pharmacist as Part of a Cystic Fibrosis Telehealth Visit, 61 J. Am. Pharmacists Ass'n e119–25 (2021).
[43] Demaerschalk et al., supra note 31.

IV HOW POLICYMAKERS CAN REMOVE BARRIERS TO HIGH-VALUE H@H PROGRAMS

While the reforms related to H@H, telehealth, and RPM created a regulatory climate that encouraged innovation in hybrid model design, they were implemented temporarily. In May 2023, the federal PHE expired. By June 2023, no state-level PHEs were in effect. While some reforms have been made permanent, the future of H@H, and hybrid care in general, remains uncertain. Yet hundreds of millions of dollars in private capital has been raised to support H@H platforms.[44] Based on our experiences, we encourage policymakers to remove barriers to developing high-value H@H care by considering the points below.

A Reimbursement and Payment Model Uncertainty

Current reimbursement uncertainty primarily affects publicly insured beneficiaries, many of whom are from marginalized populations, as patients covered by private insurance and managed care programs can receive telehealth, RPM, and H@H services that are negotiated between providers and payers and only subject to state regulations. Regarding the AHCaH waiver, which increases access to care for Medicare and Medicaid beneficiaries, Congress permitted the CMS to extend the waiver, guaranteeing payment parity for inpatient-level care provided at home with 24/7 remote clinical oversight through December 2024.[45] Congress also instructed HHS to publish a study on the outcomes and costs associated with AHCaH programs before the waiver's expiration date to evaluate the program's sustainability. While making this waiver permanent would remove one barrier to accessing H@H programs, individual state hospital licensure laws may restrict hospital participation for eligible patients residing in-state.[46] To determine what role H@H programs should play in terms of care for publicly insured patients, federal and state policymakers should consider the findings of the HHS report to determine appropriate inclusion criteria for H@H programs and patients moving forward.

Equally important to the development of high-value H@H programs, as well as postacute hybrid care models, is the temporary CMS waiver listing a patient's home as an eligible site for telehealth. During the pandemic, patients who transitioned from acute to postacute status during H@H care benefitted from continued access to covered telehealth services when their eligibility for H@H ended. As such, state and federal policymakers should make permanent or expand coverage for telehealth

---

[44] Kushal T. Kadakia et al., Omnibus Spending Bill and Hospital-At-Home: A Roadmap to Ensure Enduring Change, *Health Affs. Forefront* (January 25, 2023), doi:10.1377/forefront.20230123.822679.
[45] Eileen Appelbaum & Rosemary Batt, The New Hospital at Home Movement: Opportunity or Threat for Patient Care?, *Ctr. for Econ. & Pol'y Rsch.* (January 24, 2023), www.cepr.net/wp-content/uploads/2023/01/new-hospital-at-home-movement.pdf.
[46] Ctr. to Advance Palliative Care, supra note 9.

services associated with postacute care that have demonstrated improved patient outcomes, enabling clinicians to identify which services are most appropriate for their patient populations. Expanding access to these services can help H@H patients complete routine medication management and therapy, leading to better outcomes and fewer readmissions.

B Access to Digital Health Tools

Recent findings from the pandemic suggest that patients of all ages who are less comfortable with technology prefer using smartphones over personal computers to connect with health providers;[47] however, 29 percent of US adults aged over 65 do not have a smartphone, and patients with a lower socioeconomic status are also less likely to own a smartphone.[48] Thus, although Medicare permanently updated its definition of telehealth-eligible devices to include smartphones, barriers to telehealth services delivered as part of H@H and hybrid care models still remain.

No uniform definition for telehealth or RPM exists across states. Some states narrowly define the types of technologies eligible for use in telehealth visits or limit RPM to patients with specific diagnoses. Restricting telehealth to specific device requirements and deploying H@H programs with limited flexibility in terms of device options can potentially exacerbate health disparities for underserved populations. For example, Alaska's Medicaid program only reimburses for self-monitoring RPM services at home, a limitation potentially restricting eligible devices to those that have a patient interface and thereby excluding patients with visual disabilities or limited English proficiency.[49] These statutory definitions complicate the design of H@H and other hybrid care models by restricting telehealth and RPM offerings covered by different payers to specific devices.

After considering the findings published by the HHS report on the AHCaH waiver, policymakers should ensure their hospital licensure laws and statutory definitions accommodate the 24/7 virtual presence made possible by clinically validated emerging technologies. Since the rate of technological development outpaces the regulatory review and rulemaking process, policymakers should aim to enhance flexibility for patients and providers by taking a technology-neutral approach to defining eligible telehealth devices. Such an approach is inclusive of the digital comfort level and device availability of underserved patients by allowing providers to select software and devices able to be used by their populations, which vary by geographic location and socioeconomic status.

---

[47] Jen Lau et al., Staying Connected in The COVID-19 Pandemic: Telehealth at the Largest Safety-Net System in the United States, 39 Health Affs. (Project Hope) 1437–42 (2020).
[48] Mobile Fact Sheet, *Pew Rsch. Ctr.* (April 7, 2021), www.pewresearch.org/internet/fact-sheet/mobile/.
[49] 7 Alaska Admin. Code tit. 7 § 110.625(a)(3).

C Emerging Cybersecurity Issues

While permitting a patient's home to be an eligible site for telehealth is critical to high-value care in the digital age, deploying a H@H or hybrid care program is a resource-intensive endeavor for hospital IT departments. Both IT and clinical personnel require training in new systems and workflows; patients and family caregivers also need orientation to learn their roles in receiving care at home. Hospital IT systems must integrate security and privacy protocols for data aggregated, transmitted, and stored by RPM devices, mobile lab and imaging systems, video telehealth visits, text-based communication, and ancillary services. While HIPAA outlines privacy regulations for provider compliance, individual hospital cybersecurity protocols vary.[50]

As the HIPAA waiver, which expired at the end of the PHE, enabled providers to select platforms to deliver remote care that were not HIPAA-compliant, some providers are now transitioning to HIPAA-compliant software and RPM devices. Simultaneously, the Food and Drug Administration (FDA) offered a temporary expedited review process for digital health apps, software, and RPM devices.[51] Together, these regulatory flexibilities created a perfect storm for the adoption of insecure software products and human error related to mishandling data in remote care delivery.

Cybersecurity for clinical services enabled by RPM and telehealth software is an evolving research and operations area. As institutional cybersecurity policies are confidential, a robust analysis of the set of cybersecurity strategies employed by providers remains elusive. The lack of clarity surrounding telehealth and RPM cybersecurity affects its long-term sustainability. For instance, many patients express a reluctance to participate in remote care due to privacy and security concerns regarding third-party telehealth platforms and RPM devices, rather than about hospitals directly. Patients of low socioeconomic status, like those who lack tech savviness and English fluency, are most at risk from cyber-related exploitation via the most accessible (free or inexpensive) telehealth options. This is because low-barrier applications are the least likely to offer comprehensive data privacy and security policies, disproportionately putting underserved patients most at risk of a data breach.[52] Moreover, cybersecurity standards specific to telehealth, both in H@H and hybrid care models, are yet to be determined. A 2021 study in the *British Medical Journal* assessing digital health app privacy policies and risks found that no consistent privacy practices exist in digital health software design. Also, the privacy policies of

---

[50] Leff et al., supra note 13.
[51] US Food and Drug Admin., Digital Health Policies and Public Health Solutions for COVID-19 (April 28, 2022), www.fda.gov/medical-devices/coronavirus-covid-19-and-medical-devices/digital-health-policies-and-public-health-solutions-covid-19.
[52] Nicole Martinez-Martin et al., Ethics of Digital Mental Health During COVID-19: Crisis and Opportunities, JMIR Mental Health e23776 (2020).

many leading telehealth platforms, which may be used in home hospital models, are unclear about which associated services access what patient data.[53]

Current best practices in H@H and hybrid care cybersecurity include infrastructure audit checks and risk assessments during at-home visits. To mitigate emerging cybersecurity issues, institutional policymakers should identify concerns across administrative, physical, and technical domains for their H@H program. The expiration of the HIPAA waiver is critical to advancing a cybersecurity-conscious healthcare data ecosystem. As some reforms are made permanent post PHE, HHS should offer clarity regarding data privacy expectations and gold-standard cybersecurity guidelines for telehealth and hybrid care models like H@H, considering lessons learned during the PHE. Such an approach can assuage patient anxieties and help small-group providers, who face a shortage of skilled IT personnel, transition to HIPAA-compliant hybrid care models.

V CONCLUSION

The CMS's AHCaH waiver, combined with state and federal telehealth and RPM regulatory flexibilities, unleashed innovation in hybrid care models that can improve patient outcomes and decrease costs. To chart a path forward for H@H programs, state and federal policymakers should immediately address statutory and reimbursement issues as top priority issues, developing a framework flexible enough to deliver care during an acute episode at a distance that can help patients transition safely to outpatient status with telehealth and RPM. However, it will also be important for policymakers and those implementing H@H models to ensure a cybersecurity-conscious infrastructure. High-value home hospital programs can increase access to care, reduce costs, and enhance the quality of care, helping clinicians deliver more personalized care through a new understanding of SDoH. To overcome barriers to high-value home hospital care, we encourage government and institutional policymakers to better align statutory and reimbursement policies with updated cybersecurity guidance, facilitating the design of high-value H@H models that span the care continuum.

---

[53] Kirsten Ostherr, Telehealth Overpromises During the Covid-19 Pandemic, STAT (March 19, 2020), www.statnews.com/2020/03/19/telehealth-overpromises-during-the-covid-19-pandemic/.

13

Digitally Enabled Medicaid Home and Community-Based Services[*]

Kathryn Huber and Tara Sklar

I INTRODUCTION

Older Americans are increasingly able to receive long-term care in the home through the emergence of digital health tools, including mobile health applications, remote monitors, and video calling software for medical appointments. These digital health tools can further support older adults' preference to age in place. The demand for this type of care in the home is exemplified by the over 820,000 Medicaid-eligible Americans who sit on waiting lists – many for years – hoping to receive long-term supports and services (LTSS) through state Medicaid home and community-based services (HCBS), rather than institutional care.[1]

Medicaid HCBS includes services delivered to persons who wish to remain in their homes by providing for the full spectrum of LTSS, such as bathing, feeding, personal care, medication administration and management, and more.[2] Under Medicaid, state programs must cover LTSS in institutional settings, but HCBS are provided under section 1915(c) of the Social Security Act as a waiver program,[3] which effectively leaves hundreds of thousands without care if they wish to remain in their homes.[4] Digitally enabled HCBS could expand LTSS in the home by utilizing the digital health tools described above combined with data-driven analytics

---

[*] The authors wish to thank Slade Smith for his excellent research assistance. The authors also appreciate the opportunity to work on this chapter with the Petrie-Flom Center as part of the 2022 Annual Conference and are grateful for the editorial guidance from Julia Adler-Milstein.
[1] MaryBeth Musumeci et al., Key State Policy Choices about Medicaid Home and Community-Based Services, Kaiser Issue Brief (2020).
[2] Carli Friedman et al., Aging in Place: A National Analysis of Home and Community-Based Medicaid Services for Older Adults, 29 J. of Disability Pol'y Stud. 245 (2019).
[3] 42 USC § 1396n(c).
[4] Ryan Crowly et al., Long-Term Services and Supports for Older Adults: A Position Paper from the American College of Physicians, 175 Annals Internal Med. 1172–74 (2022). The movement toward HCBS is being driven by patient preferences and innovations in health care delivery, as well as the instrumental US Supreme Court decision in *Olmstead* v. *LC*, 527 U.S. 581 (1999), which held that the "unjustified institutional isolation of people with disabilities is a form of unlawful discrimination under the Americans with Disabilities Act."

to reduce reliance on home health care aides, an already strained workforce, and unpaid caregivers.

To illustrate this escalating demand to receive LTSS in the home, meet Cora. Cora is a 92-year-old woman who sits in her hospital bed watching plants on her windowsill collect dust, wishing she were in her home. A recent stroke has left her with moderate cognitive impairment and reduced mobility. She has been hospitalized for months while staff and family members work to identify a safe discharge plan. The new cognitive and functional impairments place her at risk for medication adherence errors and falls, precluding her from caring for herself alone at home.

The discharge dilemma that Cora, her family, and the medical team face is common for older adults when greater care at home is needed but unavailable. These distressingly difficult scenarios have been exacerbated by the insufficient home health workforce, which was decimated by the COVID-19 pandemic and continues to shrink.[5] Home health care is the largest long-term care (LTC) modality for older adults, assisting with daily living, preventing falls, and administering medication.[6] Over 1.8 million older adults in the United States are partially or completely homebound,[7] a number that will likely continue to rise with an aging population. As the homebound population increases, the need for at-home services will follow suit.

A technological response through digital health tools could enable many older adults to be safely discharged home after a hospital stay or, ideally, avoid hospitalization in the first place.[8] Cora could possibly be discharged home with a variety of new in-home devices. For example, to reduce the risk of falls, a home health agency could fit her with wearable devices and install home motion sensors and remote monitoring bed alarms. This digitally enabled approach would allow the agency to centrally monitor a larger number of patients than they could if they solely relied on in-person visits.

This chapter delineates the ethical, social, legal, and regulatory issues of implementing digital home care for a Medicaid-eligible, older adult population. The second section of this chapter describes efforts to modernize and expand HCBS

---

[5] Judith Graham, Pandemic-Fueled Shortages of Home Health Workers Strand Patients without Necessary Care, *Kaiser Health News* (2022), https://khn.org/news/article/pandemic-fueled-home-health-care-shortages-strand-patients/amp/.

[6] Lauren Harris-Kojetin et al., Long-Term Care Providers and Services Users in the United States: Data from the National Study of Long-Term Care Providers, 2013–14, 3 Vital & Health Stat. 38 (February 2016).

[7] Katherine A. Ornstein et al., Epidemiology of the Homebound Population in the United States, 175 JAMA Internal Med. 1180 (2015).

[8] Katie Adams, 5 Health Systems Recently Launched "Hospital-At-Home" Programs, *Becker's Hosp. Rev.* (January 31, 2022) (reporting a rise in the number of hospital-at-home programs), www.beckershospitalreview.com/telehealth/5-health-systems-that-recently-launched-hospital-at-home-programs.html.

by applying digital health tools and services. Ethical considerations for digitally enabled HCBS are discussed in the third section, recognizing an older population's heightened vulnerability to abuse, social isolation, and frailty in the face of concerns regarding safety, efficacy, privacy, and equitable access. The fourth section proposes recommendations for how to approach expanding digitally enabled HCBS in ways that address individual and system-level issues. Recommendations for individual-level issues focus on user consent practices and the acceptable use of collecting, sharing, and storing health data. System-level recommendations include policies to support reimbursement for remote monitoring and permanently lifting geographic restrictions around the use of telehealth so that older adults can access care from their homes. The scrutiny that follows could not be timelier, as older adults struggle to gain access to LTSS delivered in the home to safely age in place, and state Medicaid programs struggle with mounting costs, workforce shortages, and a growing aging population.

II INTEGRATION OF DIGITAL HEALTH TOOLS WITH MEDICAID HCBS

To meet the growing demand for LTC in the home, the Centers for Medicare and Medicaid (CMS) must play a prominent role in equitably expanding access to older adults. Medicaid is the primary payer for LTC in the United States, paying for about two-thirds of all LTC stays.[9] HCBS waivers are optional, but the majority of states implement them to address high-use populations with the most intensive needs, such as those aged 65 and over, because LTSS in the home is less expensive than institutionalized care and supports older adults' preference to receive care in the home.[10] States are under increasing financial pressure to meet the needs of a growing aging population and have accordingly raised Medicaid budgets to fund LTSS.[11] While the existing government policies still favor institutional care over optional HCBS for low-income older Americans, notable shifts are underway.

---

[9] Medicare, which covers about 54 million people based on age, covers only limited forms of in-home care in certain circumstances, and "doesn't cover long-term care if that's the only care you need." *Home Health Services*, Medicare.gov, www.medicare.gov/coverage/home-health-services; *Long-Term Care*, Medicare.gov, www.medicare.gov/coverage/long-term-care; Medicare – Statistics & Facts, *Statistam* www.statista.com/topics/1167/medicare/#dossierKeyfigures. Approximately, 12.3 million people are dually eligible beneficiaries for Medicaid and Medicare. *Seniors & Medicare and Medicaid Enrollees*, Medicaid.gov. www.medicaid.gov/medicaid/eligibility/seniors-medicare-and-medicaid-enrollees/index.html.

[10] Musumeci et al., supra note 1.

[11] Zachary Anderson, Solving America's Long-Term Care Financing Crisis: Financing Universal Long-Term Care Insurance with a Mandatory Federal Income Tax Surcharge That Increases with Age, 25 Elder L. J. 473, 507 (2018).

In April 2020, the CMS approved Appendix K in 1915(c) state waivers,[12] which expanded LTSS in HCBS waivers to include reimbursement for virtual assessments with providers, electronic service delivery, and other technology-related benefits to better serve beneficiaries during the COVID-19 pandemic. Furthermore, the American Rescue Plan Act, signed by President Biden in March 2021, boosted federal matching in Medicaid for HCBS, and the Infrastructure Investment and Jobs Act of 2022 provided funding to address digital health equity.[13] Highlighting the increasing value of HCBS services, the Agency for Healthcare Research and Quality recently studied the health and welfare of HCBS recipients and found significant benefits from applying emerging technologies during care.[14] The agency identified durable medical supplies and technologies, such as personal care robots, wearable fall detection devices, automated medication administrators, and assistive devices, as tools of the future that would soon be commonly used.

Yet, most Medicaid HCBS cover only assistive devices and emergency alert systems[15] and do not cover the aforementioned digital health tools. Currently, reimbursement for equipment and technology accounts for only a small portion of overall HCBS expenditures despite high usage.[16] This is partially attributable to the lengthy and uncertain process for CMS coverage of new technologies. For a new technology to be granted reimbursement, it must demonstrate significant benefit for the Medicare population beyond existing technologies or services.[17] The rate at which technologies arrive on the market often outpaces the rate of validated studies providing results to meet this high standard, thus, often limiting their use. Even if a technology is approved for reimbursement, it is up to individual states to determine which services will be covered based on needs,[18] making implementation and access to digitally enabled services heterogenous and difficult to track.

---

[12] Kaiser Fam. Found., *Medicaid Emergency Authority Tracker: Approved State Actions to Address COVID-19* (July 1, 2021), www.kff.org/medicaid/issue-brief/medicaid-emergency-authority-tracker-approved-state-actions-to-address-covid-19/.

[13] Tyler Cromer et al., Modernizing Long-Term Services and Supports and Valuing The Caregiver Workforce, *Health Affs.* (April 3, 2021), www.healthaffairs.org/do/10.1377/forefront.20210409.424254/full/; Infrastructure Investment and Jobs Act, Pub. L. No. 117–58, 135 Stat. 429 (2021).

[14] Agency for Healthcare Rsch. & Quality, *Assessing the Health and Welfare of the HCBS Population* (December 2012), www.ahrq.gov/patient-safety/settings/long-term-care/resource/hcbs/findings/find3.html.

[15] Molly O'Malley Watts et al., *State Policy Choices About Medicaid Home and Community-Based Services Amid the Pandemic* (2022).

[16] Victoria Peebles & Alex Bohl, The HCBS Taxonomy: A New Language for Classifying Home and Community-Based Services, 4 Medicare & Medicaid Rsch. Rev. (2014).

[17] Lee A. Fleisher, Medicare Coverage of Innovative Technologies, *CMS.gov* (September 13, 2021), www.cms.gov/blog/medicare-coverage-innovative-technologies-mcit.

[18] Robin Rudowitz et al., 10 Things to Know about Medicaid: Setting the Facts Straight, *Kaiser Fam. Found.* (March 6, 2019), www.kff.org/medicaid/issue-brief/10-things-to-know-about-medicaid-setting-the-facts-straight/.

Expanding reimbursement coverage for, and therefore access to, new types of devices under HCBS waivers, therefore, may reduce overall costs by supporting a shift away from labor-intensive institutional settings into the home, where more efficient LTSS care can be delivered with reduced administrative and staffing costs.[19] For example, digital tools for organizing and dispensing medications could reduce the high proportion of a home health care aide's time devoted to that task. In the scenario with Cora, rather than relying on an aide, Cora could receive reminders on her smartphone or a wearable device to take her medications, which could be dispensed through an automated cabinet. This digitally enabled approach would improve Cora's compliance and reduce medication errors.[20] Other examples of digital health tools that could reduce demand on the LTC workforce include the strategic placement of Amazon's Ring and Echo Show devices around Cora's home to help her connect via video calls to the home health care agency, when needed, and have 24/7 access to an urgent response service.[21]

Digital health tools could also benefit via the collection of data-driven analytics around the variety of services provided. Currently, state waivers for HCBS differ across the country in terms of eligibility, scope of benefits, and delivery systems.[22] It is estimated that by 2028, there will be 8.2 million HCBS job openings,[23] many of them directly impacting older adult needs. In the face of staffing shortages for personal and nursing care, many of these technologies offer low-cost solutions with reduced labor needs. States are also required to establish a quality assurance, monitoring, and improvement strategy for the HCBS benefit, yet there are no standards for this.[24] Digital health home tools could improve states' ability to monitor their LTSS delivered via HCBS through centralized data collection and analysis and through on-site monitoring of the services delivered by agencies or providers.

There are also lessons for digitally enabled HCBS to be gleaned from the recent expansion of Hospital-at-Home (H@H) practices, which use technology to provide real-time information pertinent to the monitored patient's health and needs. Examples include at-home vital signs checks and alarms for gait changes predicting falls,[25] which could be equally useful as part of HCBS. Another emerging area

---

[19] Arpita Chattopadhyay et al., Cost-efficiency in Medicaid Long-Term Support Services: The Role of Home and Community Based Services, 2 SpringerPlus, 305 (2013).

[20] Bryan C. McCarthy et al., Implementation and Optimization of Automated Dispensing Cabinet Technology, 73 Am. J. Health-Sys. Pharmacy 1531 (2016).

[21] Lea Lebar et al., The Psychosocial Impacts of E-care Technology Use for Long-Term Care Recipients and Informal Carers, 22 Int'l J. Integrated Care (2022).

[22] Musumeci et al., supra note 1.

[23] Workforce Data Center, PHI, https://phinational.org/policy-research/workforce-data-center/.

[24] Tara Sklar & Rachel Zuraw, Preparing to Age in Place: The Role of Medicaid Waivers in Elder Abuse Prevention, 28 Annals Health L. 195 (2019).

[25] Thanos Stavropoulos et al., IoT Wearable Sensors and Devices in Elderly Care: A Literature Review, 20 Sensors 2826 (2020).

includes Addison, an artificial intelligence care management tool that synchronizes across devices in a patient's home and interacts with a caregiver avatar.[26] Such technologies could be expanded to focus on core HCBS priorities, such as maintaining function by targeting the activities of daily living to help older adults eat, dress, and bathe themselves.[27] In turn, these systems can prevent the hospital admissions that lead to preventable nursing home admissions and resource inefficiencies.[28] Ideally, clinical or behavioral information from these technologies, which continuously collect data, would be available to primary care providers and other medical specialists to further support individualized care plans or chronic disease monitoring.

Despite the potential widespread benefits of integrating digital health tools into HCBS, there is a lack of federal- or state-level guidance on how to adapt digital health tools into medical and custodial care, alongside the corresponding reimbursement.[29] To date, there is little to assure quality or applicability for many digital home technologies – such as devices that monitor medication adherence and changes in the sleep-wake cycle – that will play an increasingly integral part in the care of older adults. For example, early research on automated medication cabinets and care robots is promising, but large randomized clinical trials are lacking to guide their acceptability for use among a diverse HCBS-eligible population.

As Medicaid programs increasingly look to adopt these technologies to provide LTSS in the home, beneficiaries should be engaged to determine if these proposed digital solutions are accessible and understandable. A suggested incremental approach would be for CMS to launch pilot sites with a range of state Medicaid programs to measure efficacy and to inform acceptable-use guidelines for integrating these technologies into daily care routines. Additionally, metrics around communications with digital health tools should be included to address beneficiaries' preferences, audio or visual difficulties, limited English proficiency, and lower digital-health literacy.

---

[26] Press Release, Electronic Caregiver, *Meet Addison, Electronic Caregiver's Living Avatar for Café Management* (January 3, 2023), https://ces.vporoom.com/2023-01-03-Meet-Addison,-Electronic-Caregivers-Living-Avatar-for-Care-Management.

[27] Sasha Sheppard et al., Is Comprehensive Geriatric Assessment Admission Avoidance Hospital at Home an Alternative to Hospital Admission for Older Persons? 174 Annals Internal Med. 889 (2021); Shubing Cai et al., Evaluation of the Cincinnati Veterans Affairs Medical Center Hospital-in-Home Program, 66 J. Am. Geriatrics Soc'y 1392 (2018); Roger Harris et al., The Effectiveness, Acceptability and Costs of a Hospital-at-Home Service Compared with Acute Hospital Care: A Randomized Controlled Trial, 10 J. Health Servs. Rsch. & Pol'y 158 (2005).

[28] Nicoletta Aimonino Ricauda et al., Substitutive "Hospital at Home" Versus Inpatient Care for Elderly Patients with Exacerbations of Chronic Obstructive Pulmonary Disease: A Prospective Randomized, Controlled Trial, 56 J. Am. Geriatrics Soc'y 493 (2008).

[29] Richard Schulz et al., Advancing the Aging and Technology Agenda in Gerontology, 55 Gerontologist 724 (2015).

III ETHICAL CONSIDERATIONS WITH DIGITALLY ENABLED HCBS IN AN OLDER POPULATION

Ensuring the safe, effective, and clearly regulated use of new digital health tools for the routine care of older adults requires close ethical analysis. An overarching framework to promote autonomy, safety, privacy, and equity is paramount, especially when stakeholders with such potentially differing interests are involved. In this context, stakeholders include patients and caregivers as end-users, agencies delivering HCBS, the organizations developing digital health tools, regulators, and policy makers. Below are three key considerations that consider the unique vulnerabilities of an HCBS-eligible older adult population, the autonomy and privacy concerns with continuous monitoring, and the required steps to help ensure equitable access to digital models of HCBS.

While older adults prefer to age in place and receive LTSS in the home, they are more prone to frailty, cognitive and sensory impairments, and social isolation.[30] In addition, issues of abuse and neglect are a concern among older adults and need to be taken into consideration as care moves further into the home,[31] where there may be less oversight than in institutional settings, particularly when care is provided digitally. However, if HCBS integrate more digital health tools, then the daily tracking of vital signs and other metrics could vastly improve the current oversight of Medicaid beneficiaries, which sometimes amounts to as little as quarterly phone calls from the state Medicaid office.[32]

To help illustrate the additional possible benefits from appropriate oversight, we turn back to the fictional Cora, who carries a diagnosis of chronic obstructive pulmonary disease, commonly known as COPD, and is discharged home with HCBS. Upon returning home, the home health care agency links an urgent response service to Cora's home pulse oximeter to monitor her remotely. This is a widely available monitoring device, but is not subject to standardization, safety requirements, or proof of diagnostic accuracy, and has received substantial racial and ethnic discrepancy criticism.[33] Currently, these devices are neither reimbursable by CMS nor routinely integrated into HCBS.

Yet, in the near future, this device could play a pivotal role in Cora receiving immediate care or in preventing an unnecessary hospital visit. Remote monitoring through HCBS could detect a drop in Cora's blood oxygen level and prompt her to use oxygen or an inhaler, avoiding a call to emergency medical services or hospitalization. But these interventions are only as good as the accuracy and reliability of the

---

[30] Jon Sanford & Tina Butterfield, Using Remote Assessment to Provide Home Modification Services to Underserved Elders, 45 Gerontologist 389 (2005).
[31] Nat'l Inst. on Aging, Elder Abuse, www.nia.nih.gov/health/elder-abuse.
[32] Sklar & Zuraw, supra note 24.
[33] Eric Ward & Mitchell Katz, Confronting the Clinical Implications of Racial and Ethnic Discrepancy in Pulse Oximetry, 182 JAMA Internal Med. 858 (2022); Annabel Kupke et al., Pulse Oximeters and Violation of Federal Antidiscrimination Law, 329 JAMA 365 (2023).

technology used. Currently, diagnostic error among older adults in clinical care is pervasive due to the limits around lack of data, complex conditions requiring consistent monitoring, and barriers to communication due to impairments associated with older age.[34] The above is an example of how digital health tools could diagnose in the home to intervene early, but they are only effective if the technology itself can be consistently and reliably used by this population.

In expanding access to new technologies through HCBS waivers, issues of digital health equity may be addressed. Many Medicaid-eligible older adults lack the internet or data services needed to support digitally enabled tools in the home and related access to home telehealth to manage their medical needs.[35] Federal and state government investments in broadband infrastructure and continued reimbursement for home telehealth are essential for this group.

IV INDIVIDUAL AND SYSTEM-LEVEL CONSIDERATIONS FOR MODERNIZING HCBS

For digitally enabled HCBS to become a reality, stronger regulatory oversight is needed to ensure the safe and effective deployment of the enabling technologies. The promise of such an approach aligns with the goals of HCBS waivers to reduce LTC costs and ensure high-quality care in the home, particularly for older adults with unique needs, preferences, and vulnerabilities. To support the integration of digital health tools in HCBS, we make the following practice and policy recommendations. These recommendations include focusing on individual user consent practices, as well as system-level advocacy for policies that support payment parity for remote patient monitoring and telehealth.

To date, there are two key issues with digitally enabled services: (1) Inconsistent, difficult-to-interpret consent practices that do little to empower users and (2) ambiguity around device company practices with respect to device monitoring, data collection, use, and security. Both of these are controlled at the company level but could be subject to change when utilized for HCBS care. In studies examining the acceptability of home monitoring and surveillance among caregivers and persons with dementia, many users (or future users) hoped for technologies that would provide peace of mind, safety, and support in the home, with the primary goal of promoting safe aging in place.[36] Yet, the digital health tools used today in the care of

---

[34] Christine Cassel & Terry Fulmer, Achieving Diagnostic Excellence for Older Patients, 327 JAMA 919 (2022).

[35] Sarah Nouri et al., Commentary, Addressing Equity in Telemedicine for Chronic Disease Management During the Covid-19 Pandemic, NEJM Catalyst (May 4, 2020), https://catalyst.nejm.org/doi/full/10.1056/CAT.20.0123.

[36] Mira Ahn et al., Supporting Aging-in-Place Well: Findings from a Cluster Analysis of the Reasons for Aging-in-Place and Perceptions of Well-Being, 39 J. Applied Gerontology 3 (2020); Sebastiaan T. M. Peek et al., Older Adults' Reasons for Using Technology while Aging in Place, 62 Gerontology 226 (2016).

older adults, such as wearables, in-home cameras and care robots, often use a one-off, click-through process with dense, hard-to-understand terms to obtain consent, if any. These consents are typically presented during initial use or when new users access app-based technologies and fail to account for changes in user preferences over time or, in the case of older adults, changes in cognition and capacity to consent to their use.

Secondly, there is a lack of transparency around how device companies will use and provide security around the data collected from these digital health tools. The proposed recommendations aim to simplify instructions to promote improved understanding among users and delineate privacy and security risks about how health data will be collected, used, shared, and stored to encourage the trust and, ultimately, utilization of these tools.[37] If digitally enabled HCBS are to become widely adopted, then stricter standards around data use and maintenance by device companies must protect patient's privacy by not sharing identifiable health information that would be required by covered entities, namely providers and insurers, under the Health Insurance Portability and Accountability Act (HIPAA).[38]

Currently, many of the device companies who have access to health data are considered non-covered entities (NCEs) under HIPAA, meaning patients or residents have little access to and control over how their health information is handled and shared with unauthorized users, including marketers. Expanding the reach of HIPAA to include these companies as covered entities could encourage more older adults to view digitally enabled HCBS as secure and trustworthy. NCEs could also voluntarily comply with HIPAA to encourage uptake, which would encompass establishing safeguards, such as a firewall, encryption, and two-step authentication, among other steps to protect user privacy.

In addition, a more transparent, formalized process of disclosure and consent can be implemented so that older Medicaid beneficiaries may better understand to what extent their personal data is being collected and how it may be used. Discussions about home surveillance and monitoring devices provide patients and their families with opportunities to make informed decisions about whether to use these technologies given all the factors involved – from data risks to the benefits of continuous monitoring. Requiring transparency and disclosure by device manufacturers provides another step in the right direction. For example, model privacy notices (MPN), akin to FDA nutrition facts labels,[39] allow for clear communication around data use and security practices that cater to a broad range of user understanding and health literacy. Transparency and disclosure requirements for digitally enabled

---

[37] Peek et al., supra note 36 (addressing that tendency requires clearly communicating that at-home test kits have imperfect diagnostic capability and that this carries implications for decision-making).
[38] Health Insurance Portability and Accountability Act of 1996, Pub. L. No. 104-91, 110 Stat. 1936.
[39] *Model Privacy Notice (MPN)*, HealthIT.gov, www.healthit.gov/topic/privacy-security-and-hipaa/model-privacy-notice-mpn.

technologies at the same level of oversight as covered entities (CEs) under HIPAA offer two salient options for improvement on existing practices.

Taking the case of Cora, shared decision-making – around her comfort with in-home surveillance, with cameras or a wearable continuously monitoring her activity – may reveal preferences for sharing information or, alternatively, restricting its use to only certain times or circumstances. Using information readily accessible and understandable through the devices' MPN, Cora and her family could make informed decisions about which devices to use and how. They use a redesigned consent form that explains how companies may use her data when employed through HCBS to keep her safe and independent at home. Under existing HCBS Community Transition Services, for example, Cora would be given some agency in determining which services align with her values, activities-of-daily-living (ADL) needs, and environmental adaptations at the time of her transition to home. Folding digitally enabled services into these decision points would offer greater opportunities for more tailored and personalized care, as well as a seamless integration of custodial-type services with her medical care. Expanding control over how, when, and where these technologies and their derivative data are used may allow older adults to meaningfully drive individually tailored care under their HCBS that better aligns with their specific values around privacy or confidentiality.

System-level tactics that support policies providing access to remote patient monitoring and home telehealth through payment parity would provide another driver for digitally enabled HCBS to become a reality. These broader access issues connect with HCBS to support the ability of Medicaid-beneficiaries to safely age in place by receiving remote management of their chronic or acute conditions. The Consolidated Appropriations Act of 2023 continues to lift telehealth geographic restrictions and allow for payment parity of home telehealth so that those visits are reimbursed by Medicare until December 31, 2024, at the same rate as in-person visits.[40] Medicare also provides reimbursement for remote monitoring so that providers can review data and manage treatment plans for patients without in-person visits. These national trends speak to the rising attention to and support for patient preference and need to remain in place, as well as the value of expanded access to care via in-home technology.

V CONCLUSION

The greater personal capacity for older adults to maintain function and autonomy in their daily routines via digital health tools with less in-person human assistance would allow for more older adults to safely age in place. Combining these technologies with Medicaid HCBS also serves to advance digital health equity for an older population group with limited resources. Under a person-centered care model, such

---

[40] Consolidated Appropriations Act, 2023, Pub L. 117–328.

as the one that HCBS strives to deliver, regulators can align user values and preferences with the models used by agencies delivering these services.

Ensuring equitable access, the mitigation of risks, and supported decision-making around digitally enabled HCBS is central to the success of these new models in the care of older adults. The heightened physical and social risks many older adults face when left to struggle at home without support can be significantly reduced for all older adults with these technology-assisted options. State Medicaid programs are in an unsustainable fiscal situation, struggling with an increasing aging population and shrinking long-term care workforce. Through the recommendations posed here, digitally enabled HCBS pose one avenue forward to address the older population's needs and preferences as well as to expand access in a forward-looking health technology supported world.

14

EU In-Home Digital Diagnostics – Cross-Border Patient Reimbursement under Threat?

Kaat Van Delm

I INTRODUCTION

Telemedicine has boomed over the last ten years thanks to new digital technologies, such as the extended use of the Internet and the availability of increasing amounts of data.[1] The virtual offering of new data-driven health care increases its accessibility to physically distant patients, including patients from other countries. In the European Union ("EU"), cross-border healthcare triggers specific reimbursement queries. A legal framework was developed over time to coordinate the various national reimbursement schemes in cases of cross-border care, which also explicitly regulates the reimbursement of cross-border telemedicine. This chapter assesses whether, in an EU cross-border context, patients have the same cross-border reimbursement rights for one form of telemedicine – digital diagnostics – as for receiving such health care in person, and the consequences thereof.[2]

This introduction describes the EU context, the applicable EU reimbursement legislation, and the limitations in scope. The second section compares the situation of a patient receiving cross-border care in person, and a patient receiving cross-border telemedicine services while residing in their home country, highlighting the resulting reimbursement opportunities and limitations. The third section assesses the consequences of the described legal framework from the point of view of the patient, the telemedicine solutions providers, and the EU member states.

A EU Context

Digital diagnostics qualify as "telemedicine" under the EU legal framework applicable to cross-border reimbursement. Even though no official definition is available under EU health law, the European Commission provides the following indicative definition: *"The provision of healthcare services at a distance through the use*

---

[1] European Commission, Directorate-General for Health and Food Safety et al., *Market Study on Telemedicine* 23, 78 (October 2018), https://bit.ly/EC-marketstudy-telemedicine.
[2] This chapter reflects doctrinal research, with an internal comparative approach.

of ICT, e.g., *teleconsultations, telemonitoring, telesurgery,* … ."[3] Digital diagnostics constitute, depending on the circumstances, teleconsultations or telemonitoring, and, therefore, qualify as telemedicine. A 2018 market study on telemedicine of the European Commission stated that in almost all member states, reimbursement for telemedicine remained vague or even non-existent.[4] At the cross-border level, the report notes that the reimbursement issue is even more problematic.

The reimbursement struggles stem from the fact that public benefits still vary significantly among the member states.[5] The EU member states have parallel public and private health coverage. Most member states provide near-universal health coverage for a core selection of health care.[6] However, the amount of coverage varies.[7] These disparities in coverage make it impossible to grant EU citizens an unconditional right for receiving reimbursable health care in another member state. Therefore, it remains up to the member states to decide on both the "basket of health care" to which patients are entitled, specifically, the health care which is reimbursed, and the related financing mechanisms.[8] To safeguard the national social security systems, the EU legal framework strictly coordinates the reimbursement options for cross-border care, without touching upon the question of which type of health care falls within patients' basket of health care. It clarifies which member state bears the financial burden for the cross-border care, and when the patient must request prior authorization to qualify for reimbursement. One aim for the codification of the current legislative framework was "modernising and simplifying" the "complex and lengthy" preceding rules.[9] Initially, the establishment of this framework, both via case law and via legislation, created a convergence among the national social security systems. However, among other reasons, the aging of the EU population, costly technology, and the economic crisis put this convergence under pressure.[10]

B *Cross-Border Health Care Law*

Where a patient receives EU cross-border health care, the patient can choose between two legal bases for claiming reimbursement from the EU member state

---

[3] European Commission, *Glossary for Good Patient Information Provision in Cross-Border Healthcare* 6 (2019), https://health.ec.europa.eu/system/files/2019-12/2019_ncptoolbox_ncp_glossary_en_0.pdf.
[4] European Commission, Directorate-General for Health and Food Safety et al., supra note 1, at 94–95.
[5] Id. at 211 fig.7.10.
[6] OECD & European Union, *Health at a Glance: Europe 2020 – State of Health in the EU Cycle* 208 (December 2020), https://doi.org/10.1787/82129230-en.
[7] Id. at 211 fig.7.10.
[8] Council of the European Union, Council Conclusions on Common Values and Principles in European Union Health Systems OJC 146/01, at 2 (June 22, 2006).
[9] Regulation (EC) No. 883/2004 of the European Parliament and of the Council of 29 April 2004 on the Coordination of Social Security Systems, OJL 166, at Recital 3 (April 30, 2004).
[10] European Commission, *Communication on Enabling the Digital Transformation of Health and Care in the Digital Single Market; Empowering Citizens and Building a Healthier Society* 1, COM (2018) 233 final (April 25, 2018).

concerned. Regulation 883/2004 "on the coordination of social security systems"[11] (the "Regulation")[12] provides the first reimbursement basis. The Regulation stems from the free movement of persons, one of the four fundamental freedoms of the EU.[13] Its aim is to ensure equality between citizens of the providing member state and EU patients receiving care in that member state, by treating EU patients as if they were insured under the providing member state's public health care system.[14] The reimbursement right embedded in the Regulation co-exists with another reimbursement right, based on the free movement of goods and services, two other fundamental freedoms of the EU.[15] The European Court of Justice (ECJ) established this second reimbursement route via case law which has eventually been codified in Directive 2011/24/EU "on the application of patients' rights in cross-border healthcare" (the "Directive").[16] The aim of the Directive is to ensure that patients are entitled to treatment and reimbursement in other EU member states as if they were receiving the treatment in their own competent member state.[17] If both reimbursement routes are available, by default, the Regulation applies over the Directive.[18] However, patients may request otherwise if they prefer to receive reimbursement based on the Directive, if they deem this basis to be more advantageous for their situation.

As the Regulation and the Directive are based on different free movement rights, and as they consequently have different aims, it should be of no surprise that their scope, conditions for admissibility, and procedure also differ. For example, whereas the Regulation only concerns treatment covered by public health care, the Directive can also cover private health care. Hence, the potential interest for patients to opt for one or the other reimbursement basis. The following Table 14.1 provides a general overview of the differences relevant for cross-border telemedicine, which Section II analyses further in detail.

Overall, the number of patients receiving cross-border care under the Regulation or the Directive, although rising every year, remains low. In 2016, a report estimated that cross-border health care under the Directive and the Regulation cost, respectively, 0.004 percent and 0.1 percent of the EU-wide annual health care budget.[19]

---

[11] Regulation No. 883/2004, supra note 9.
[12] A "regulation" is binding EU law, which is, as such, directly applicable in the EU member states.
[13] Initially aiming for a "free movement of workers," though over time growing into a broader free movement of persons. (See, e.g., A v. *Latvijas Republikas Veselības ministrija*, case C-535/19, 2021 ECJ, (ECLI:EU:C:2021:595) (concerning access to member states' public sickness insurance schemes for economically inactive Union citizens).
[14] Regulation No. 883/2004, supra note 9, at art. 4.
[15] Directive 2011/24/EU of the European Parliament and of the Council of 9 March 2011 on the Application of Patients' Rights in Cross-Border Healthcare, Recital 2, OJL 88, April 4 2011; A "directive" is EU law, which all EU member states need to implement into national law.
[16] Id. at art. 10.2.
[17] Id. at art. 7.7.
[18] Id. at art. 8.3.
[19] European Commission, *Report on the Operation of Directive 2011/24/EU on the Application of Patients' Rights in Cross-Border Healthcare* 8, COM (2018) 651 final (September 21, 2018).

TABLE 14.1 *Regulation versus directive: Differences relevant for telemedicine*

	Regulation 883/2004	Directive 2011/24/EU
Scope	Free movement of persons	Free movement of goods and services
Reimbursement tariff	From providing member state	From competent member state
Upfront payment by patient	Generally not, only co-payment	Often
Prior authorization request by patient	Always	Depending on (1) care and (2) choice of competent member state
Recourse[a]	83.5 percent	16.5 percent
Success rate[a]	86 percent	75 percent

[a] European Commission, Directorate-General for Health and Food Safety et al., Data on Cross-Border Patient Healthcare Following Directive 2011/24/EU – Reference Year 2020 (December 2021), https://bit.ly/Directive-data-2020; European Commission, Directorate-General for Employment, Social Affairs and Inclusion et al., *Cross-Border Healthcare in the EU under Social Security Coordination: Reference Year 2020* (October 2022), https://data.europa.eu/doi/10.2767/714637; see also infra Sections II.B to II.D.

In 2019, this increased slightly to 0.01 percent and 0.3–0.4 percent, respectively.[20] Although increasing patient mobility as such is not a goal in itself in the EU, the fostering of cross-border eHealth solutions is.[21] This includes telemedicine. Where these cross-border telemedicine solutions increase, implicitly patient mobility also increases. Despite the low market percentages, it is therefore very relevant to assess a patient's virtual cross-border reimbursement rights.

C Limitations

The EU cross-border reimbursement framework solely concerns insured patients receiving health care crossing an *internal* EU border. The EU framework does not concern care provided outside of the EU, as the EU has no competence thereto.[22] As for physical health care, care providers using in-home digital diagnostics not established in the EU therefore depend on the reimbursement legislation of the member states individually.[23]

The legal framework applies differently to unplanned health care – for example, falling ill during a holiday abroad – and planned health care – for example, going

---

[20] European Commission, *Report on the Operation of Directive 2011/24/EU on the Application of Patients' Rights in Cross-Border Healthcare* 9, COM (2022) 210 final (May 12, 2022).
[21] European Commission, *eHealth Action Plain 2012–2020 – Innovative healthcare for the 21st century* 40, COM (2012) 736 final (December 6, 2012).
[22] For the sake of completeness: The Regulation also covers Norway, Liechtenstein, Iceland, and Switzerland, and in limited circumstances the Directive also covers third country nationals.
[23] A company is established in the EU if it has its "registered office, central administration or principal place of business within the [European] Union" (Art. 54 Treaty on the Functioning of the European Union).

abroad for more qualitative dental care. Under EU law, the more interesting comparator is the situation of planned care, as the outcome in reimbursement options vis-à-vis in-person care is more divergent. Therefore, this contribution focuses on the rules concerning planned cross-border health care, such as a situation where a care provider monitors a patient who is located abroad for potential arrhythmias, using wearables to transfer the relevant heart rate data.

II REGULATION V. DIRECTIVE: REIMBURSEMENT IMPLICATIONS FOR DIGITAL DIAGNOSTICS

A *Various Situations*

In the context of in-home digital diagnostics, there are two main EU cross-border health care situations: Patients residing in the member state where they are insured (situation 1, stagnant patient), and patients residing in a different member state from where they are insured (situation 2, patient insured abroad). In both situations, the patients stay at home to receive virtual diagnostic services from a health care provider established in another member state. To understand the legal consequences thereof, one should distinguish between the "competent member state,"[24] the "member state of residence" and the "member state of treatment" (see Table 14.2).

Table 14.3 demonstrates what these concepts imply for both situations.

The different scopes of the Regulation and the Directive have direct consequences for telemedicine. Whereas the Directive explicitly includes telemedicine in its scope,[25] guidance published on the website of the European Commission states that the Regulation does not apply to telemedicine, which directly limits the reimbursement opportunities for patients.[26] However, considering both the situations of stagnant patients and patients insured abroad, this conclusion should be nuanced to fully reflect all possible scenarios. For situation 1, concerning stagnant patients, the Regulation indeed does not apply, as the patients did not exercise their free movement of persons. Stagnant patients can therefore only rely on the Directive for receiving potential cross-border reimbursement. However, in situation 2, patients do exercise their free movement of persons as they took up insurance in one member state and residence in another member state. This triggers the application of the Regulation. Consequently, contrary to stagnant patients, a patient insured abroad receiving digital diagnostics may qualify for reimbursement both

---

[24] The Directive also refers to the "member state of affiliation." For the situations described, the member state of affiliation always coincides with the "competent member state" under the Regulation.

[25] Directive 2011/24/EU, art. 3(d) and art. 7.7.

[26] Ecorys et al. for European Commission, *Manual for National Contact Points – Reimbursement of Cross-Border Healthcare 2* (2019), https://health.ec.europa.eu/system/files/2019-12/2019_ncptoolbox_ncp_manualncp_en_0.pdf.

TABLE 14.2 *Member state functions*

Concept	Definition
Competent *member state*	Where the patient is insured.
Member state of **residence** = **Home** *member state*	Where the patient habitually resides.
Member state of **treatment** = **Providing** *member state*	Where the patient receives treatment (for in-person care) OR where the care provider is established (for telemedicine).[a]

[a] Directive 2011/24/EU, art. 3(c) and (d).

TABLE 14.3 *Stagnant patient versus patient insured abroad*

	Competent member state	Home member state	Providing member state	Example
Situation 1 (stagnant patient, receiving telemedicine)	– Competent member state = home member state: Patients have insurance in the member state where they habitually reside. – Patients do not travel to another EU country to receive diagnostic services.		Where the digital diagnostics provider is established.	Patient living and insured in France, monitored for arrhythmias by a care provider established in Italy.
Situation 2 (patient insured abroad, receiving telemedicine)	Where the patients are insured.	– Patients reside in another member state than where they are insured. – Therefore, a cross-border component is in place, even though the patient does not travel to another EU country for receiving diagnostic services.	Where the digital diagnostics provider is established.	Patient living in France but insured in Germany, monitored for arrhythmias by a care provider established in Italy.

TABLE 14.4 *Situations triggering application of regulation and/or directive*

	Regulation	Directive
Understanding of "cross-border" health care	Free movement of persons	Free movement of services: "healthcare provided or prescribed in a Member state other than the [competent] Member State."
Situation 1 (stagnant patient)	Does not apply	Applies
Situation 2 (patient insured abroad)	Applies	Applies
Patient receiving physical cross-border care	Applies	Applies

under the Regulation and the Directive. This outcome is similar for physical cross-border health care, where patients can enjoy both legal bases for reimbursement (see Table 14.4).

As situation 2 triggers the same legal outcome as for patients receiving physical cross-border health care, this chapter hereafter does not discuss situation 2 separately. The following subsections therefore focus on the comparison between the reimbursement options for in-home digital diagnostics for stagnant patients and for similar in-person diagnostics services, by analyzing the differences in scope and procedure of the Regulation and the Directive. This comparison allows for an assessment as to whether there are potential barriers to cross-border digital diagnostics.

B Price

The Directive generally requires a patient to pay all costs concerning the health care upfront, whereas, under the Regulation, the competent member state generally pays the providing member state directly.[27] Consequently, a patient receiving in-person care may solely be required to pay the co-payment, while a stagnant patient is more at risk of having to pay for the full treatment at the outset. The latter may be problematic concerning expensive treatments.

Depending on the type of health care sought, patients may have an advantage relying on the Regulation or the Directive, as both legal instruments calculate reimbursement rates on another basis. Under the Regulation, the tariff of the providing member state applies, whereas under the Directive, the tariff of the competent member state applies. As stagnant patients cannot receive reimbursement for telemedicine based on the Regulation, stagnant patients cannot benefit from potentially preferential reimbursement rates available in the providing member state, whereas

---

[27] Id. at 4, 8.

patients having recourse to the exact same diagnostic services in person do have access to such rates. Where a patient receiving in-person treatment can perform forum shopping based on the Regulation, a stagnant patient cannot.

C Procedure

Both under the Regulation and the Directive, the competent member state may require a patient to seek prior authorization to receive reimbursement for cross-border care. At first sight, the prior authorization scheme under the Regulation seems stricter than the one under the Directive. Specifically, under the Regulation a patient must always request prior authorization, whereas under the Directive a member state can only require a patient to ask for prior authorization regarding specific types of health care. Currently, twenty of the EU member states have such a limited prior authorization scheme in place under the Directive.[28] Regarding telemedicine, some of these prior authorization bases of the Directive may apply more easily: For example, a member state could argue that, because of the distance, telemedicine presents "a particular risk for the patient" or gives rise "to serious and specific concerns [regarding] the quality or safety of the care."[29] Also, a third category of justifications for requesting prior authorization may be relevant. The Directive allows a member state to require prior authorization to control costs and avoid waste of resources for care requiring "highly specialized and cost-intensive medical infrastructure or medical equipment." A member state may, therefore, refuse the reimbursement of digital diagnostics to ensure the valorization of its national health care investments. At EU or member state level, there is no uniform approach regarding the definition of "highly specialized and cost-intensive medical infrastructure or medical equipment."[30] However, a 2022 study indicated that, half of the time, member states harness this justification for requiring prior authorization regarding expensive imaging techniques, such as CT and PET scans, MRI, angiographies, or gamma knife.[31] Although such imaging techniques currently cannot be replaced by digital alternatives, they could serve as inspiration for the protection of other cost-intensive traditional imaging techniques. Therefore, where digital diagnostics are introduced to replace imaging

---

[28] European Commission, Directorate-General for Health and Food Safety et al., *Study on Enhancing Implementation of the Cross-Border Healthcare Directive 2011/24/EU to Ensure Patient Rights in the EU – Final Report* 30 (February 2022), https://data.europa.eu/doi/10.2875/92318.

[29] Directive 2011/24/EU, art. 8.2.

[30] European Commission, Directorate-General for Health and Food Safety et al., *Literature-Based Approach to Defining the Concept of "Highly Specialised and Cost-Intensive Medical Infrastructure or Medical Equipment" – Final Report* 32 (April 2014), https://data.europa.eu/doi/10.2875/574887.

[31] European Commission, Directorate-General for Health and Food Safety et al., *Study on Enhancing Implementation of the Cross-Border Healthcare Directive 2011/24/EU to Ensure Patient Rights in the EU: Mapping and Analysis of Prior Authorisation Lists: Analytical Report* 28 (February 2022), https://data.europa.eu/doi/10.2875/378986.

techniques, the probability increases that other member states will require prior authorization, trying to limit the financial risk of stagnant patients seeking recourse to these virtual diagnostic services over traditional imaging techniques. The protection of the health care system, indeed, is the main reason for member states to implement a prior authorization scheme. In conclusion, telemedicine seems to fulfill the justifications under the Directive more easily, rendering it easier for member states to request prior authorization for such health care. Specifically, regarding digital diagnostics that would replace traditional imaging techniques, member states may fear for the waste of their national health care resources as cross-border health care increases in the EU. They may, therefore, increasingly try to request prior authorization for digital diagnostics under the Directive, as a barrier against such financial risk.

The Regulation and the Directive also have different procedures for refusing such prior authorization. Under the Regulation, the competent member state cannot refuse authorization if the national public health care of the home member state includes the health care requested, and if that care "cannot be given [...] within a time limit which is medically justifiable."[32] Under the Directive, the potential grounds for refusal are similar and formulated the other way around: A member state is only allowed to refuse authorization for specific, limited reasons. In a telemedicine context, a member state could again argue that the provision of health care at a distance raises concerns regarding the quality thereof, relying on the justification that the patient may be exposed to a "patient-safety risk that cannot be regarded as acceptable" or that the health care raises serious and specific concerns regarding national standards and guidelines on quality of care and patient safety. Furthermore, as for the Regulation, a member state can rely on the fact that it can provide the health care "within a time limit which is medically justifiable." For the latter ground for refusal, reimbursement depends on the interpretation of the concept of a "medically justifiable time limit" for providing diagnostic services. Both the Directive and Regulation stipulate, in line with the case law of the ECJ, that such assessment should focus on the individual situation of the patient, considering the patient's current state of health and the probable course of the illness, and the Directive specifies that restrictions should be limited to what is necessary and proportionate.[33] The proportionality test will include the availability of digital diagnostics, and the outcome of such an assessment will determine how far a member state is allowed to protect its investments when they are surpassed by more innovative techniques in other member states.

Even though, at first sight, the Regulation's prior authorization scheme may seem stricter, as it is mandatory for all cross-border care, eventually, everything depends on the approach of the competent member state. First, although the reimbursement

---

[32] Regulation 883/2004, art. 20.2.
[33] Directive 2011/24/EU, recital 44.

route via the Directive may seem more accessible as, contrary to the Regulation, it does not always require prior authorization, member states may impose prior authorization under the Directive more swiftly for telemedicine – for example, where digital diagnostics would replace traditional imaging techniques – to protect their national health care investments. Second, member states can refuse authorization on similar grounds under the Regulation and the Directive, namely that the competent member state can offer the treatment within a time limit that is medically justifiable. Third, although the Directive does also list other potentially relevant refusal grounds (namely, where digital diagnostics qualify as an unacceptable patient-safety risk or as raising serious and specific concerns regarding respecting national standards and guidelines on the quality of care and patient safety), member states may take such refusal grounds into account under the Regulation too, even though the Regulation does not explicitly refer to them. In conclusion, the criteria adopted by the member states determine whether the prior authorization scheme of the Regulation or Directive is more lenient for patients requesting cross-border care. Where the criteria under the Regulation would be more lenient than those of the Directive, the reimbursement disparity between stagnant patients and patients receiving in-person diagnostics becomes bigger.

D In Practice

Analyses of the recourse made to the Regulation and the Directive in the past years consistently demonstrate that patients submit far more prior authorization requests under the Regulation than under the Directive.[34] For example, two reports from the European Commission describing the EU cross-border health care landscape under the Directive and Regulation in 2020 specify that member states reported 5,409 requests under the Directive,[35] compared to 27,386 requests under the Regulation.[36] Consequently, only around 16.5 percent of the reported prior authorization requests are based on the Directive. This discrepancy stems partially from the fact that the Directive does not always require prior authorization. However, an analysis of the EU-wide annual health care budget shows that in 2016, the EU spent twenty-five times more budget under the Regulation than under the Directive,[37] figures unrelated to whether patients have to ask for prior authorization or not. As

---

[34] For further background: The Directive requires member states to have in place "National Contact Points for cross-border healthcare," to facilitate the exchange of information regarding the cross-border reimbursement options available. In practice, decisions regarding granting permission or not generally go via the health insurance funds, as each citizen – mandatorily – has a certain degree of public health insurance.
[35] European Commission, Directorate-General for Health and Food Safety et al., supra note a in Table 14.1 at 23.
[36] European Commission, Directorate-General for Employment, Social Affairs and Inclusion et al., supra note a in Table 14.1 at 64.
[37] See infra Section III.C.

discussed, a priority rule is in place favoring the application of the Regulation over the Directive.[38] This default application of the Regulation may partially explain the discrepancy in recourse toward the different reimbursement routes. However, such a priority rule also implies that the advantages of the Regulation set out in this section apply automatically to patients receiving in-person treatment, anchoring their added value even more compared to cross-border health care for stagnant patients excluded from the scope of the Regulation.

The success rate for prior authorization requests for the two reimbursement routes is more comparable: In 2020, 75 percent of the requests were authorized under the Directive,[39] while under the Regulation, 86 percent of the requests were authorized.[40] Still, there is an 11 percent higher success rate in favor of the Regulation procedures, which in absolute numbers is considerable, given the Regulation's wider applicability.

Finally, it is worth comparing the reasons for refusal of authorization, even though the reports state that not many member states were able to provide such details. Both under the Regulation (53 percent) and the Directive (71.4 percent) the main reason for which member states refused authorization was that the cross-border treatment applied for could be provided in the home or competent member state, respectively, within a medically justifiable time limit.[41] Further, member states only rarely refuse because of quality and safety concerns: They only reported one such case in 2022 under the Directive, and the report covering the Regulation does not even mention this refusal ground. Time will tell whether the member states will attempt to rely on such refusal grounds when telemedicine becomes more prominently available.

For stagnant patients, this implies that they have no access to the most frequented reimbursement route. The remaining reimbursement route is also less successful. Furthermore, member states refuse more frequently on the basis that they can provide treatment within a medically justifiable time limit, which is of importance for the example of cross-border digital diagnostics competing with traditional imaging techniques.

III PRACTICAL IMPLICATIONS

This section describes the potential consequences of the rules set out in Section II for the various stakeholders involved: The patients, the telemedicine providers, and the EU member states.

---

[38] Directive 2011/24/EU, art. 8.3.
[39] European Commission, Directorate-General for Health and Food Safety et al., supra note a in Table 14.1 at 23.
[40] European Commission, Directorate-General for Employment, Social Affairs and Inclusion et al., supra note a in Table 14.1 at 64.
[41] European Commission, Directorate-General for Employment, Social Affairs and Inclusion et al., supra note a in Table 14.1 at 65; European Commission, Directorate-General for Health and Food Safety et al., supra note a in Table 14.1 at 27.

A Patient Perspective

The EU health framework takes a different approach toward stagnant patients and patients receiving cross-border care in person. Stagnant patients cannot select the most favorable rate among all potential providing member states, while patients crossing a border for the same care in-person can, even if it concerns the exact same diagnostic service. This is a disadvantage for elderly patients and severely ill patients, who are less mobile. In addition, there is a higher burden for stagnant patients to get access to care, as generally they must pay the full cost of the health care upfront. The Regulation generally does not require patients to pay upfront. Therefore, telemedicine will be less accessible for less wealthy patients. They may not be able to pay the full price upfront under the Directive, and they neither have the means to cover travel costs upfront for receiving the care physically in another country under the Regulation.

At first glance the procedure under the Directive may seem more favorable as the Directive does not always require prior authorization. However, everything depends on the criteria imposed by the member states. The grounds for refusal of prior authorization also depend primarily on the approach of the competent member state. Furthermore, the default application of the Regulation pursuant to the priority rule combined with the higher success rate reinforces the weaker reimbursement position of stagnant patients. As telemedicine solutions are booming, the discrepancy in reimbursement options between a stagnant patient and a patient receiving in-person cross-border diagnostics will become more apparent.

B Telemedicine Solution Providers' Perspective

The EU spectrum of telemedicine solution providers is diverse: The main actors are telecom companies, Big Tech companies, medical device manufacturers, pharma companies, and start-ups.[42] Their development of telemedicine solutions holds great potential for society as it can create a scale advantage: A 2018 European Commission study concluded that "the higher the share of telemedicine, the more cost-effective wide-scale deployment becomes."[43] The increased use of telemedicine reduces the total cost of the patient journey and the mortality rate, and increases life quality. Telemedicine can lead to the integration of, for example, e-visits to doctors for routine investigations, but could also create a market for innovative or niche treatments, as it enables reaching a crucial minimum number of patients. However, the 2018 study states that reimbursement is key to speeding up success.[44] Therefore, the EU cross-border reimbursement challenges are a de facto limitation of the potential

---

[42] European Commission, Directorate-General for Health and Food Safety et al., supra note a in Table 14.1 at 61.
[43] Id. at 12, 128.
[44] Id. at 128.

scale advantage for telemedicine solution providers. A lack of interoperability across a fragmented EU health care market reinforces this limitation.[45]

Consequently, if a company develops a diagnostics solution and releases it on the EU market, contradictorily, it may have a greater reach if offered physically in the member state which approved such reimbursement, rather than virtually. This way the Regulation is applicable too, and EU patients can access the diagnostic services in a more diverse, reimbursable way. The existing EU reimbursement system may therefore have a retarding effect on the development of the telemedicine market in the EU.

C EU Member State Perspective

The competent member state can decide to exclude cross-border in-home digital diagnostics from reimbursement because of budgetary concerns. When arguing against reimbursement for cross-border health care, member states traditionally state that the measure is necessary for "safeguarding the financial balance of the social security system."[46] Cross-border telemedicine may indeed cost money. However, telemedicine may also be cost-effective for the member state.[47] When assessing whether cross-border reimbursement decisions compromise the sustainability of the social security system, member states should consider whether the advantages of cross-border digital diagnostics counter the potential cost of opening the reimbursement system further. Even though opening up the reimbursement scheme to certain cross-border telemedicine solutions requires the dedication of extra budget for that telemedicine solution, the solution provided could be substantially more cost-effective than the existing in-person alternatives – for example, analysis via data captured by a wearable instead of an expensive scan. Therefore, the overall balance for the member state could be positive, despite covering the reimbursement of both the in-person solution and the telemedicine alternative. The 2018 telemedicine market study noted that "a lack of willingness to adopt new solutions is a barrier to innovation."[48] The member states' adherence to known solutions could therefore hinder the integration of telemedicine solutions in the reimbursed "basket of health care."

In addition, as mentioned in the introduction, the number of patients requesting health care under both the Directive and the Regulation remains low. Therefore, the real-life impact of telemedicine on the financial balance of a member state's social security system is still low, even though patients are becoming more independent

---

[45] Id. at 78.
[46] For example, *Nicolas Decker v. Caisse de Maladie des employés privés*, case C-120/95, 1998 ECJ, (ECLI:EU:C:1998:167) §§39–40; Gabriella Berki, *Free Movement of Patients in the EU* 47 (2018).
[47] European Commission, Directorate-General for Health and Food Safety et al., supra note 1, at 12.
[48] Id. at 75.

and increasingly look for care options across borders. The surge of telemedicine and digital diagnostics will require member states to perform thorough assessments regarding their financial benefits and risks, including cost effectiveness. If cross-border patient numbers remain low, the member states should also consider this more limited impact when assessing reimbursement feasibility.

IV CONCLUSION

In-home digital diagnostics are a form of telemedicine. The reimbursement of cross-border telemedicine constitutes specific reimbursement challenges in the EU. Patients insured in their home member state only qualify for reimbursement of cross-border telemedicine under Directive 2011/24/EU, whereas patients receiving the same care in person abroad qualify for reimbursement both under Directive 2011/24/EU and under Regulation 883/2004. Opting for one reimbursement basis or the other has an impact on the flexibility regarding the price of the health care sought, the potential upfront payment, and the prior authorization procedure which they must follow. Consequently, exclusion of the scope of the Regulation may disadvantage patients receiving telemedicine, as they have less reimbursement options. In addition, the Directive is the less frequented and less successful reimbursement route. Telemedicine solution developers too may face challenges, as the current reimbursement system deprives them partially of the scale advantages linked with telemedicine. Finally, the EU member states need to scrutinize whether they will reimburse in-home digital diagnostics or not, considering the cost-efficiency of telemedicine and the limited recourse made to telemedicine by patients. The overall EU cross-border reimbursement framework has again become "complex and lengthy," especially when considering both in-person care and telemedicine. The legislator will need to consider whether the increase in telemedicine will again necessitate a modernizing and simplifying effort for this legal framework.

Printed in the United States
by Baker & Taylor Publisher Services